AN APOLOGY FOR POETRY

ore

OLD & MIDDLE ENGLISH TEXTS
General Editor G. L. Brook

SIR PHILIP SIDNEY

An Apology for Poetry

or

The Defence of Poesy

Edited by
GEOFFREY SHEPHERD

MANCHESTER UNIVERSITY PRESS

BARNES & NOBLE BOOKS · NEW YORK
(a division of Harper & Row Publishers, Inc.)

First issued 1965
by Thomas Nelson & Sons Ltd

This edition 1973
© Geoffrey Shepherd
issued by
MANCHESTER UNIVERSITY PRESS
316–324 Oxford Road
Manchester MI3 9NR

ISBN 0 7190 0516 7

Published in the U.S.A. 1973 by
HARPER & ROW PUBLISHERS, INC.
BARNES & NOBLE IMPORT DIVISION

Printed in Great Britain
by Butler & Tanner Ltd
Frome and London

ACKNOWLEDGMENTS

I wish to thank Viscount De L'Isle, V.C., for permission to consult the text of William Temple's Analysis of the *Apology*.

The title page on p. 93 is reproduced by courtesy of the Librarian of Edinburgh University Library.

Many people have helped me in the preparation of this edition, and I thank them all : especially my colleagues at Birmingham, Mrs E. E. Duncan-Jones, Mrs Joan Rees, Professor T. J. B. Spencer, Dr Stanley Wells, and members of the Shakespeare Institute ; Professor Ellis Waterhouse of the Barber Institute of Fine Arts; and Professor Philip Edwards of the University of Essex.

I gratefully acknowledge special debts to Dr D. S. Brewer, to Dr E. G. Stanley of Queen Mary College, London, to Mr W. T. McLeod of Edinburgh, and to Dr Katharine Davies who has given me constant help and guidance.

CONTENTS

ABBREVIATIONS

Ad Her.	*Rhetorica ad Herennium*, ed. Caplan (Loeb Library)
Cook	A. S. Cook's edition of *The Defense of Poetry*
CP	*Classical Philology*
Curtius	E. R. Curtius, *European Literature and the Latin Middle Ages*
EETS	Early English Text Society Publications
ELH	*Journal of English Literary History*
Fr	French
Gilbert	A. H. Gilbert, *Literary Criticism: Plato to Dryden*
Gk	Greek
Hathaway	Baxter Hathaway, *The Age of Criticism*
Herrick	M. T. Herrick, *The Fusion of Horatian and Aristotelian Criticism, 1531–1555*
HLB	*Huntington Library Bulletin*
HLQ	*Huntington Library Quarterly*
Ital.	Italian
JEGP	*Journal of English and Germanic Philology*
JHI	*Journal of the History of Ideas*
JWCI	*Journal of the Warburg and Courtauld Institutes*
Lat.	Latin
ME	Middle English
Med. Lat.	Medieval Latin
MLN	*Modern Language Notes*
MLQ	*Modern Language Quarterly*
MLR	*Modern Language Review*
MnE	Modern English
MnFr	Modern French
MPh	*Modern Philology*
NED	*New* (or *Oxford*) *English Dictionary*
OE	Old English
Olney	Olney's text of the *Apology*

1a

PL	*Patrologia Latina*, ed. Migne (quoted by volume and column)
PMLA	*Publications of the Modern Language Association of America*
Poems	*The Poems of Sir Philip Sidney*, ed. William Ringler
Ponsonby	Ponsonby's text of the *Apology*
PQ	*Philological Quarterly*
RES	*Review of English Studies*
Shuckburgh	E. S. Shuckburgh's edition of *The Defence of Poesie*
Smith	G. Gregory Smith, *Elizabethan Critical Essays*, 2 vols.
SP	*Studies in Philology*
Spingarn	J. E. Spingarn, *A History of Literary Criticism in the Renaissance* (2nd ed.)
Tilley	M. P. Tilley, *A Dictionary of the Proverbs of England in the 16th and 17th centuries*
Wallace, *Life*	M. W. Wallace, *The Life of Sir Philip Sidney*
Weinberg	Bernard Weinberg, *A History of Literary Criticism in the Italian Renaissance*, 2 vols.
Works	A. Feuillerat's edition of *The Complete Works of Sir Philip Sidney*, 4 vols.

SELECT BIBLIOGRAPHY

Only titles of works or articles directly relevant to the study of the *Apology* or of general importance for its understanding are listed. Further bibliographical information can be obtained from the *Cambridge Bibliography of English Literature*, ed. F. W. Bateson, vol. 1 (Cambridge, 1940) and *Supplement*, ed. George Watson (Cambridge, 1957) ; from the Introduction, notes and footnotes of William Ringler's edition of *Poems of Sir Philip Sidney* (Oxford, 1962) ; and from S. A. Tannenbaum, *Sir Philip Sidney; a Concise Bibliography*, Elizabethan Bibliographies, 23, (New York, 1941).

Many modern texts of the *Apology* are available. These are not listed.

I EDITIONS

The Complete Works of Sir Philip Sidney, ed. Albert Feuillerat (4 vols., Cambridge).
I *The Countesse of Pembrokes Arcadia* (1912).
II *The Last Part of the Countesse of Pembrokes Arcadia ; Astrophel and Stella*, etc. (1922).
III *The Defence of Poesie ; Political Discourses; Correspondence ; Translations* (1923).
IV *Arcadia : the original version* (1926).

The Poems of Sir Philip Sidney, ed. William Ringler (Oxford, 1962). Indispensable.

An Apology for Poetrie (1595), ed. Edward Arber (London, 1868). Reprint of Olney's text.

The Defence of Poesie (1595). Noel Douglas Replica (London, 1928). Reprint of Ponsonby's text.

The Defense of Poesy, otherwise known as An Apology for Poetry, ed. Albert S. Cook (Boston, 1890). Modernised text, excellent notes.

The Defence of Poesie, ed. E. S. Shuckburgh (Cambridge, 1891).

An Apology for Poetrie, in G. Gregory Smith, *Elizabethan Critical Essays* (Oxford, 1904), vol. 1, pp. 148–207. Some good notes.

An Apology for Poetrie, ed. J. Churton Collins (Oxford, 1907).

A Woorke concerning the trewnesse of the Christian Religion, by Philip of Mornay, Lord of Plessie Marlie, Begunne to be translated into English by Sir Philip Sidney and finished by Arthur Golding (London, 1587).

The Correspondence of Sir Philip Sidney and Hubert Languet, ed. S. A. Pears (London, 1845).

II STUDIES OF SIDNEY
(i) LIFE AND LITERARY CAREER

BOAS, F. S. *Sir Philip Sidney: his Life and Writings* (London, 1955).

BOURNE, H. R. FOX. *A Memoir of Sir Philip Sidney* (London, 1862). Extensive collection of material.

BUXTON, JOHN. *Sir Philip Sidney and the English Renaissance* (London, 1954).

GREVILLE, FULKE, BARON BROOKE. *Life of Sir Philip Sidney,* ed. Nowell Smith (Oxford, 1907).

MOFFET, THOMAS. *Nobilis, or a view of the life and death of a Sidney,* ed. V. B. Heltzel and H. H. Hudson (San Marino, California, 1940).

MYRICK, KENNETH O. *Sir Philip Sidney as a Literary Craftsman* (Cambridge, Mass., 1935). Good.

OSBORN, JAMES M. *Young Philip Sidney* (New York & London, 1972).

POIRIER, M. *Sir Philip Sidney, le chevalier poète élisabéthain* (Lille, 1948).

SIEBECK, BERTA. *Das Bild Sir Philip Sidneys in der englischen Renaissance* (Weimar, 1939).

VAN DORSTEN, J. A. *Poets, Patrons, and Professors : Sir Philip Sidney, Daniel Rogers, and the Leiden Humanists,* Publications of the Sir Thomas Browne Institute, II (Leiden, 1962).

WALLACE, M. W. *The Life of Sir Philip Sidney* (London, 1915). Standard.

WILSON, MONA. *Sir Philip Sidney* (London, 1931).

ZANDVOORT, R. W. 'Sidney in Austria', in *Anglistische Studien* as *Wild Festschrift, Weiner Beiträge zur englischen Philologie* **66** (1957), 227–45.

(ii) STUDIES RELEVANT TO THE APOLOGY

BARROWAY, I. 'Tremellius, Sidney and Biblical Verse', *MLN* **49** (1934), 145–9.

BRONOWSKI, JACOB. *The Poet's Defence* (Cambridge, 1939).

CAMPBELL, LILY B. 'The Christian Muse', *HLB* **8** (1935), 29–70.

CAMPBELL, LILY B. "Sidney as 'The Learned Soldier'", *HLQ* **7** (1944), 175–8.

CAWLEY, R. R. 'Areytos in the *Defence of Poesie*', *MLN* **39** (1924), 151–3.

DOWLIN, C. M. 'Sidney's Two Definitions of Poetry', *MLQ* **3** (1942), 573–81.

DOWLIN, C. M. 'Sidney and "Other Men's Thought"', *RES* **20** (1944), 257–71.

GOLDMAN, M. S. 'Sidney and Harrington as Opponents of Superstition', *JEGP* **54** (1955), 526–48.

HAMILTON, A. C. 'Sidney and Agrippa', *RES* N. S. **7** (1956), 151–7.

HAMILTON, A. C. 'Sidney's Idea of the "Right Poet"', *Comparative Literature* **9** (1957), 51–9.

HEARSEY, MARGUERITE, '*The Defence of Poesie* and Amyot's Preface in North's *Plutarch*', *SP* **30** (1933), 535–50.

KROUSE, F. M. 'Plato and Sidney', *Comparative Literature* **6** (1954), 138–47.

MALLOCH, A. E. '"Architectonic" Knowledge and Sidney's *Apologie*', *ELH* **20** (1953), 181–5.

MONTGOMERY, ROBERT L. *Symmetry and Sense: the Poetry of Sir Philip Sidney* (Austin, Texas, 1961).

NEWELLS, KLEMENS. 'Eine spanische Übersetzung der *Defence of Poesie*, von Sir Philip Sidney', *Anglia* **72** (1954), 463–6.

PADELFORD, F. M. 'Sir Philip Sidney's Indebtedness to Sibilet', *JEGP* **7** (1908), 81–4.

PHILLIPS, J. E. 'George Buchanan and the Sidney Circle', *HLQ* **12** (1948), 23–55.

RIBNER, IRVING. 'Sir Philip Sidney on Civil Insurrection', *JHI* **13** (1952), 257–65.

SAMUEL, IRENE. 'The Influence of Plato on Sidney's *Defense of Poesie*', *MLQ* **1** (1940), 383–91.

SPENCER, THEODORE. 'The Poetry of Sidney', *ELH* **12** (1945), 251–78.

TATLOCK, J. S. P. 'Bernardo Tasso and Sidney', *Italica* **12** (1935), 74–10.

THALER, ALWIN. *Shakespeare and Sir Philip Sidney: the Influence of the Defence of Poesy* (Cambridge, Mass., 1947).

THORNE, J. P. 'A Ramistical Commentary on Sidney's *An Apologie for Poetrie*', *MPh* **54** (1957), 158–64.

WHITNEY, LOIS. 'Concerning Nature in the Countess of Pembroke's *Arcadia*', *SP* **24** (1927), 207–22.

III LITERARY HISTORY

(i) GENERAL

BUNDY, MURRAY, W. *The Theory of the Imagination in Classical and Medieval Thought*, University of Illinois Studies in Language and Literature, XII, 2–3 (Urbana, Ill., 1927).

CURTIUS, E. R. *European Literature and the Latin Middle Ages* (English trans. W. R. Trask) (London, 1953).

GILBERT, ALLAN H. *Literary Criticism: Plato to Dryden* (New York, 1940).

LEWIS, C. S. *English Literature in the Sixteenth Century, excluding Drama* (Oxford, 1954).

WIMSATT, WILLIAM K., and BROOKS, CLEANTH. *Literary Criticism: a Short History* (New York, 1957).

(ii) RENAISSANCE CRITICISM

(*a*) Texts

ASCHAM, ROGER. *The Scholemaster*, ed. J. E. B. Mayor (London, 1863).

BACON, FRANCIS. *The Advancement of Learning*, ed. W. A. Wright (Oxford, 1900).

BOCCACCIO, GIOVANNI. *Boccaccio on Poetry, being the Preface and the Fourteenth and Fifteenth Books of Boccaccio's Genealogia Deorum Gentilium*, ed. and trans. Charles G. Osgood (Princeton, 1930).

CASTELVETRO, LODOVICO. *Poetica d'Aristotele vulgarizzata et sposta* (Basel, 1576).

CASTIGLIONE, BALDASSARO. *The Book of the Courtier*, trans. Sir Thomas Hoby, Everyman's Library, 807 (London, 1928).

ELYOT, Sir THOMAS. *The Boke Named the Governour*, ed. H. H. S. Croft (2 vols, London, 1883).

FRACASTORIUS, G. *Naugerius*, trans. Ruth Kelso, introduction by M. W. Bundy, University of Illinois Studies in Language and Literature, IX, 3 (Urbana, Ill., 1924).

FRAUNCE, ABRAHAM. *The Arcadian Rhetorike* (1588), ed. Edith Seaton, Luttrell Society Reprints, IX (Oxford, 1950).

GOSSON, STEPHEN. *The Schoole of Abuse*, ed. E. Arber (London, 1868).

HARVEY, GABRIEL. *Ciceronianus*, ed. Harold S. Wilson and Clarence A. Forbes, University of Nebraska Studies in the Humanities, IV (Lincoln, Nebraska, 1945).

HOSKINS, Sir JOHN. *Directions for Speech and Style*, ed. H. H. Hudson (Princeton, 1935).

LYLY, JOHN. *Euphues: the Anatomy of Wit; Euphues and his England*, ed. M. W. Croll and Harry Clemons (London and New York, 1916).

MERES, FRANCIS. *Poetrie*, ed. Don Cameron Allen, University of Illinois Studies in Language and Literature, XVI, 3–4 (Urbana, Ill., 1933).

MINTURNO, ANTONIO. *De poeta libri sex* (Venice, 1559).

MINTURNO, ANTONIO. *L'arte poetica* (Naples, 1725).

MULCASTER, RICHARD. *The First Part of the Elementarie* (1582), ed. E. T. Campagnac (Oxford, 1925).

PUTTENHAM, GEORGE. *The Arte of English Poesie*, ed. Gladys D. Willcock and Alice Walker (Cambridge, 1936).

RAINOLDS, JOHN. *Oratio in laudem artis poeticae* (1572), ed. William Ringler, trans. W. Allen, Princeton Studies in English, XX (Princeton, 1940).

ROBORTELLO, FRANCISCO. *In librum Artistotelis de arte poetica explicationes* (Florence, 1548).

SALUTATI, COLUCCIO. *De laboribus Herculis*, ed. B. L. Ullman (2 vols., Turin, 1951).

SCALIGER, JULIUS CAESAR. *Poetices libri septem* (Heidelberg, 1617).

SMITH, G. GREGORY (ed.). *Elizabethan Critical Essays* (2 vols., Oxford, 1904).

VIVES, LUIS. *De tradendis disciplinis* (1531), trans. Foster Watson, *Vives on Education* (Cambridge, 1931).

WILLS, RICHARD. *De Re Poetica*, ed. A. D. S. Fowler, Luttrell Society Reprints, XVII (Oxford, 1958).

WILSON, Sir THOMAS. *The Arte of Rhetorique* (1560), ed. G. H. Mair (Oxford, 1909).

(*b*) Modern Studies

ATKINS, J. W. H. *English Literary Criticism: the Renascence* (London, 1940).

BALDWIN, CHARLES S. *Renaissance Literary Theory and Practice* (New York, 1939).

BALDWIN, T. W. *William Shakspere's Small Latine and lesse Greeke* (2 vols., Urbana, Ill., 1944). On range and content of a literary education in the 16th c.

BOAS, F. S. *University Drama in the Tudor Age* (Oxford, 1914).

CAMPBELL, LILY B. *Divine Poetry and Drama in Sixteenth Century England* (Cambridge and Berkeley, 1959).

CHARLTON, H. B. *Castelvetro's Theory of Poetry* (Manchester, 1913).

CLARK, D. L. *Rhetoric and Poetry in the Renaissance* (New York, 1922).

CLEMENTS, ROBERT J. *Critical Theory and Practice of the Pléiade* (Cambridge, Mass., 1942).

CRANE, W. G. *Wit and Rhetoric in the Renaissance* (New York, 1937).

HALL, VERNON. *Renaissance Literary Criticism: a Study of its Social Content* (New York, 1945 : reprinted Gloucester, Mass., 1959).

HATHAWAY, BAXTER. *The Age of Criticism: the Late Renaissance in Italy* (New York, 1962). Important.

HERRICK, MARVIN T. *The Fusion of Horatian and Aristotelian Criticism, 1531–1555* (Urbana, Ill., 1946).

HOWELL, WILBUR S. *Logic and Rhetoric in England, 1500–1700* (Princeton, 1956).

JONES, RICHARD FOSTER. *The Triumph of the English Language* (Stanford, California, 1953).

RUBEL, VERÉ L. *Poetic Diction in the English Renaissance from Skelton through Spenser* (New York, 1941).

SASEK, LAWRENCE A. *The Literary Temper of the English Puritans*, Louisiana State University Studies, Humanities Series, IX (Baton Rouge, 1961).

SPINGARN, J. E. *A History of Literary Criticism in the Renaissance* (2nd ed., New York, 1908).

SWEETING, ELIZABETH J. *Studies in Early Tudor Criticism* (Oxford, 1940).

THOMPSON, JOHN. *The Founding of English Metre* (London, 1961).

TUVE, ROSAMUND. *Elizabethan and Metaphysical Imagery* (Chicago, 1947).

WEINBERG, BERNARD. *A History of Literary Criticism in the Italian Renaissance* (2 vols., Chicago, 1961). Full, difficult.

IV INTELLECTUAL AND ARTISTIC BACKGROUND

BOLGAR, R. R. *The Classical Heritage and its Beneficiaries* (Cambridge, 1954).

BUSH, DOUGLAS. *The Renaissance and English Humanism.* The Alexander Lectures (Toronto, 1939).

BUXTON, JOHN. *Elizabethan Taste* (London, 1963).

CASSIRER, ERNST. *Individuum und Kosmos in der Philosophie der Renaissance* (Berlin : Leipzig, 1927).

GOMBRICH, E. H. *Art and Illusion* (London, 1960).

HAYDN, HIRAM C. *The Counter-Reformation* (New York, 1950).

HILL, CHRISTOPHER. *Society and Puritanism in Pre-revolutionary England* (London, 1964).

KRISTELLER, PAUL O. *Renaissance Thought: the Classical, Scholastic and Humanistic Strains* (New York, 1961).

ONG, WALTER J. *Ramus, Method and the Decay of Dialogue* (Cambridge, Mass., 1958).

PANOFSKY, E. *Idea, ein Beitrag zur Begriffsgeschichte der älteren Kunsttheorie*, Studien der Bibliothek Warburg (Leipzig and Berlin, 1924).

RICE, EUGENE F. *The Renaissance Idea of Wisdom* (Cambridge, Mass., 1958).

ROSENBERG, ELEANOR, *Leicester, Patron of Letters* (New York, 1955).

SARGENT, R. M. *At the Court of Queen Elizabeth* (London, 1935).

TOFFANIN, GIUSEPPE. *La fine dell' umanesimo* (Naples, 1933).

WOODWARD, W. H. *Studies in Education during the Age of the Renaissance* (Cambridge, 1906).

YATES, FRANCES A. *The French Academies of the Sixteenth Century*, Studies of the Warburg Institute, XV (London, 1947).

INTRODUCTION

A FOREIGNER studying the intellectual and political habits of the English during the past few centuries might well recall that the great Earl of Chatham was said to have made himself master of only one book—Spenser's *Faery Queen*. It may seem an unlikely choice for a politician's *vade-mecum*. William Pitt was a politician, not an aesthete; yet he could move men's minds with his words, he formulated the second British empire and his designs are still visible on the maps of the world, though some of the colouring has changed. His addiction for Spenser's poem is typical. Other nations may entrust themselves with more or less success to the guidance of economists, or technocrats or columnists, to savants or generals or oracles; this country in the past has been happy enough to discover its hidden moral springs of political action in poems.

Sir Philip Sidney's *Apology for Poetry* is still the best analysis and the most persuasive justification of this peculiar notion—that a sensible and comprehensive control over human affairs can be learnt from splendid poems. To acquire something of this attitude towards life and letters has been part of the regular education of English poets; and the assumption of its usefulness has worked its way into and along all the educational system of England. The notion is still powerful. It lives even in its perversions.

Sidney died in 1586. In 1595 Henry Olney of St Paul's Churchyard published *An Apologie for Poetrie* by the right noble, vertuous, and learned Sir Phillip Sidney, Knight (see title-page). In the same year, perhaps a little earlier, appeared THE DEFENCE of Poesie, by Sir Phillip Sidney, Knight, LONDON Printed for *William Ponsonby* 1595.

The circumstances of publication suggest an amicable rivalry between two parties of Sidney's friends, each in possession of a MS of the *Apology*. Both Olney's text and Ponsonby's are good, carefully printed texts, independently

1

intelligible. The fairly numerous minor variations between them rarely affect the general meaning and seem often to depend upon small changes in emphasis or rhythm, some perhaps rather the results of over-carefulness than of carelessness in preparing MSS of the *Apology*. At Penshurst there is a MS text of the *Apology* in a late sixteenth-century hand, again with its own minor variants, but often agreeing with Olney's text. No doubt several handwritten texts were in fairly wide circulation before publication. The *Apology* was frequently reprinted during the seventeenth century in Sidney's collected works, but none of the trivial variants in these texts of the *Apology* seems to have any authority.[1]

In this edition an attempt is made to present a text which will make the sense of the *Apology* as apparent as possible. In general it is based on Olney's text. Olney's punctuation is rhetorical and his paragraphing designed to show as much the flow as the stages of argument. In this edition the punctuation and paragraphing have been modified and the spelling modernised. Textual variants of any interest or substance are recorded in the Notes.

It is not possible to determine exactly when the *Apology* was written. Sidney published nothing during his lifetime, but he had permitted his works to be circulated among his courtly acquaintances. If we read the *Apology* as an integral composition, then it cannot have been finished before the publication of Spenser's *Shepherd's Calendar*, which was entered at Stationers' Hall, 5 December 1579.

From the time of the publication by Thomas Zouch in 1808 of *Memoirs of the Life and Writings of Sir Philip Sidney*, it has been commonly supposed that the *Apology* was intended as answer to Stephen Gosson's *School of Abuse*, published late 1579, which was dedicated, apparently without permission, to Sidney. Spenser recorded that Sidney received the work with some scorn (Smith, vol. i, p. 89), but whether

---

[1] A. Feuillerat in his edition of Sidney, *Works*, vol. iii, pp. 377–85, prints variants in editions up to 1674 Folio edition. Much information about the texts of Sidney's works is given by W. Ringler in *Poems*, but without specific attention to the *Apology*; but see his article, *PQ* **29** (1950), 73, and B. Juel-Jensen, *The Book Collector*, **12** (1963), 199–200.

the scorn was directed towards the writer, the manner of writing, or the argument, we cannot tell. Even by this time Sidney was a friend, correspondent, and something of a patron to some of the most eminent men of letters in Europe. He had no cause to feel much honour in receiving the dedication of a pamphlet, put out apparently with the direct backing of the City Fathers of London, by an Oxford hack, a failed playwright turned moralist; nor would one suppose that he had much interest in replying to it. Moreover, what Gosson was attacking, Sidney is not defending. Gosson dealt with the social inconveniences and dangers of the new popular stage plays. Sidney deals with this subject only in passing, and his attitude seems to be much the same as Gosson's. Sidney was as much, or as little, a Puritan as Gosson (who ended his days in 1615 as Rector of St Botolph's, Bishopgate, with some reputation as an anti-Puritan controversialist).[1]

The *Apology* was written after Sidney had become, in his own words, ' a paper-blurrer '. It is likely that he had written verses from his schooldays onwards. Some of the sonnets in *Astrophil and Stella* were probably composed before 1578, when the masque *The Lady of May* was presented at Wanstead, Essex. It is usually assumed that the first draft of *Arcadia* was begun in 1580. According to the letter prefatory to the first printed text of 1590, the romance was written on loose sheets, and given directly to his sister, the Countess of Pembroke. Fulke Greville, writing in November 1586, immediately after the death of Sidney, asserts that the original version of *Arcadia* (*viz.* the *Old Arcadia* which did not appear at all in print until the present century) was completed ' four or five years since ' which would be in 1581 or 1582. Fulke Greville in 1586 had in his possession the copy of a revised version of much of *Arcadia*. This revision provided pretty certainly the text which appeared in 1590 apparently under Greville's supervision as *The Countesse of Pembrokes Arcadia*, published by William Ponsonby. Between

---

[1] W. Ringler, *Stephen Gosson* (Princeton, 1942), argues that the *School of Abuse* prompted the *Apology*; but the evidence is not conclusive. Verbal parallels adduced between the two works are insignificant; see notes on **96**/16; **116**/34; **123**/14; **126**/14.

this new version of the *Arcadia* and the *Old Arcadia* there
is a great difference in style and intention. It looks as if
Sidney in revising the work was attempting to compose a
full heroical poem. The *Old Arcadia* on the other hand has
the appearance of a simply constructed, if lengthy, Elizabe-
than romance. The stimulus towards this change may well
have been given by the composition of the *Apology*. In that
case we may think that the *Apology* was written after 1580
(when the first version of *Arcadia* was begun). The likeliest
date appears to be during the years 1581 to 1583 (and see
notes on **131/16**).

THE AUTHOR

A great deal is known about Sidney's life; good modern
biographies are numerous. Here there is no need to do more
than sketch his career as it illustrates his authorship of the
Apology. Philip Sidney was born at Penshurst in Kent on
29 November 1554, the eldest son of Sir Henry Sidney, who
was for many years Lord-Deputy of Ireland and one of
Elizabeth's most faithful and least rewarded soldiers and
servants. Philip's mother was the Lady Mary, eldest daughter
of John Dudley, Duke of Northumberland, sister to Robert
Dudley, Earl of Leicester, Elizabeth's favourite, and Philip's
uncle, friend, and lord.

Sidney and Fulke Greville, who was to be Sidney's life-
long friend and eventually his biographer, started school
together at Shrewsbury in 1564, under Thomas Ashton, a
humanist and a Calvinist. The statutes of the school pre-
scribed the study of Cicero, Caesar's *Commentaries*, Sallust,
Livy, *Dialogues* drawn out of Cicero and Vives, and Virgil,
Horace, Ovid, and Terence. In Greek, which Sidney seems
never to have known well, the set books were the New Testa-
ment, Isocrates' *ad Demonicum* or Xenophon's *Cyropaedia*.
By 1568 Sidney was at Christ Church, Oxford. One of his
tutors was Thomas Cooper, already the author of the great
Anglo-Latin dictionary; his contemporaries included Fulke
Greville still, William Camden the antiquary, Richard Carew
(who on one occasion disputed academically with Sidney),
Richard Hakluyt the historian, Walter Raleigh, Henry Savile,

Richard Hooker, John Lyly, Edmund Campion (who before he became a Jesuit was to write *A History of Ireland* for Leicester), and Richard Stanihurst, who translated the *Aeneid*. Sidney presumably followed the normal Arts course, which still concentrated on the medieval trivium, Grammar, Rhetoric, and Logic. Academic distinction was achieved by proficiency in formal disputation. Much of the training was merely verbal. In 1580 Sidney warns his brother that the chief fault of teaching at Oxford in both logic and rhetoric is that it concentrates on words and neglects things. Sidney adds ' so you can speak and write Latin not barbarously, I never require great study in Ciceronianism' (*Works*, vol. iii, p. 132). But whether or not Sidney was satisfied with what he himself acquired at the University, it is unlikely that the earnest young man whom Fulke Greville remembered was ever entirely at the mercy of a syllabus: ' His talk ever of knowledge, and his very play tending to enrich his mind ' (*Life*, p. 6). . . . ' His end was not writing, even while he wrote; nor his knowledge moulded for tables, or schools; but both his wit, and understanding bent upon his heart, to make himself and others, not in words or opinion, but in life and action, good and great. In which Architectonical art he was such a Master, with so commanding, and yet equall waies amongst men, that whersoever he went, he was beloved and obeyed ' (*Life*, p. 18).

After leaving Oxford, Sidney may well have passed some months at Cambridge, but to complete his education he went to France in 1572 in the train of the Earl of Lincoln, a few months before the Massacre of St Bartholomew. This bloody disaster to the Protestant cause seems permanently to have insulated Sidney from French culture in general and at the same time to have rendered him highly sympathetic with the thought of a number of individual Huguenots, some of whom in 1572 he probably met for the first time, the Protestant nobleman Philippe du Plessis-Mornay, the learned lawyer François Hotman, Théophile de Banos, the first editor of the works of Ramus, and Hubert Languet. He kept in touch with these men for the rest of his life. With Languet, scholar, theologian, and diplomatist, ambassador for the

Elector of Saxony, Sidney was to enter a tutelary friendship which was to last and glow across the years in unremitting correspondence and occasional encounter until Languet's death in 1581. Probably this friend Languet had more influence than any man on Sidney, teaching not only the theory of statecraft, but also an equanimity of spirit in public affairs and the stoical pursuit of virtue. We may guess that what Sidney learnt from Languet he had found in the man himself,

> Languet, the shepheard best swift Ister knewe,
>   For clerkly reed, and hating what is naught,
> For faithfull hart, cleane hands, and mouth as true:
> With his sweet skill my skillesse youth he drewe,
>   To have a feeling tast of Him that sitts
> Beyond the heaven, far more beyond your witts.
>
> *(Poems*, ed. Ringler, p. 99)

In the autumn of 1572 Sidney was at the house of the printer Andreas Wechel in Frankfort, and the next summer he was in Languet's company at Vienna, having stopped a while on the way at Heidelberg, where he won the friendship of the printer and scholar Henri Estienne, who, beginning with a Greek New Testament, was to dedicate a series of books to the young Englishman; and at Strasburg, where he met the humanist John Sturm, the counsellor and correspondent of Roger Ascham. At the Imperial court at Vienna Sidney won many admirers among the learned, some of whom were to remain his correspondents for years. From Vienna he made excursions into Hungary accompanied by Greville and into Italy, to Venice, and Padua, returning to Vienna in the autumn of 1574. He took his way back through the Low Countries to England in 1575.

Rarely has a young Englishman made so grand a tour of the Continent as this. Sidney's birth gave him entry into the great courts, but his curiosity and his intelligence won him the attention of the learned. He met not only the princes and nobles but the great executives of policy and the political thinkers of Europe, as well as the artists and craftsmen of many countries.

Leicester introduced Sidney at court, where he was to distinguish himself in many customary exercises in pageantry and gallantry. He resided for most of the time at Leicester House, in company with Sir Edward Dyer, the poet, Leicester's secretary, and with many literary and professional men, including Spenser and Abraham Fraunce, both in Leicester's service. Sidney was the centre of a learned literary group, an unconstituted academy which was investigating the resources of the English language for high literary purposes.

He was also becoming involved in the policies of the northern European powers seeking to establish the *foedus evangelicum*, a Protestant League. Henceforward most of his political efforts were devoted to this cause. Indirectly to the same end, from 1576 he promoted the voyages of the English explorers. But in all his political schemes he was frustrated of the harvest. As he wrote unhappily to Languet in March 1578: ' To what purpose should our minds be directed to various kinds of knowledge unless there is opportunity for putting it into practice so that public advantage may be the result, which in a corrupt age we cannot hope for ? ' Throughout his career Sidney's interests were identified with Leicester's faction, which although it served Leicester's personal ambition developed a state policy and a temper of its own: it was nationalist, sober, practical, puritan, mercantile. It gave a cast to personal culture as well as to national policy. It was opposed to another, probably more subtly influential, temper of the court, which Languet saw and considered ' somewhat less manly than I could have wished, and most of your noblemen appeared to me to seek for a reputation more by a kind of affected courtesy than by those virtues which are wholesome to the State'[1] ; an aesthetic and irresponsible affectation of valour and culture which Sidney saw personified in the Earl of Oxford.

In 1580 Leicester's fortunes and his policies were under a cloud. In this year Sidney wrote an astonishingly frank letter to the Queen opposing her avowed intention of marrying Alençon, the brother of the French king. About the same time occurred the famous quarrel at tennis with the

---

[1] *The Correspondence of Sir Philip Sidney and Hubert Languet*, ed. S. A. Pears (London, 1845), p. 167.

Earl of Oxford in view of the French ambassadors. Sidney was obliged to withdraw from the Queen's court, probably to Wilton, the seat of his sister Mary, the Countess of Pembroke. He was back in London in 1581 and became Member of Parliament and later a joint Master of Ordnance. He was in the escort accompanying Alençon to Antwerp, where Languet had died in 1581. In the years that followed, militant Protestant policies were in the ascendant and Sidney was employed in the administrative affairs of an England preparing for the eventual contest with Spain. But his political capacities were still unfulfilled. In 1583 he was knighted by the Queen to provide an escort of rank to his friend Count Casimir. Later in the same year he married Frances, daughter of Sir Francis Walsingham, a secretary of state. Early in 1585 Elizabeth came to realise the inevitability of conflict, and with it the necessity of helping the Low Countries against Spain and of assuming the leadership of a loosely co-ordinated Protestant league. Sidney was stayed on the very point of embarking with Drake for Spanish waters, and appointed Governor of Flushing. He left England for the Low Countries in November 1585, holding a comparatively minor appointment in the English expedition which was put, after many royal hesitations, under the command of Leicester. On 22 September 1586, occurred a militarily insignificant skirmish between Alva's forces and a surprised and highly select force of the English at Zutphen. Sidney received ' a sore wound upon his thigh, three fingers above his knee '. He died twenty-two days later, shortly before his thirty-second birthday. During this period, he made his will, talked and wrote to his friends, prayed much, and read the Bible. On the morning of his death he said farewell. ' Love my memory, cherish my friends. . . . But above all govern your will and affection by the will and word of your Creator; in me, beholding the end of this world, with all her vanities. All things in my former life have been vain, vain, vain.' [1] He was buried in St Paul's in February 1587. All England mourned, and much of Europe.

[1] From Mr Giffard's account, printed in T. Zouch, *Memoirs of the Life and Writings of Sir Philip Sidney* (York, 1808), pp. 267–78.

The virtue and valour of this man remain unassailable. Though he himself may have often enough found existence a vanity, his powers unrealised, his learning unapplied, with great works of war and letters beating unachieved in his brain, yet looking back we see an integrity and completion in his career, a unity of splendid ambition, generosity, intelligence, grace, and piety. His ambition was political in the fullest sense. It was directed to the whole of life, it rested on a notion of human perfection, which, though forlorn generations may at times reject it, is as noble and compelling as that of any mystic, philanthropist, or pacifist. But we cannot ever hope to understand the way in which Sidney attracted men of his own time. The face a man shows to his own time is even less clearly discerned than the mind which writes his books.

It was not only the eager pursuit of virtue that gave Sidney an attractive grace. His intellectual curiosity was irresistible. He was concerned with all the arts of war and peace. And he was well informed about them. In an expansive age of European learning this young man was a highly promising, gifted, and diligent scholar. Though he used, judiciously, other men's epitomes, indexes, and aids to learning, he read, marked for himself, and learned from a wide range of books, in Latin and in the vernacular languages. He knew French and Italian; Spanish, German, and Greek less well. He read where he needed in vernacular translation. What works containing literary judgments he consulted for the *Apology* we cannot be sure, apart from Scaliger's *Poetices*, Elyot's *Governour*, Cornelius Agrippa's satire *De vanitate et incertitudine scientiarum*, Landino's Preface to Dante, Horace's *Art of Poetry*, and something of Plato and Aristotle; but the *Apology* is the product of much wider reading than literary criticism. Most humanist writing was accessible to him. He read in Petrarch, Boccaccio, Tasso, Mantuan, Pontanus, Sannazzaro, Erasmus, More, Ascham, Ramus, Bembo, Patrizi, Bodin, Buchanan, Ronsard, du Bartas. He knew the old Roman poets, historians, moralists, and dramatists well. Certain books and authors were particularly congenial to him: Plutarch notably, and the Bible; also Xenophon, Virgil, and Seneca.

Some of Sidney's interests have never been fully assessed. We know of his studies abroad in mathematics and astronomy and of his friendships with the botanist Clusius, the physicians Camerarius and Crato von Krafftheim, and later with the philosopher Bruno. With Sir Edward Dyer he learnt some chemistry from Dr John Dee, who at his home at Mortlake had collected a large library of scientific works which were made freely available to experimenters. It seems unlikely that Sidney was uninterested in the projected Gresham College; and from the time of his appointment as a Master of Ordnance he was at the centre of the remarkable movement of scientific inquiry which was to involve most of the men of Gresham: among them, Thomas Bedwell, a mathematician and engineer, keeper of ordnance stores at the Tower of London; Thomas Digges, son of the celebrated mathematician Leonard Digges, himself an astronomer and geographer who served as muster-master-general in the Netherlands with Sidney; Thomas Blundeville, a member of Leicester's household, a writer of text-books not only on horsemanship and government but also on navigation and astronomy. Leicester indeed was patron to many men of this type: learned, serious-minded men of Puritan convictions interested in developing the technology of colonisation, sea-captains, merchants, and government officials. The first fruits of these activities was the victory over the Armada. Others ripened more slowly; some were gathered by seventeenth-century colonists to the Americas; others by the scientists of the Royal Society.

We may assume that it was in the years after he had written the *Apology* that Sidney became most intimately involved in this circle of new learning. We should not expect to find in that work evidence of the young official who was to spend much of his last few years supervising the production of maps and cannon and gunpowder for the queen's ships. The *Apology* is on another plane. Yet it should be no surprise to find in it many anticipatory echoes of the methodological problems upon which Bacon worked in *The Great Instauration*. Much of the *Apology*, particularly where it deals with history as a descriptive record of events, can be read as a

preliminary meditation on Baconian themes (see notes
104/3f; **106**/14; **110**/24; **111**/22. The more closely the
Apology is studied the more astonishing appears Sidney's
sensitivity to contemporary intellectual development, in the
arts, in religion, in politics, and in science.

His conscious ambitions were always practical. The ideal
he cast for himself was as a man of war, a man of affairs, as a
useful courtier, as only an amateur scholar. The nonchalant
gentlemanliness of his passion for learning catches the *sprez-
zatura* of Castiglione's ideal courtier—that kind of ' Recke-
lesness to cover art withall ' which does everything without
apparent effort. His mind was rather like that of an ideal
editor of a serious review of our own time, serious so far as
seriousness does not inhibit liveliness. He knew the direction
in which currents of thought flowed even if he had not the
scholarship or the time to identify the solid shapes on the
stream. The learned men of Europe who found him worth
talking to no doubt also found him an unusually good
listener, with remarkable assimilative gifts—the open-minded
receptivity of Shakespeare, but probably at a more purely
intellectual, and certainly at a more directly political level.
As a result nothing that Sidney writes is trivial. His articula-
tions are moments of European self-consciousness. Slight
and deceptively easy though the *Apology* may appear, it is
written by a man who knows what is going on in life and
letters and what is at stake in Europe. It is the fundamental
seriousness of the great issues crowding on the margins of
elegance which gives the pages of the *Apology* a characteristic
density. We should not underestimate Sidney's dexterity in
evoking in the *Apology* an intellectual and distinctly marked
milieu with which he does not deal directly. And this may
account in part for the common experience in reading the
Apology. It is easy to read and evokes in reading admiration
and assent, and yet it is not easy to remember as an argument.

THE FORM OF THE APOLOGY

It is helpful to recognise what the *Apology* was intended to
be. It is not a discursive essay on a selection of critical matters

to which observations on the contemporary situation are loosely appended. The intention is manifested in a highly artificial form and this form maintains a clear intelligible line of argument.[1]

The *Apology* conforms to a type of oration well known to the ancients, as a variety of the laudatory oration adapted to the justification of philosophy or an art, and controlled by the conventions of a counsel's speech for the defence. In order to actualise these conventions and the fictitious situation which precipitates them, we should imagine Sidney delivering the *Apology* in reply to a prosecutor's speech in which poetry has been charged with being a worthless and time-wasting activity. No more than with Milton's *Areopagitica*, also composed as an oration, is there need to think that the *Apology* was ever composed for oral delivery on a specific occasion. Though much of the phrasing and syntax, as well as the general method of ordering and constructing the arguments, conform to conventions originating in the requirements of forensic delivery, the fine finish of the piece, the marmoreal completeness as well as some revealing phrases, suggest beyond much doubt that the *Apology* was written, not spoken, and was intended for private though not invariably silent reading.

As an oration laudatory of an art, a kind of composition familiar to the ancient, medieval, and Renaissance worlds of letters, the *Apology* follows the normal rhetorical recipe in construction. A modern eye will observe that it falls into three sections: (i) a commendation of the dignity of poetry (**95–120**), (ii) a defence of poetry against a variety of charges (**120–131**), (iii) a review of the contemporary situation (**131–142**). This is fair observation, and each of the three parts may be profitably examined to disclose how Sidney develops an argument. But this analysis into three parts does not clearly indicate the unity of the whole, nor does it do justice to Sidney's skill and care in following traditional methods. The following scheme shows the lines on which Sidney himself

[1] Kenneth O. Myrick, *Sir Philip Sidney as a Literary Craftsman* (Cambridge, Mass., 1935), pp. 46–83, has an excellent chapter on the *Apology* as a classical oration.

organised the *Apology*, and shows how devotedly he followed
the recommendations of the ancient and traditional rhetorical
theory. It falls into seven parts with the addition of a digres-
sion. A construction in seven parts is not an invariable recipe
for such an oration; the more usual recommendation in
Ciceronian rhetoric is for construction in five parts, and Aris-
totle observes that the essentials are but three, narration,
proposition, and proof. But treatment under seven heads
is to be found in the systems of many rhetoricians, most
interestingly as far as Sidney is concerned, in the *Arte of
Rhetorique* by Thomas Wilson, whom Sidney had known per-
sonally and whose books in the 1580s were according to
Gabriel Harvey in every man's hands.

I EXORDIUM (**95**/1–**96**/7)
   (Employs a recognised method of indirect approach to
   the case and seeks to capture the goodwill of the audience
   by humorous anecdote, mock expostulation, and modesty
   formulas. The anecdote adumbrates the concern of the
   Apology with the relation between the theory and prac-
   tice of an art.)

II NARRATION (**96**/8–**101**/33)
    (Relates the facts which give dignity to poetry.)
    Brief transitional argument to lower the personal credit
    of the opponents of poetry (**96**/8–16)
    Facts indicating worth of poetry
    (*a*) its superior antiquity (**96**/16–**97**/30)
    (*b*) the universality of poetry (**97**/31–**98**/15)
    (*c*) its names and etymology (**98**/16–**101**/27)
        (i) title of *vates* (**98**/120–**99**/27)
        (ii) title of ' maker ' (**99**/28–**101**/27)
    Transition (**101**/28–32)

III PROPOSITION (**101**/33–6)
    That poetry is to be commended and approved for what
    it essentially is—Imitation
    (This is the central issue of the controversy and sums up
    what is about to be discussed step by step.)

IV DIVISION (**101**/37–**103**/38)

(Shows the way in which the facts averred in the NARRA-
TION are going to be systematically interpreted to prove
the PROPOSITION.)

Poetry classified according to

(*a*) its subject matter or fable

    (i) religious themes (**101**/37–**102**/13)

    (ii) philosophical themes (**102**/14–20)

    (iii) strictly imitative themes (**102**/21–**103**/8)

(*b*) its form (**103**/9–37)

DIVISION ends with ENUMERATION of the parts of the
CONFIRMATION (**103**/38–**104**/2)

V CONFIRMATION or PROOF (**104**/2–**120**/11)

(*a*) by examining the ' works '—the nature and effects of
poetic imitation

    (i) the essential function of human arts (**104**/2–37)

    (ii) claims of philosophy to be the supreme discip-
line (**104**/38–**105**/19)

    (iii) claims of history (**105**/20–**106**/9)

    (iv) comparison of poetry with other disciplines
(**106**/10–**114**/32)

    (v) examples showing value of poetic imitation
(**114**/33–**115**/26)

    (vi) conclusion (**115**/27–34)

(*b*) by examining the ' parts '—the character and effects
of the different kinds of poetry (**115**/35–**120**/11)

[SUMMARY of the whole argument up to this point (**120**/
12–26) leading to the conclusion that poetry is the
worthiest of all disciplines.]

VI REFUTATION (**120**/37–**130**/31)

(Deals with the specific charges against poetry which
the prosecution is assumed to have made.)

(*a*) personally discrediting attack on those who defame
poetry (**121**/4–30)

(*b*) objections against poetic form answered (**121**/31–
122/38)

(c) objections against poetic material listed (**123**/1–16)

   (i) fallacy of argument that poetry is unprofitable exposed (**123**/17–27)

  (ii) assertion that the poet is a liar rebutted (**123**/28–**125**/1)

 (iii) assertion that poetry is the nurse of abuse rebutted (**125**/2–**128**/7)

 (iv) Plato's condemnation of poets answered (**128**/8–**130**/30)

[SUMMARY of favourable points from REFUTATION (**130**/31–**131**/2), which by leading to the conclusion that poetry should be the more honoured turns the REFUTATION into a corroboration of the PROOF.]

[DIGRESSION (**131**/3–**141**/20)
(Indicates the ways in which contemporary English writers disgrace the ideal of poetry set out in the rest of the *Apology*, and how they should amend. The DIGRESSION has the structure of an independent oration.)

I NARRATION giving an account of situation

  (i) great men in the past honoured poetry (**131**/11–25)

 (ii) even in England poetry was once honoured (**131**/25–31)

(iii) poetry now despised and produced by base writers (**131**/31–**132**/17)

II PROPOSITION that poets must seek to know what to do and how to do it, if poetry is to be esteemed properly (**132**/18–29)

III DIVISION indicating the need for art, imitation, and exercise, followed by ENUMERATION of matters to be discussed (**132**/29–**133**/16)

IV CONFIRMATION by consideration of
(a) subject-matter or fable

  (i) deficiencies in past practice (**133**/17–36)

 (ii) defects in drama (**133**/37–**137**/23)

      in disregard of unities (**134**/5–**135**/29)

      lapses in decorum (**135**/30–**137**/23)

(iii) defects in the other kinds (**137**/24–**138**/5)

VII PERORATION of the whole   (**141**/7 to end)

The main ideas in the *Apology* are not peculiar to Sidney though the arrangement of the argument is his own. It is a product of his own intelligence, his own intellectual *milieu*, and its critical inheritance. He gives to poetry a function we have forgotten. He sees it as a work of the practical intellect, designed to teach what ought to be known. It is best to avoid the verbal difficulties which would arise if we sought to understand what Sidney has to say in terms of later critical theory —of the creative imagination, and poetic sensibility. Terms such as these are confusing anachronisms when applied to the *Apology*, and we shall do better to give full meaning instead to the terms which Sidney himself used in talking about poetry.

The *Apology* is not epoch-making, but it is epoch-marking. Of course Sidney was unaware of what vernacular English poets were to achieve within the next generation or so, and yet what he intends is triumphantly authenticated by their achievement. Part of the meaning as well as part of the importance of the treatise is lost if we refuse to interpret it forwards. We shall often understand better what Sidney was implying and towards what ends he was working if we have grasped what his successors in poetry, Spenser, Ben Jonson, Milton, and Pope, achieved when they wrote at the top of their bent. It is the peculiar character of the *Apology* that it serves for us as the initial manifesto of what persists as the central tradition of English poetry into the late eighteenth century, a manifesto which prognosticates if it does not control the course and temper of this line. As with most successful and influential pieces of writing, the *Apology* adapts the remote past and the immediate past to the present to serve the needs of the future.

THE MEDIEVAL INHERITANCE

Medieval theory, inheriting from classical antiquity, gave the poet two rôles: either he was a writer in verse, or he was a maker of stories. Often these activities were thought of separately. Usually they were conceived quite simply, and neither was rated highly as an intellectual exercise. A poem was marked off from other kinds of discourse first by its form, by being composed in measured language, then by its story which made no claim to be considered true. This division runs right through the *Apology*. In the Middle Ages the writing and reading of poems were in the main the concern of junior schoolmasters. Some would make richer use of this material than others, but all used it for grammar and composition lessons, for social occasions, and for inculcating proverbial morality. Such an attitude to poetry is not, we may reflect, altogether unfamiliar to us today. We may wonder indeed whether poetry in the Middle Ages was not slightly better off than it is with us, for the men of the Middle Ages retained a powerful respect for the art of words and a dim sense of the prestige of literature in the Roman world. Moreover, for as long as Latin remained the medium for all thoughtful and official communication in church and state, Latin had to be taught in the classrooms and some Latin authors studied by every aspiring child. Of course there were excellent medieval poets, and some of their audience were mature and appreciative listeners, but their interests rarely modify the dominant educational scheme. In the main men whom we should call literary figures were esteemed on extra-literary grounds: Virgil was honoured particularly as a prophet and magician, Seneca and Cato Minor were yoked as moralists, the reputation of Dictys the Cretan stood above that of Homer. It was not that the intellect was despised in medieval times; but a poem considered simply as metrical composition was the work of a fairly low-grade craftsman. If the poem had any intellectual value it was the product of what it was about, not of what it was in itself. The form aided the memory, but in so much as form diverted the attention from the matter, poetry even at best was no more than second-class material from a strictly intellectual point of view; and this was as true in reading Chaucer as in hearing the worst doggerel. The very prejudice of intellectual disesteem tolerated the production of an immense amount of verse in which no literary, apart from a formal, distinction could be made between serious and trivial work.

Men of the Middle Ages could identify ' a poem '. The more learned among them knew what the ' art of poetry ' was: it often meant little more than skill in manipulating metres and figures of speech. But they did not have the term ' poetry ' as a group name for a type of writing different in quality as well as in form from other types of verbal discourse. They did not distinguish ' classics ' from school text-books. Nor did they isolate a continuum called ' literature '. Only in the sixteenth century in Europe are these concepts established. The distinctions that were made then may seem pedantic, but they were important.[1] You cannot have a history of literature or poetry, or a criticism of poetry, until the subjects are recognised as having an independent intellectual existence. Neither literature nor poetry had this independence in the Middle Ages.

The medieval attitudes died hard, particularly in England among the countries of Europe, and particularly in the universities of England, the centres of English intellectual life. When John Colet at Oxford in the last decade of the fifteenth century treated the *Epistle to the Romans* in a modern way,

---

[1] See J. Spingarn, *Literary Criticism in the Renaissance* (New York, 1908), p. 27 note ; E. R. Curtius, *European Literature and the Latin Middle Ages* (Eng. trans. London, 1953), pp. 152ff. On Sidney's use of *poetry* and *poesy* see note on **99**/18.

and instead of hacking the epistle into a succession of autonomous texts provided a continuous interpretation of the whole book, he was called ' poet ' by the traditionalists, his detractors. He had forfeited, so they judged, his title of a serious theologian. In Sidney's lifetime, Puttenham indicates that, among academics, ' poet ' was still being used as a term of derision.

HUMANISM

Colet had applied to Scripture ideas which he had acquired in Italy. There during the late fourteenth and fifteenth centuries—and even earlier, as Dante's career indicates—literary activities had been pursued in a way which medieval England never knew. A great line of intelligent critics formulated theories about literature. Individually these theorists were never very influential in England, but by the sixteenth century the weight of their testimony was irresistible. England was still slow to react. Not that Englishmen had slower minds; it was rather that the traditional studies in England and Italy were different. Italian schooling had throughout the Middle Ages set greater store by rhetorical exercises. In England the prestige of scholastic logic was stronger. From Petrarch onwards the Italians thought of British logicians as prime agents in the intellectual world which the new attitude to letters which we know as humanism was resolved to conquer. Scholasticism in England was supported by the whole apparatus of ecclesiastical power in the state and in the universities. Humanism in England could be effective only as it was emancipated by, and in turn became an instrument of, political and religious change.

When the humanists pushed literature and sometimes poetry forward into the front rank of intellectual disciplines, there was necessarily a good deal of confusion, much pushing and shuffling, much changing of the ground upon which all the disciplines of knowledge stood—some prospect even of ' civil war among the Muses '. Part of the esteem poetry acquired was from the new company it kept. On the other hand, other intellectual disciplines were regarded differently as a result of this assertion of poetry. The general European debate on the value of the arts and sciences which we see taken up in the first part of the *Apology* was concerned with much more than the destiny of European poetry.

From a literary point of view the centre of humanism lay in its belief that the method and articulation of inquiry is as important as the field in which the inquiry is conducted, that knowledge without communication is worthless. The humanists thus opened up again the old quarrel fought in ancient Greece between the philosophers and the sophists. It is usual to assume that the philosophers deservedly won that day, and associating ourselves with the victors we tend still to misunderstand what was at issue. For the contention was not, as the philosophers would have us believe, between honest inquirers and dishonest word-spinners: it was rather between those who believed that the method of truth is by analysis, by logically testing the validity of thought, and those who believed that truth, by virtue of its nature, requires exemplification and finds its confirmation only in the complexity of existence. The typical protagonists of this quarrel are not so much Plato and the sophist Gorgias, as Aristotle and Isocrates—and Isocrates was much read in the sixteenth century: he was in the syllabus of Shrewsbury school. We would do well to entertain the notion that the opposition between philosopher and rhetorician can appear much less like a quarrel between a high-souled intellectual and a low publicity agent, and much more like the tension which exists in this country today between the sciences and the arts.

Broadly speaking, from antiquity until the Renaissance, philosophy held the upper hand, and, as we know very well, Aristotle the prince of the philosophers established his dominion ever more securely. In seeking to dethrone Aristotle the humanists reasserted the cause of Isocrates and the old rhetoricians. Indeed, in Italy, but only in Italy, the rhetoricians had never been completely and utterly routed, and it is becoming increasingly evident that the Italian humanists are the direct heirs and successors to the professors of the art of letter-writing in the medieval Italian city schools and universities.[1]

[1] See P. O. Kristeller, *Studies in Renaissance Thought and Letters*, (Rome, 1956), pp. 559ff, especially pp. 565–74.

The protracted campaign that went on in western Europe from the fifteenth century well into the eighteenth century between Philosophy (later treated as science), and Rhetoric (later treated as ancient classical learning in general) was fought over many fields. The forces were too large ever to be deployed in one mass encounter. As far as England is concerned, the emergence of a native literature of high quality with an unrestricted range such as we get from the sixteenth century onwards would have been impossible unless the grip of medieval Aristotelianism on the forms and sources of intellectual energy had been broken. If the term Renaissance as applied to English literature of the sixteenth century has any usefulness at all, it lies in applying it to the consequences of the assertion made at that time that Eloquence and Wisdom are indivisible. The argument of the *Apology* rests on this assertion.

THE IDEA OF WISDOM

But in order that Eloquence and Wisdom could be brought together in such a programme as Sidney proposed, not only had poetry to be exalted far above the station it had held in medieval times, but the old ideas of wisdom had to be transformed.

The late-medieval scheme of knowledge, although resolutely Aristotelian in its methodology, had given a Platonic cast to the view of wisdom. Only theology working with the tools of Aristotelian logic was empowered to investigate first causes. But wisdom in its highest forms was a contemplative virtue, and the highest life of which man was capable was a life of religious contemplation. With the Renaissance the general position was reversed. The methodology of medieval Aristotelianism was rejected, but the human centre of Aristotle's own inquiries reasserted. Cicero, the Stoics, and St Augustine become more important. Wisdom acquires a much more practical cast; for Petrarch, taking up Augustine's words, ' Wisdom is piety '—it is the humble, intellectual recognition of the acts of power and love of God in this life. And this in the main, though in a different cultural setting, is the attitude of Erasmus and of the English

Reformers in the sixteenth century. The highest wisdom is knowing how to be good; and being good is taken to imply having the power of doing good. Since it is impossible to know God fully, but possible to love and serve Him, so the eye of contemplation must be recognised as half-blind at best. ' The active life, in so far as it is to be distinguished from the life of contemplation, is to be preferred in all ways to contemplation, both on earth and in heaven.' [1]

The primacy of the active life was a cardinal belief of most of the humanists, and certainly of those of the North. They had become suspicious of all attempts to provide final and formal definitions about the nature of things. Socrates, who sat in the market-place and asked questions about daily life and human behaviour, whom Augustine had regarded as the very type of the active life, replaces Aristotle, the logician of the schools, whom some late scholastics had attempted to canonise. Wisdom takes a new path. The humanists were concerned with human conduct, with social and civic behaviour, with the potentialities of good and evil in man, with the pursuit of virtue. They held that true philosophers were to be regarded not as scientists, as the medieval theologians had been, but as practical moralists. *Prudentia*, the practical aspect of wisdom, became the key virtue. There was a glorification of the life consciously devoted to corporate social ends. Just as philosophy was thought of differently, so history acquired a completely new importance. The proper study of mankind is man, man in history and in society and man in the solitary companionship of his conscience. Let it be emphasised that this was no irreligious programme, although it is totally and vigorously opposed to the scholastic way of thinking. But the new bias of humanist inquiry made the mind of man a much more important field of study than it had been before. There is more interest in the process of thinking, in mental analysis, in biography and autobiography. There is a prime emphasis in Renaissance thought on concept-making. A penetrating analysis of this

[1] Coluccio Salutati, *De nobilitate legum et medicinae*, ed. E. Garin (Florence, 1947), p. 192; and see Eugene F. Rice, *The Renaissance Idea of Wisdom* (Cambridge, Mass., 1958), pp. 36ff.

conceptualising process is provided by the Frenchman, Charles de Bovelles, in *Liber de Sapiente* (Paris, 1511).[1] Knowledge for Bovelles is an activity. The mind manufactures its own intellectual species. It mirrors the whole sensible world and itself makes the images of the things which God created, in the same way as God's creations are themselves images of God's knowledge. This doctrine of the mind as a *speculum vivens*, creating the forms of its own contemplation, has obvious similarities with Sidney's suggestions concerning the ' other nature ' fabricated by the poet (see p. 61 below). But Bovelles is not alone in this respect. Similar suggestions can be found among the neo-Platonists of the Florentine Academy, and indeed behind these neo-Platonists in medieval Augustinian thought, especially among the Franciscans. Again, these cosmological speculations have their effect on sixteenth-century artistic thought.

The new attention to the mind of man and the nature of human thinking was bound to produce new attitudes in faith and worship. Of course there were many other influences, doctrinal, social, and political, working in the same direction.

But whether a Renaissance writer turned his attention to the problems of human *prudentia*, or rode the Platonic forms high towards the uncreated essence, in both cases he succeeded in emphasising the otherness of God. The planes might be parallel, but they did not meet, for ' between the Creator and the Creature there is no proportion at all ' (*Works*, vol. iii. p. 313). A writer might be led to a belief in the utter depravity of man, or, even within the same system, towards an assertion of a limited competence in man. He might be tempted to shut God out from human affairs, with far-reaching consequences for human thought. If there were men who became Epicureans and looked upon virtue as no more than ' a school-name ' (114/25), there were more who found nothing but shame in discovering that man was so completely estranged from God. Most men of the sixteenth century really felt themselves to be in the position most convincingly described by Calvin, who, as a humanist turned

[1] Printed by E. Cassirer, *Individuum und Kosmos in der Philosophie der Renaissance* (Berlin : Leipzig, 1927), pp. 299–412.

theologian, became a profound dissector of the contemporary human heart. The will of man was hopelessly infected after the Fall, but through God's mercy man lives in a constant crisis, struggling for virtue. Man is both God and slave: in the familiar words of Pope (often one of the best mediators to the modern mind of advanced sixteenth-century thought), the glory, jest, and riddle of the world.

The fierceness with which men of the sixteenth and seventeenth centuries maintained this paradox may seem nonsensical to us now. Matthew Arnold, repudiating in the name of English culture much of the legacy of Puritanism with what appears a wilful uncomprehendingness, has made it difficult for us to realise the response of moral fervour and moral anguish which made Calvinist theology so compelling. But most men then as now solved their dilemmas by living them out. Some aspired to Faustian visions, some to the sweet fruition of an earthly crown, some to pluck bright honour from the moon; but their aspirations might equally well be to stand on the Delectable Mountains or even to claim a martyr's crown shining over the fire of the stake. On the one hand, men acknowledged deep in their brains and blood the absolute and terrible sovereignty of God; on the other, they saw quite plain the sordid demands made by the human body and an embattled world to keep society going. By stretching the mind to the fullest possible recognition of the majesty and strength of God, an astounding energy was released for the prosecution of human affairs. These habits of thought could make cruel men, but even their cruelty was often a travesty of a divinely sustained courage; they could make hypocrites, but less self-deluding hypocrites than the late Middle Ages had produced; they were eventually to produce Arnold's Philistines, but even these were less assertive Philistines than the medieval ' barbarians ' whom Lorenzo Valla and Erasmus had denounced.

SIDNEY'S RELIGIOUS AND POLITICAL BELIEFS

Sidney did not have to study and distinguish the various strands of Aristotelian or neo-Platonic or Calvinistic humanism: he lived in the sixteenth century and felt where they touched him. If we have to abstract from actuality and life, we can see that he stands in succession in England to such men as John Colet and Sir Thomas Elyot, Roger Ascham and Thomas Wilson. Like them he links wisdom with book-learning (**127**/2), like them he links learning and an English Reformation. Running through all these men's thoughts is a comprehensive patriotism, which is intellectual, literary, religious, as well as political.

In Europe generally during the sixteenth century the arts of eloquence were considered to have a direct usefulness in promoting policies and doctrines. The Reformation, the Counter-Reformation, and the nationalist wars were fought out not only with fire and sword, but also with documents, with innumerable pamphlets and libels, almost all of which lie now as motionless and heavy as the culverins and halberds of those ancient cruel wars. The achievement and the astonishing busyness of English, French, Italian, Dutch, and Spanish writers, the insistence of all Protestants on the primacy of the Bible, the foundation of the Jesuit schools, all testify to the unwonted importance attached to the sermocinative arts during the sixteenth century. Politics and religion are dominated by the power of the word.

Sidney had a European perspective. In his dealings with foreigners (such as Giordano Bruno), and with sectarians (such as Edmund Campion) he displayed a friendly tolerance and a generosity of spirit in disagreeing. But in matters of state policy his position was unequivocal. He was a royalist, an absolutist within limits (cp. **108**/23 note), a firm nationalist. Patriotism is not just a colouring, it is an assumption always present behind the argument of the *Apology*. It is visible in details: quite coolly he adds Agincourt and Poitiers to the list of battles which shaped the world. As coolly he almost completely ignores contemporary French poets, whose achievements in exalting France he is certainly eager to emulate. For as Thomas Wilson believed that an English logic and an English rhetoric served the cause of England, so Sidney believed that an English poetry could be part of the national strength. Those who have marvelled that Sidney should have left the future so unread as to find no Shakespeare there could better have reminded us how sure Sidney was that a fully developed English literature was possible and how infectious this confidence was to prove. We are probably right in seeing in Spenser's *Shepherd's Calendar* the first work in which an English poet is bold enough to stand before the tribunal of European tradition and claim judgment on equal terms with writers of classical antiquity now rediscovered and reassessed. But behind Spenser's work stand the arguments of Sidney. And nobody could have accused Sidney after his return from the Continent in 1574 of uninformed insularity or of indifference to the value and dignity of foreign literature and scholarship.

His religious beliefs matched his political opinions. In religion, he can be termed a Puritan, but a first-generation Puritan, of the years before Cartwright gave English Puritanism its later doctrinaire complexion. He was no anti-episcopalian, it would appear. He stood with Roger Ascham, the Queen's tutor, with Thomas Wilson, Arthur Golding, with Spenser, with Leicester. Although many of Sidney's friends and correspondents on the Continent were Calvinists, there is no need to think that he himself was formally a Calvinist in belief. In anachronistic, and perhaps slightly acrobatic terms, he was a low-church Anglican, slightly left of centre along Elizabeth's middle way. His position was then more or less like Bishop Jewel's or Archbishop Grindal's.

Even if we can assess the political importance to Sidney of religion we can still know little concerning the intimacies of his religious life. The temper and range of his own religious spirit is reflected probably in the discourse *On the Treweness of the Christian Religion* which he in part translated from the French of du Plessis-Mornay. It was a learned, well-written, sweet-tempered book, the work of a humble and devout Platonic-minded Protestant, soberly excited by the beauty of the world, the work of human hands, and the grasp of the human mind. But in his own compositions too, Sidney everywhere shows himself ' a passionate lover of that unspeakable and everlasting beauty to be seen by the eyes of the mind only cleared by faith ' (**99**/19ff). His character, his way of life, and his theory of poetry grow out of a sense common enough among the English throughout the medieval centuries, of the discrepancy between the ideal and actual. It could induce in him moods of melancholy and quietism which at times worried Languet. The shadow of the perfection of which we cannot know the substance in this sublunary world haunted his life and writings. It appears in the famous sonnet *Leave me O love*; secularised, it is the very air they breathe in Arcadia. The beauty of the earth is lovely indeed, yet laid beside that other heavenly perfection, all insubstantial and ' too-much-loved '.

With his sister, the Countess of Pembroke, Sidney translated the Psalms. Most European poets of the sixteenth century concerned with the emancipation and exaltation of vernacular literatures attached importance to the Psalms: Baïf's Academy in France, for example, was preoccupied with their moral and religious duty of providing a vernacular version. Most poets believed with Sidney that musical utterance could inculcate virtue directly, as Plato had taught, and also that the Psalms as spiritual songs offered the finest exemplar of religious poetry.

According to tradition and the testimony of Sylvester, Sidney towards the end of his life was engaged in translating the *First Week* of the French Huguenot poet, Salluste du Bartas. We can assume that Sidney admired du Bartas's poetry. We know that du Bartas admired Sidney's person and corresponded with him. Both poets were entangled during the 1580s in the literary and political affairs of King James VI of Scotland. Sidney's relations with du Bartas suggest the lines on which his thought as a writer was developing in his latter years. Poetry would have become an active member of the Protestant alliance.

But even in the *Apology* Sidney's religious temper exercises a control upon his theory of poetry. Poetry, he acknowledges, cannot enter the supernatural domain of religion, which has its end beyond all human learning (**106**/17ff). Poetry is no more than the highest human skill (**106**/16); yet it is ultimately justified by true religion. It is, moreover, a skill that can be made use of for sacred ends, it is exemplified

in the Psalms of David (**99**/7), it was not disdained by the
Saviour Himself (**120**/31). With conviction then, Sidney can
assert that against poetry properly grounded, ' none will
speak that hath the Holy Ghost in due holy reverence '
(**108**/37ff).

THE DEBATE ON THE ARTS

In selecting poetry as supreme among the verbal arts, as an
art most useful to men and possessing a divine sanction,
Sidney is, of course, justifying his own ' unelected vocation '.
A man may legitimately proclaim the faith which in him pro-
duces works. But having declared his interest Sidney pre-
sents an excellent and reasoned case. He draws upon many
arguments which had become traditional by his time.

The inter-relationships and comparative importance of the
different arts had been much discussed. Many of the Italian
humanists as university professors had urged the merits of
their own particular subjects or interests, whether it was law,
or medicine, or the arts of war, and so on. Thus a long
tradition of discussion, highly pedagogical (and somewhat
self-advertising) in original intent lies behind the *Apology*
in its comparison of the arts; and all these discussions serve
as rehearsals for Bacon's *Great Instauration*. Sidney embeds
his claim for poetry within a favourite field of Renaissance
debate.[1]

The low medieval estimate of the intellectual status of
poetry had been early rejected by some Italian writers, im-
plicitly by Dante and Petrarch, emphatically and at some
length by Boccaccio and Coluccio Salutati. Boccaccio in *De
genealogia deorum* sought to lift poetry out of its medieval
haunts of schoolroom and tavern, and so he cut out of con-
sideration all the products of the ragged rhymers, the porno-
graphers and the mere tale-tellers, and denied that what such
men wrote was in any way poetry. And this indicates the
approach made by Elizabethan men of letters and their suc-

[1] See the texts in E. Garin, *La Disputa delle Arti nel Quattrocento*
(Florence, 1947). For the debate on the status of poetry, see Bernard
Weinberg, *A History of Literary Criticism in the Italian Renaissance*
(Chicago, 1961), vol. i, chap. 1.

cessors in identifying poetry. It comes to be accepted axiomatically that true poetry is serious, high-toned, and thoroughly artificial work, written by wise and learned poets. Low writing on low subjects is by simple exclusion not poetry at all.

With Boccaccio serious poetry is still not justified by any intrinsic literary qualities. True poetry is an excellent thing because it is still fundamentally a sort of theology, a veiled theology. He calls in the medieval scheme of knowledge to legitimise a new approach. Theology for Boccaccio as for all other genuine medieval intellectuals is the queen of the sciences. If poetry is theology, and the poet a theologian, then poetry merits acclaim and the poet demands prestige. Coluccio Salutati, one of the great early advocates of a high theory of poetry, in *De laboribus Herculis*, had taken Boccaccio's argument a step further. He agreed that the poet was not only a craftsman but claimed that he was a true philosopher on his own account. Poetry has a superior value as a moral discipline to philosophy generally in that it presented truth more vividly and impressively. The Scriptures themselves are poetry.

Such theories, maintaining that poetry is primarily religious allegory and that the poet covers his truth with a delightful veil, were to prove immensely influential and supply the great solvent of medieval notions about poetry and the underlying justification of poetry for some centuries. Bacon elaborates an allegorical theory of poetry; Sir John Harington, in his preface to the translation of *Orlando Furioso*, following, but simplifying the argument of the *Apology*, sets it out in its traditional form. But it is not a theory to which Sidney pays much attention in the *Apology* (see **142**/1ff). It did not offer any explanation why poetry should so disguise itself under the veil of allegory. Boccaccio in exalting poetry had reduced it to serious fable-making and, following the medieval notion of poetry, had re-defined it as fable-making with a quasi-theological import. The ultimate sanction of poetry lay thus outside poetry itself, in theology, which Sidney excludes from consideration in the range of human sciences. Inevitably when the rôle of theology in the domain of the arts and sciences was changed, this theory of poetry as allegory needed re-examining. When poetry had acquired some dignity it no longer needed to creep into the circle under the cloak of theology. When Eloquence came to be recognised as the inseparable form of Wisdom, poetry emerged as a very strong candidate in its own right for primacy among the arts.

Sidney takes up the debate by recognising that the final end of knowledge is to lead and draw us to as high a perfection as our degenerate souls are capable of (104/6 ff). To this end some cultivate astronomy, natural philosophy, music, or mathematics. But these in Sidney's eyes are all ' serving sciences '; that is, they concern external, fragmentary sectors snipped for specialist examination off the universe in which the humanist finds himself at home. The only worthy and relevant knowledge commensurate with man's position amid the multiple relationships in the universe is the knowledge of a man's self in ' the ethic and politic consideration with the end of well-doing ' (104/29). True knowledge, then, is not concerned with the investigation of the nature, structure, proportions, and quantities of the external world, except in so far as these are relevant to man. Nor for that matter is human knowledge properly concerned with speculation about an unknowable God. Here we must rest on revelation through the Scriptures and through God's daily dealings with us. The study of divinity has its originating force and its rewards outside man. In seeking to know about the nature of man himself, whose end is virtuous action, Sidney finds that the ordinary syllabus of learning offers three disciplines— law, history, and moral philosophy.

Leicester House, where Sidney lodged for some years, lay beside the Inns of Court. The importance of the Inns of Court as a centre of literary activity is well known. But we should remember that they were also, properly enough, the scene of profound professional studies. It was a great age for practising and theorising lawyers, including Bacon and Sir Edward Coke (1552–1634), author of the *Institutes*, and earlier in the reign Sir Thomas Smith (1513–77), author of *De republica anglorum* (1578), and Walter Haddon (1516–72), who was, like Ascham, one of the Queen's tutors, and also

professor of Civil Law and international defender of the
Protestant faith. In Leicester's party the study of the law
stood in high esteem. Walter Haddon and Thomas Wilson
in the 1560s had both exhorted Leicester to the study of law
as preparation for his great career in national affairs. It is
as certain that Sidney was involved in professional talk about
the law at Leicester House as that many a young lawyer
went there for literary gossip. Sidney knew as well as
Castiglione and all the courtiers whom Castiglione had in-
structed that Justice was the chief virtue of a Prince, and
accordingly, in the world of politics, the chief of virtues (**106**/
21 and note). But not ' in the ethic consideration ', Sidney
commented: not in the realm of conscience which determines
personal action. The realisation in the sixteenth century
that virtue could not be enforced by law was a shred of the
vast load of responsibility that Protestant theology was to
throw on the shoulders of the individual Christian. Sidney
had too much sympathy with the ethical standpoint of Calvin
to acquiesce in having no care so a man be a good citizen,
how bad a man he be (**106**/25 f). So the law fails to offer the
highest human discipline of learning. We can observe that
later (**124**ff) in denying that poetry can be condemned for the
misuse bad men make of it, Sidney is tacitly asserting the
conviction of his time that the measure of virtue depends upon
the purity of will and intention. This ground of private
morality does not count for much in law.

The more central debate in the early pages of the *Apology*
is concerned with the claims of history and philosophy.
Though neither study can be considered vocational, as is law,
yet looked at through studious humanist spectacles, both
were pretty extensive, as we can see from Bacon's scheme in
the *Instauration*. History meant the record of what had
happened in this world. Thus it could be understood as
including what we should call experimental science. The
facts of science are things that happen. History could include
everything about man, the world, and God, which could be
approached empirically and handled by the memory—sacred
history and natural history as well as human history. Phil-
osophy on the other hand embraced all that could be

approached conceptually. It was concerned not with happenings and the actuality of things but with their causes and principles. Natural philosophy, which developed as a synonym for science, was in that Elizabethan age an activity of rational judgment concerning itself with causes and first principles, not with experimental observation.

It is not easy to give an account of what Sidney or what his contemporaries meant by philosophy. In any modern history of philosophy it is usual to assume that as far as reputable philosophy is concerned there is a gap between the late-medieval scholastics and Descartes in the seventeenth century, a gap ornamented but not occupied by Ficino, Pico, Bruno, Bacon. And this is true as far as metaphysics is concerned. Nevertheless a fine mist of metaphysical thought hangs over all the serious literary activity of the sixteenth century. And in logic and in some branches of applied philosophy, in the philosophy of religion, of history, of law, of medicine, great changes and advances were made: much of Renaissance achievement lay in diffusing over all human activities the intense, highly specialised acquisitions of philosophical thinking in medieval times. In a long perspective of intellectual development, the function of the Renaissance was to distribute the hoard, to spread knowledge, to secularise, to raise the general standard. It was an advance in education, and its great representative men were pedagogues: Vittorino da Feltre, Erasmus, Vives, Ramus, Bacon, Comenius.

And even the changes in logic, profound and far-reaching in their effects, were pedagogical in character. In the fifteenth century the growing dissatisfaction with scholastic logic had been most influentially expressed by the German, Rudolph Agricola (1444–85).[1] In his De inventione dialectica, Agricola had met the scholastic insistence that the art of logic was aimed at formal and scientific certitude by denying that demonstrable and probable knowledge required distinct logical techniques. Such a move could be seen as an attempt to reduce science to a sort of literary and impressionistic approach to truth, and is thus often represented nowadays,

[1] On Agricola's work and influence, see Walter J. Ong, Ramus, Method and the Decay of Dialogue (Cambridge, Mass., 1958), chap. 5.

as indeed it was by those who plodded in the rearguard of scholasticism in the sixteenth century. Agricola himself was not concerned to change any fundamental philosophical positions. He was more interested in the instrument than the end. He required first of a logic that it should be useful to both teacher and pupil in discourse. It was of less interest to Agricola that the form of a statement should command assent by the validity of its form than that the discourse should be able to seize a pattern of meaning out of the confusion of existence and set it out intelligibly. The new attitude to logic invaded the universities of Europe. At Cambridge from 1535 Agricola's dialectic was studied. Change came slower, as usual, at Oxford. In 1583 Bruno still found it, to his disgust, a stronghold of Aristotelian logic, where in dispute a pedantic doctor stumbled ' fifteen times over fifteen syllogisms, like a hen amongst the stubble '.

But the process of re-defining the scope of logic in European thought had been taken further at Paris by Ramus, who in some quarters has become almost as controversial a figure in our own time as he was in his own [1]; in dealing with Sidney, he cannot be ignored. Pierre de la Ramée was born in 1515 in Picardy. The thesis which he maintained when he took his master's degree in 1536, that ' whatsoever propositions were declared by Aristotle must be accounted " fabricated " ' (commentitia), indicates the tenor of what he was to teach, even if it did not signalise a complete revolution of studies in the university of Paris. In 1551 Ramus was made Regius Professor of Eloquence and Philosophy. In the 1560s he declared himself a Protestant, and he perished in the Massacre of St Bartholomew. He was primarily a logician, but his profession was teaching and he reorganised all the recognised field of learning with the aid of the new logical

[1] Perry Miller, *The New England Mind* (New York, 1939), showed the importance of Ramus in seventeenth-century American thought; Rosamund Tuve, *Elizabethan and Metaphysical Imagery* (Chicago, 1947), his influence on poetic practice; Walter J. Ong, *op. cit.*, laboured to show his intrinsic insignificance: Ong's Bibliography is valuable. The best treatment of Ramism in England is in W. S. Howell, *Logic and Rhetoric in England, 1500–1700* (Princeton, 1956). See also Neal W. Gilbert, *Renaissance Concepts of Method* (New York, 1960).

instruments which he continued to sharpen up to his death. He disliked the muddle and redundancy which he observed in the traditional arts syllabus where each discipline had had its content assembled haphazardly through centuries of usage and development. He attempted to establish the different subject matters by an examination of the general wisdom behind a given use. He reorganised logic and rhetoric so that each concerned only that which properly belonged to its own specialist province. And similarly with the other arts.

Of Sidney's knowledge of and interest in Ramus there can be no doubt. With Languet, who knew Ramus personally, he promoted Ramism in learned circles outside the universities in England and on the Continent. In the early 1580s Abraham Fraunce put together the *Shepheardes Logike* (out of Ramus and Spenser) and dedicated it to ' his verye good Master & Patron, Mr. P. Sydney '; and in his better known *Lawiers Logike* (1589), Fraunce reveals that he had entered on these works ' when I first came in presence of Sir P. Sydney ', and that ' these small beginnings drew both him to a greater liking of & myself to a further trauyling in the easy explication of Ramus his Logike '. William Temple, who was to become the leading Ramist of his generation in England, dedicated his commentary on Ramus, *Dialecticae Libri Duo* (1584), to Sidney. It was after this date that Temple became his secretary and good friend and wrote the strict Ramist analysis of the *Apology*.[1] On Protestant scholars in England and later in America Ramus's influence is beyond doubt. Milton, who based his own book of Logic on Ramus, notes that Sidney like himself considered Ramus the best of the logicians. There are indeed traces of Ramism in the *Apology* (see notes 100/11, 15; 133/5; 139/6), and the very arrangement of the material suggests Ramist teaching; so for that matter does the general success that Temple, as a professed disciple of Ramus, had in applying the Ramist analysis to the *Apology*.

But Sidney had not been strict enough for Temple. For

---

[1] See J. P. Thorne, *MPh* 54 (1957), 158–64. The text of Temple's analysis is in the possession of the Viscount De L'Isle and Dudley of Penshurst.

Ramus despite his own uncertainties inculcated into many of his followers a rigidity of method which in practice denied his own premises. Ramistry, in England at least, could all too easily become, as Hooker observed, a superficial technique which worked to inhibit inquiry into the nature of a complexity. Sidney would have the intelligence to perceive the danger. His Ramism is revealed rather by coincidence of sympathies than by a following of any of the recognisably Ramist schemes. The influence is pervasive, not specific.

Gabriel Harvey's brilliant inaugural oration at Cambridge, *Ciceronianus* (1577), shows how the general influence of Ramus was absorbed. Sidney, like Harvey, rejected a false Ciceronianism which valued words more than content. Harvey's exhortation to unite dialectic with knowledge and rhetoric, thought with language, shows how the tendency initiated by Rudolph Agricola has gathered momentum. By being made practical and serviceable to a teacher, all logic has become a sort of rhetoric; and the general field of knowledge in which this sort of rhetoric can work seems to be taken as more or less coterminous with philosophy. This is the same unfencing of fields that we have met before. Every comprehensive humanist theory of knowledge assumed this unity, a completed circle of the sciences, a creative harmony among the Muses. Every great humanist took like Bacon all learning for his province; and the supreme instrumental art was always to be looked for in persuasive discourse.

The pure or mere philosopher is thus ousted from office by humanism. He is replaced by the rhetorician with high moral principles, by the man of letters. Sidney in the *Apology* thinks of philosophy as the kind of mental activity that an intelligent, well-educated man indulges in when he thinks or writes about moral problems or quotes Plato and Aristotle. As a result the figure of the philosopher which he presents in the *Apology* is rather a man of straw, the humanist's superannuated bogyman. Throughout the *Apology* Sidney appropriates Plato and Aristotle and any other philosopher on matters of substance for his literary argument; but the Philosopher whom he presents as contender with the Historian and the Poet is rudely clothed, identified by externals only. Philosophic discourse is conducted in ' words of art ' 113/14), by means of definitions, divisions, and distinctions; it is hard of utterance, misty, or thorny (106/36ff). The substance of philosophy is only vaguely indicated as the abstract and the general. In its most particularised form it is plain that Sidney is thinking only of moral philosophy (cp. (105/8ff, 106/15). In fact an attempt to reconstitute from the *Apology* the Philosopher as the opponent of the Poet discloses an imaginary hybrid Stoic, Cynic, or Epicurean using scholastic terminology.

Sidney's attitude towards philosophy in the *Apology* is very similar to the Second Brother's in Milton's *Comus*.

> How charming is divine Philosophy!
> Not harsh and crabbed as dull fools suppose,
> But musical as is Apollo's lute. . . .

The Wisdom that the moral philosopher professes to teach is the supreme wisdom; but it is best taught by poetry. Spenser is a better teacher than Aquinas, as Milton asserts, because his methods were better. The traditional forms of philosophic discourse, ' the obscure, squalid and bloodless terms ' of the scholastics deprive the noblest themes of all their nobility.

THE DEBATE WITH HISTORY

The more substantial debate about the primacy of the arts concerns history. As we have suggested already, in the humanists' search for the discipline which should most successfully promote the perfection of the *activa vita*, history was an obvious favourite. Many humanists wrote *artes historicae*, Valla, G. Pontanus, Robortello, Patrizzi among them. Usually their chief concern is with the rhetorical character of historiography—with the style, with the use of description and oration, with the general effectiveness and dignity of the writing; their criteria are almost exclusively literary and moral.[1]

---

[1] See John L. Brown, *The Methodus ad facilem Historiarum Cognitionem of Jean Bodin: A critical study* (Washington, 1939), chap. 3.

Many of these writers make a comparison of the different arts. Jacques Amyot has a discourse of this kind in his Preface to his translation of Plutarch's *Lives*. Sidney we know read the translation and used the Preface. A more substantial comparative discussion of the arts is introduced by Lorenzo Valla before his *Historiæ Ferdinandi Regis Aragoniæ* (1520). Valla argues that although philosophers claim a primacy for philosophy on grounds of its antiquity, history must be considered as the foundation of all learning and of all the verbal arts. Philosophy and poetry both stem from this same source; but Valla, displaying the same constant humanist bias against the philosophers, finds that poetry has in truth a greater antiquity, a greater authority and dignity than philosophy. ' Why should poets who are worthy of the name of philosophers be thought inferior to philosophers, seeing that poets originated philosophy, and secondly that where they differ from philosophers is in philosophising better ? '

But all the advantages of poetry belong to history also. The antiquity of history is highly respectable. Were not Moses and the Evangelists really historians ? Valla concludes that history is to be preferred to philosophy on grounds of antiquity and rational usefulness; in addition, history offers a somewhat firmer and more solid discipline than poetry. In its supreme manifestations historical writing must arouse admiration and wonder, not simply display rhetorical skill; it must exhibit the highest degree of judgment, insight, and intellectual penetration.[1]

We may note that Valla, Amyot, and Sidney in turn seem to take quite seriously the question as to which of the disciplines is of greatest antiquity. Temple in his careful analysis of the *Apology* thinks Sidney's argument here worth disputing on point of fact. The importance of antiquity and the authority attached to the testimony of the ancients rise in part from the humanist insistence on the study of the splendid past as providing the measure of human achievement; but it was also generated by the inability of medieval and most

[1] For an account of Valla as an historian, see F. Gaeta, *Lorenzo Valla* (Naples, 1955), pp. 169–92, from which the quotations are taken.

Renaissance thinkers to believe that any human knowledge
could have been attained without an initial revelation such as
God gave to Adam in Genesis 2:19–20. Any increase in
knowledge marked not a progression, but a restoration, a
return towards the perfection of knowledge before the Fall.
Thus, arguments from antiquity, which in itself is venerable
(**96**/26), had for Sidney and his contemporaries an intellectual
strength which we cannot admit.

It will be agreed from such treatments as Valla and Amyot
provide that the humanists blur the distinction between
history and poetry. This merging of the disciplines can be
found even in humanist treatments of strict literary theory;
it accounts in part for the importance given to heroic poetry
in the sixteenth and seventeenth centuries. Castelvetro
argues that if we possessed an art of history, then it would be
unnecessary to write an art of poetry; the arts run parallel
throughout. Poetry itself may be defined as ' a resemblance
or imitation of history '. The difference between them for
Castelvetro is simply that between a true story and a made-
up story, and also between the prose medium and verse;
indeed, we have here the same old medieval notions of the
nature of poetry which were academic commonplaces in
Europe from the time of Isidore of Seville. The difference
is that in the sixteenth century history is thought capable of
exhibiting something of the persuasive power of poetry.

The positions Valla, Amyot, and others take up are in
part, no doubt, the result of a wish to avoid or moderate
the old conflict between philosophy and rhetoric. History is
offered as a third force, possessing those aspects of both con-
tending parties which appear most useful in providing a
course in wisdom and virtue. To put Valla's or Amyot's
discussion alongside Sidney's casts a good deal of light on
humanist aims and methods. Sidney's and Amyot's desired
end is the same: instruction in virtue. The elements and
the methods of their arguments are the same: they are hand-
ling more or less the same material, more or less in the same
terms. Yet the conclusions are opposed. Amyot asserts that
the arguments show history the supreme discipline; Sidney
that the same arguments show poetry supreme. The common

element is the belief in the importance of persuasive writing. But the whole discussion considered as a treatment of a question of substance may seem to afford such a case of colouring arguments and weighting words as men like Locke at the end of the seventeenth century found irritating beyond endurance in humanist controversy. Is the *Apology* in this part of its argument engaged in a trifling and elegant variation on a stock theme of humanist discussion?

Not altogether; for in the late sixteenth century a new dimension is added to these discussions. This was brought about chiefly by the reforming and rationalising scholars working in northern Europe, most notable of whom is Jean Bodin, whose work Sidney brought to the attention of his brother Robert in 1581. Bodin attempted to introduce *method* (the use of the word recalls the programme of Ramus) into an objective study of the past. With Bodin himself, with Languet, and with many thoughtful historians on both sides the Channel, the study of history was approached in this new spirit largely as a result of the attempts which were being made to see man in society as a constant, above the flux of time and place, and in this way to grapple with the consequences of an emerging *jus gentium*. Many legal studies acquired an historical basis; More and Bacon were not the only lawyers with humanist sympathies who turned historian at some time or other in their careers.

In Elizabethan England the writing of history was taken very seriously. There was a developing emphasis on factual truth, and yet at the same time a more conscious and prouder arrangement of material than medieval historians had sought, with the intention of bringing the material into conformity with the writer's deepest convictions about the nature of man and the purposes of God in the world. History was written and read as a spur to patriotism, as the ground of Protestantism, as a text-book of private and public virtue and national prosperity. An unending stream of histories and translated histories appeared under the patronage of the politicians. Burleigh, for example, received the dedications of an edition of the translation of the *Mémoires* of Commines, of Holinshed's *History*, and of Camden's *Britannia*; and

Leicester seems to have been the special patron of historians.[1]
On all levels of society, history was recognised as a main arm
of Protestant education and propaganda. Archbishop Parker
and Bishop Jewel as well as Burleigh and Leicester were
fully aware of its importance. History reading was enjoined
on the common people in the Book of Homilies.

An earlier but purposeful handling of history and one
directly relevant to Sidney's treatment is to be found in Sir
Thomas Elyot's *Governour* (1531), a book which ' treateth of
the education of them that hereafter may be deemed worthy
to be gouernours of the publike weale'. The wisdom that
such men will require comes largely by experience, and ex-
perience comes in two fashions: first from practice and
second by example. It is experience gathered by example
which constitutes history (*Governour*, Bk. III, xxv–xvi). The
scope of history, as Elyot presents it, is large. It includes all
things that it is necessary to put into the memory—physio-
logy, anatomy, all descriptive science in fact, most of the
Old Testament and the Gospels and the Acts. It seems likely
that Elyot knew Valla's discussion on history; it is pretty
certain that Sidney knew Elyot's eulogy of its study (see notes
108/7ff). Once again we find that Sidney turns arguments
which he had found applied to another discipline into argu-
ments for poetry. Elyot like Amyot had urged that the
wisdom of experience could be picked up even in unlikely
places, even in histories ' interlaced with leasings '; Sidney
argues instead that the admixture of the poetic in the histori-
cal shows that poetry is the more fundamental discipline. And
this is his opinion too in a letter he wrote to his brother
Robert (*Works*, vol. iii, p. 130). History, he tells Robert, is
either to be taken as a simple story with straightforward
chronology, or as a treatise ' which adds to the chronology
many things for profit and ornament: thus Xenophon,
Thucydides, Herodotus, Diodorus Siculus. In treatises you
have principally to note the examples of virtue or vice etc.
Beside this, the Historian maketh himself a discourser for
profite and an oratour, yea a Poet sometimes for ornament.'

[1] See Eleanor Rosenberg, *Leicester, Patron of Letters* (New York,
1955), chap. 3.

Sidney in instructing his brother does not entirely commend this diffused amateurishness of the historian, who ' not professing any art, as matter leades him, he deals with all arts '. ' And that it is which makes me and many others rather note much with our penn than with our minds.' Sidney considers the prime use of histories as mines from which to quarry ' wittie words ', ' sentences ', similitudes, stratagems, and examples. Many passages of the *Apology* show material of this kind which Sidney had himself collected.

The advice to his brother was delivered in haste but seems to contain Sidney's considered judgment. And by the 1580s he was no beginner in historical studies. Greville's *Life* shows how thoroughly Sidney mastered the historical background to contemporary politics of Europe. Many years earlier in advising him, as Sidney was now advising his brother, Languet had thought it superfluous to ' speak to you of reading history, by which more than anything else men's judgments are shaped, because your own inclination carries you to it and you have made great progress in it '.[1]

Sidney as a politician and as a member of Leicester's party can have had no doubt as to the good sense of encouraging the study of history in order to win public support for nationalist and Protestant policies. But the letter to Robert and the *Apology* suggest that he had a theoretical distrust of any over-insistence on the value of history. He is a little suspicious of the superficial, opportunist, and flatly utilitarian character of many historical studies (and we may recall that history included many records of observations which now form part of science). The historian is tied to ' the particular truth of things and not to the general reason of things, that his example draweth no necessary consequence' (**107**/4ff). History does not give sufficient scope for a genuinely intellectual analysis of cause and effect. Its study cannot easily incorporate knowledge into the personality: the historian ' better knowing how this world goeth than how his own wit runneth ' (**105**/26). If the act of knowing could be a certain act, or if all that were required in knowing were the knowledge of ascertainable fact, then history were sufficient.

[1] *Correspondence*, ed. Pears, p. 26.

But history, as Sidney knew it, dealt in the main with the unknown and the unknowable: the historian guesses his way through what can only be a selection of past events and then presents his story deceptively as an arrangement of facts. But in many cases what Sidney calls ' fortune ' (110/30) is invoked to account for the apparent muddle that past events present to an honest recorder. The real causes and pattern of events can never be laid bare. A residual scepticism about the value of history Sidney probably shared with other men of the late sixteenth century. He could have found traces of it in Amyot; it is best known in Montaigne; he would have heard it proclaimed more harshly and nearer at hand by Fulke Greville. But with Sidney those doubts are not so much a part of the total uncertainty of life and of a sense of the vanity in all knowledge which Greville experienced but spring rather from a faith that the true centre of understanding lay not in experience or in memory but in the generalising reason. He anticipates something of the scepticism about the value of history that Swift and Bolingbroke display. He suspects its haphazardness, its absorbing triviality, its lack of guiding rational principle; and it is this lack, Sidney believes, that poetry can supply.

THE DISCIPLINE OF POETRY

So far we have considered poetry in relation to the whole field of knowledge. But plainly poetry has also a history and an economy of its own, which can be regarded with some degree of independence, though always there are incursions from and into other fields of knowledge. Three main traditions of thinking about poetry, and hence of composing poems, mingle in Sidney's time and Sidney's thought: the Horatian, the Ciceronian, and the Platonic.

Horace is by far the most influential and representative single writer on the poetic art as far as the Middle Ages and the Renaissance were concerned. His *Epistle to Piso*, often referred to as the *Art of Poetry*, a work written it would appear for a particular set of literary circumstances in Augustan Rome, touched so skilfully and so generally the whole literary field of its time that it came to be regarded as a body of carefully considered and organised literary precepts. If to a modern reader lacking the inner threads of relevance the *Art* looks something of a jumble, for earlier generations of Europeans it had the character of a book of definitive judgments stamped with the authority of a great poet and with the achievement of antiquity.

In considering the opinions of any sixteenth-century critic or writer we should start with the *Art*, realising that the great shape of Aristotle looms behind Horace in support but is not yet regarded as an ultimate oracle in his own right.[1] Throughout western Europe the beginnings of critical literary analysis are signalled by the rendering into the vernaculars of Horace's *Art of Poetry*. Archdeacon Drant (d. 1578 ?), the originator of those rules for English verse which Spenser and Harvey discussed (Smith, vol. i, pp. 90ff), produced the first English version in 1567; Ben Jonson produced another. On the Continent the first translations of Horace were quickly supplemented by translations and commentaries of Aristotle's *Poetics*, of which Alexander Paccius had produced a Latin text at Venice in 1536. Several commentaries on Aristotle appeared in Italy in the next twenty years, of which Francisco Robortello's (Florence, 1548) is the most important. With the learned critics of the middle and end of the sixteenth century, with Minturno, J. C. Scaliger, Castelvetro, and so on, the profundities of Aristotle are used to weight the elegancies of Horace. Aristotle's *Poetics* is still being approached and understood by means of Horace's *Art*. English criticism so far as it concerns itself with fundamental theory, which it does only to a limited extent, offers a very thin distillation of all this Continental theorising. We cannot be sure that Sidney had read much in the commentaries on Aristotle's *Poetics* (he was more interested in Aristotle's *Ethics* and *Rhetoric*), but he had acquired some knowledge of what Italian critics thought were Aristotelian poetic principles. He certainly knew Horace's *Art of Poetry* and the familiar topics of Horatian criticism.

[1] See Marvin T. Herrick, *The fusion of Horatian and Aristotelian literary criticism, 1531–1555* (Urbana, 1946).

There was a second spirit from antiquity powerfully at work. Right through the Middle Ages the influence of Ciceronian rhetoric lived on, somewhat feebly at times it is true, often strangely transformed or applied, but as an intellectual force which can be felt through all accomplished writing on every subject. When Cicero becomes the humanists' special darling, poetry tends to be subsumed under rhetoric and is regarded, however respectfully, as a metrical and highly ornamented variant of prose. This seems to be the way in which Roger Ascham and Thomas Wilson think of poetry. One of Sidney's aims is to liberate poetry from an absolute dependence on rhetoric without denying it all the benefits of dignity which it had recently acquired from an intimate association with an exalted rhetoric. The essential difference in status between them, as Sidney saw it, is that rhetoric, considered strictly, is another of the ' serving sciences '; it is ' compassed within the circle of a question ' (100/14), whereas poetry is open and uncircumscribed. But the area of discourse governed by Ciceronian rhetoric was too broad and well organised for any writer to escape from completely, and Sidney shows no desire to do so. Cicero was the humanists' ideal not simply because he used the Latin language supremely well, but still more because his conception of the art of letters was all-inclusive, ranging over all fields of knowledge, and on comfortable terms with moral philosophy. Systematising Cicero, Quintilian had provided in the *Institutes of Oratory* full instruction in the arts of speaking, and thereby, he believed, a full education in wisdom and in virtue. This programme the humanists made directly or indirectly their own. Gabriel Harvey in *Ciceronianus* (1577) re-stated it. And often, in consequence of the origins of Cicero's own moral and philosophic interests, contact was made with Plato.

Plato and the medieval and Renaissance Platonisers make up the third force in criticism, and this band of diverse spirits includes Boethius, Augustine, the late-medieval mystical writers, Ficino and other members of the Florentine Academy. Throughout the Middle Ages the orthodox philosophy of beauty was essentially Platonic, but as its context was almost exclusively theological, it scarcely provided a practical aesthetic for any human artistic activity. The beauty of which medieval Platonisers speak is essentially the divine beauty. Things of matter and sense are clogs to the mind seeking to contemplate the unspeakable and perfect essence. To rest the mind in beautiful things made by men is to be checked by dangerous and worthless illusions. But with Ficino and with many of the neo-Platonists of the sixteenth century, especially those who concern themselves with the arts and in particular with the art of painting, the illusionism which is condemned by Plato and by the medieval Platonists is accepted as a means of ascending to God, if it can provide an ideal image.[1] We have noted a formulation of such a theory in Bovelles; we shall find similar notions elaborated with an artistic application in Zuccaro and Lommazo. A part of Sidney's mind responded very easily to these notions.

We must see, if we cannot yet clearly distinguish, these three strains (the Horatian, the Ciceronian, and the Platonic) working in Sidney. His understanding of the nature of poetry is Horatian in main character and derivation, but it is reinforced by a firmer if still mainly indirect knowledge of Aristotle than had been possessed by any earlier theoriser on poetry in England; it is enriched still further with high Platonic notions about ideal forms in art which still retain religious overtones; and it is supported throughout by the technical instructions and moral insistences from an unbroken line of rhetoricians stretching back through the humanists to Quintilian, Cicero, and Isocrates. This is the critical *milieu* we could expect of a man of Sidney's intelligence and interests, placed in his chronological position. For us perhaps it appears an intricate inheritance, a complex of traditions which is almost as difficult to unravel as to see whole.

But Sidney was no Italianate Englishman. He learned much abroad, but what he learned he engrafted sensibly upon English habits and an English education. And there were many things he could have learnt about poetry without crossing the seas. Though English vernacular writing had had few serious intellectual pretensions since the Norman

[1] See André Chastel, *Marcel Ficin et l'art* (Geneva-Lille, 1954), pp. 64ff.

Conquest there was a rich repertory of verbal skills. Comments in the *Apology* as well as the verbal character of Sidney's own poetry show that he was well aware of these native traditions. He was by no means the first Englishman to look at them critically. Although the early humanists were chiefly concerned with the general problem and importance of verbal discourse and concentrated their interests on Latin prose, they were not unmindful of poetry. More wrote poems in Latin and in English. Stephen Hawes, Skelton, Wyatt, and Nicholas Grimald all worked within a humanist frame. A generation and more before Sidney, poetry had been learnedly discussed in England. It had been treated in print at some length by Sir Thomas Elyot and by Luis Vives, for some years after 1523 a Fellow of Corpus Christi, Oxford. Roger Ascham and his Cambridge friends had many ' pleasant talks ' on poetry together; discussing the drama, they adduced ' the precepts of Aristotle and Horace, with the examples of Euripides, Sophocles and Seneca '.

The claims of poetry had been formally put forward in the universities. John Jewel, who was to become the great apologist of the Elizabethan Church, lectured on poetry at Christ Church *c.* 1548. A typical if undistinguished academic oration in humanist style is John Rainolds' *Oratio in laudem artis poeticae*. More elaborate and learned is Richard Wills' *Disputatio de re poetica* (*c.* 1573) with its debts to Vives and Scaliger. Such academic pieces are important. They are cast in the same oratorical form as the *Apology*. They are also reasoned defences of poetry covering many of the same arguments. Sidney's reflections on his own practice as a poet as well as his application of contemporary Continental theory are presented in the *Apology* in a form and mode and context of thought which had long been familiar to educated men in England.

THEORY OF POETRY

Sidney gives two definitions of poetry. ' Poesy therefore is an art of imitation, . . . that is to say, a representing counterfeiting, or figuring forth—to speak metaphorically, a speaking picture—with this end, to teach and delight ' (**101**/ **33–6**). This is the thesis which he examines in the *Apology* to prove the usefulness of poetry. He re-states the proposition again (**103**/28–31): ' it is that feigning notable images of virtues, vices, or what else, with that delightful teaching, which must be the right describing note to know a poet by '.

The definitions are rich in associations. Nearly every phrase could form a text on which to hang an historical discourse drawing on the literary theory and practice of centuries. A writer who used such phrases had his head full of theory and of interpretations whose origins were submerged by repetition. The kernel of both of Sidney's definitions is that poetry is essentially imitation. A theory of poetry as imitation has little currency nowadays except in literary history: it was destroyed, as De Quincey observed, during the early years of the nineteenth century.

✗ IMITATION

In part the theory of imitation is a rationalisation of a naïve response to art, a response which we can still observe in the satisfactions popularly expressed in representational accuracy, in catching a likeness in portraiture for example, or in the verisimilitude of a story or play. Obviously this is imitation in the sense of establishing a convincing illusion of what is represented, and imitation of this kind remains continually satisfying to many people in a way which some theories of art during the last hundred years have been unwilling to admit. Aristotle, to whom we may turn first for a theory of art as imitation, does not disregard this element of naïve illusionism. Art is an elaboration of the instinct of imitation. ' Imitation is natural to man from childhood . . . he is the most imitative creature in the world, and learns at first by imitation. And it is also natural for all to delight in works of imitation. . . . Imitation, then, being natural to us . . . it was through men's original aptitude, and by a series of improvements for the most part gradual on their first efforts, that they created poetry out of their improvisations ' (*Poetics*, 4).

Let it be admitted that exactly what Aristotle meant by

imitation still baffles his commentators. An imprecision in understanding does not matter much here. His full teaching on the subject was presumably not preserved, and even the actual drift of it seems not to have been understood in antiquity by Horace. When the art of letters fell into the clutches of the schoolmasters of the Roman world, a much looser and broader notion of imitation becomes current. Horace usually thinks of imitation as copying what is already created (the common analogy for poetry is with the copy that painting or sculpture makes of a visible object). Moreover, the endless discipline of the schools in marking and re-examining the beauties of their standard texts gave a further thrust to that inescapable tendency of all schools to turn life into contents of books. Often enough imitation comes to be spoken of not as a representation of life but simply as an imitation of life in books—a copying of old authors. Roger Ascham begins his Book on Imitation in the *Schoolmaster*: ' All the workes of nature in a manner be examples for arte to follow. But ' he goes on ' to our purpose '; and his purpose is to show that imitation is a method of learning in school by examining and following earlier writers. In Sidney's time this verbal dependence on old authors is rising into greater prominence in European literary theory. Scaliger shows that in copying Virgil a poet is copying a second Nature. Later, ' following the ancients ' becomes a cry of orthodoxy. Already much of Sidney's argument is based on the belief that the old writers of Greece and Rome provide us with our most reliable models (see **133**ff).

But Sidney throughout is also grappling with the more profound conception of imitation. And men who thought about the arts in the sixteenth century found it necessary to re-forge the whole doctrine and give it a new edge. The question that sought an answer was what, if poetry is an imitation, does poetry imitate ? The answer we should be ready with— that surely the arts in so far as they are imitative imitate the appearances of things or the actuality of events—is certainly to be found in some Renaissance writers. Sidney suggests this when he speaks of the superiority of poetry to philosophy in providing a true lively knowledge (**107**/**13**ff), or when he

commends the forcibleness of a writer (**138**/2). He has no
doubt that a picture of an elephant or a rhinoceros, or a model
of a palace, would immediately be comprehended by the be-
holder (**107**/18ff). But photographic representation or de-
tailed accurate description would not have satisfied him.
Indeed, most Renaissance writers on art (perhaps Leonardo
da Vinci is an exception) would have been puzzled and
depressed by the non-human, non-moral character of photo-
graphic accuracy. No art that they knew was like this: all
arts had their origin and reference in human understanding
and human intention. The modes of apprehending reality
that they had inherited from the Middle Ages would make
them suspicious. And Aristotle, whose theory of art as
imitation rested ultimately on his metaphysics, would confirm
them in these suspicions.

For Aristotle a thing is most accurately represented in the
fullest development of its potentiality. A man is essentially
a man in his prime. The local and temporary disfigurements,
the immediate surroundings, the momentary mood, the acci-
dents of light and shade—all the individual modifications that
contribute to successful photographic realism—these have
no necessary place in Aristotelian imitation. ' We in our way
should follow the example of good portrait-painters, who
reproduce the distinctive features of a man, and at the same
time, without losing the likeness, make him handsomer than
he is ' (*Poetics*, 15). In art then we represent a man in the
likeness of Man. Imitation gives the essential character, not
the surface copy.

A poet best achieves this effect not by description but by
exemplifying how a man behaves. The object of poetic
imitation is actions (*Poetics*, 9). So the poet although he
represents men in his poems does not base his imitation on
the appearance or behaviour of particular men, but on
generalised Man behaving in a characteristically representa-
tive way. Robortello, commenting on Aristotle's *Poetics*, 15,
puts it well. A poet will use imitation properly ' if he does
not consider the actions and behaviour bit by bit of the
character he is presenting; but rather his description will
depend upon a consideration of nature itself and of the whole

pattern of actions and behaviour. So if he wants to make an imitation of an angry person, he will not consider a particular angry man, but the nature and absolute pattern of anger.' This is the same distinction Sidney makes (**102**/25ff). The poet is released from establishing exact correspondence with a distorting actuality. It is on these grounds that the poet's imitation is to be counted in generalised truthfulness superior to an historian's narration: the poet presents not what has happened, but the kind of thing that might happen—' what is possible, as being probable or necessary ' (*Poetics*, 9).

Imitation is the essence of poetry. This is Sidney's thesis. He agrees with Aristotle that it is imitation not versification that distinguishes a poet's writings from all other writings. So ' Homer and Empedocles . . . have really nothing in common apart from their metre; so that, if the one is to be called a poet, the other should be termed a physicist rather than a poet ' (*Poetics*, 1; cp. **102**/16 note).

UT PICTURA POESIS

Aristotle explains the imitative process by comparison with pictorial arts. Such comparisons are common with the ancients (see **102**/25ff), and not unknown to writers of the Middle Ages. But with the great expansion of all artistic activity at the Renaissance the implications of these parallels . between the verbal and the visual arts are worked out much more systematically. The phrase of Horace, *ut pictura poesis* (*Art*, 361), entirely innocent of theory in the original context, comes to underpin the artistic practice and specula- tion of European writers and painters into the nineteenth century.

In the *Apology* Sidney frequently makes recourse to illus- trations drawn from the visual arts. He was himself inter- ested in all the arts. ' There was not a cunning Painter, a skillful Engineer, an excellent Musician, or any other Artificer of extraordinary fame, that made not himself known to this famous Spirit and found him his true friend without hire ' (*Life*, p. 34). References in the *Apology* (**102**/30; **125**/30ff; **126**/34) may well be to pictures he knew in Italy, Austria, or

England. We may recall that he himself was painted by Paul Veronese and met Tintoretto in Venice. Many descriptions in *Arcadia* indicate how satisfying he found the world as spectacle. Art sets forth nature as in a play (**100**/1). The poet spreads a rich tapestry of beauty (**100**/29).

An analogy from the visual arts occurs at several crucial points of his argument: when he is distinguishing the character of ' right poets ' (**102**/25); when he is emphasising the particular force of poetical teaching (**107**/18); in making the distinction between literal accuracy and a true pattern of perfection (**109**/38); on the nature of delight (**136**/32). And they are analogies which support his arguments convincingly.

But we must be careful lest we attach too much meaning to them. It would be as untrue to say of Sidney, as has been all too commonly suggested of Spenser, that poetry for either of them is a surrogate for painting. In his definition of poetry, Sidney has quoted Simonides' dictum of ' a speaking picture '; but he introduced it with the words ' to speak metaphorically ' (**101**/35). And if we take any of his analogies to pieces we shall see that the use of terms of visual sense-perception is metaphorical. When Sidney speaks of the effigy of a just empire provided by Xenophon (**103**/20), or ' that picture of love ' provided by Heliodorus (**103**/24), it is evident that he refers to no visual impressions. Always, the real comparison is not between poetry and the painting which represents what the eye sees but between poetry and a sort of painting which shall shew what the eye ought to make of what it sees (cp. **102**/25ff). It is not in its ability to produce likenesses of sense-impression that poetry has common ground with painting. The common ground is in their method of forming concepts in the mind. It is the conceptualising activities of both which authenticate the parallels between them.

NATURE

All considerations of imitation turn back to one ground. The poet imitates nature. Sidney like every other innovator in the course of English poetry requires the poet to return to a truer knowledge of what he is to imitate. He affirms that all human arts are constituted and tied to nature (**99**/37ff). The imitation of poetry ' hath the most conveniency to nature of all other ' (**114**/5f). What imitation implies obviously depends upon the meaning and the function given to nature.

The word had a great network of meanings, some of which remained in combination to give us our modern ideas of nature; but in the sixteenth century they presented a general configuration and pattern very different from our own. Nature was still thought of as the common mother of us all. It was also the creative and sustaining force in the universe. It was also the part of that force individuated in each man, a man's faculty or ' genius '. It was also the sum or a representative part of what was produced by the generating force in the universe. The concept of nature is then an amalgam of meanings, classical, Stoic, medieval, pagan, and Christian.

As the sum of the created and creating forces in the universe, nature could be spoken of almost as if it stood outside the dominating categories of Christian theology. This was immensely useful. Most medieval writers found themselves in great difficulty when they wished to treat at the ordinary level of society themes concerned with human behaviour and human destiny. The notion of nature, often personified as the goddess Natura, served as a useful working hypothesis in conducting this sort of inquiry.

Nevertheless, in medieval thought only the supernatural world presented a fully intelligible order. The realm of the goddess Natura was subrational: here, blind forces harnessed by necessity worked to unforeseen ends; in this inscrutable process, cruel games with human lives were played by Fate, or Fortune, or Chance.

Perhaps the great intellectual achievement of Christendom in the sixteenth century was that it made the invasion and conquest of the whole natural order by intelligence and rationality credible and acceptable not only to theologians but to ordinary people. However we regard the exploitation in later times of this conquest over the irrational by the rational, the achievement itself in the sixteenth century made possible a fuller Christianisation of life than the Middle Ages ever knew. It released men from the fearful tyranny of fate. It made all creation eloquent of God. It exalted the natural order with the supernatural into one divine order.

It is this new and emergent vision of nature that Sidney holds before him. He believed most firmly that this nature, this ladder of existing forms reaching down from the heavens to man and below, was the product of design not chance. His religious faith and his poetic theory rest on the belief that intelligent design, not chance, is inherent in nature itself. It is from this position that Sidney urges that poetry can provide what history cannot guarantee (cp. **41–2** above), a grasp of the universal design and order; for poetry can make Fortune the well-waiting handmaid of virtue (**111**/28).

What nature meant to Sidney and what he considered the relation of nature and art is set out in the new *Arcadia*, in the dispute between the cruel scheming queen Cecropia and her virtuous captive Pamela (*Works*, vol. i, pp. 402ff). Pamela is embroidering when Cecropia enters; and Pamela in her needlework as in her own appearance was ' paying the tribute of undeceyving skill to so high perfections of Nature ' (p. 403). She ' was woorking uppon a purse certaine Roses and Lillies, as by the finenesse of the work, one might see she had borrowed her wittes of the sorow that owed them, & lent them wholy to that exercise. For the flowers she had wrought, caried such life in them, that the cunningest painter might have learnt of her needle. . . . But the colours for the grounde were so well chosen, neither sullenly darke, nor glaringly lightsome, and so well proportioned, as that, though much cunning were in it, yet it was out to serve for an ornament of the principall woorke' (p. 402). (Here we can learn a good deal of what Sidney thought should be the proper relation between thought and word in a poem.)

Cecropia ' sate down by Pamela: and taking the purse, and with affected curiositie looking upon the worke, Full happie is he (saide she) at least if he knewe his owne happinesse, to whom a purse in this maner . . . is dedicated. In faith he shall have cause to account it, not as a purse for treasure, but as a treasure itselfe. . . .' Pamela dissents. She insists on thinking of things according to their true nature and use; she thinks of what she is making ' even as a verie purse '. Though Cecropia goes on to urge that it is ' the right nature of Beautie to woorke unwitting effectes of wonder ', Pamela will not agree that Beauty is ' but a pleasaunt mixture of naturall colours, delightfull to the eye, as musicke to the eare, without any further consequence ' (p. 403). A purse is still ' a verie purse '. The beauty of a beautiful thing is not simply aesthetic. Woman is beauty, Cecropia argues, as the schoolmen before, and James Joyce since argued; and woman, Cecropia affirms, conquers merely by exhibiting herself, she commands without authority, she persuades without speaking. Pamela becomes very cross at this. The consequences of this aestheticism, as Pamela and Sidney see it, are Epicurean, libertine, atheist, and determinist. ' Each effect hath a cause ', Pamela retorts, even the effect of beauty. Not even beauty is self-originating or self-proclaiming, or else it would have to be explained in the last resort as the work of chance. The discussion on beauty takes a moral turn and the debate on art is swallowed up in the next few pages of the *Arcadia* in Pamela's impassioned argument on divine causality in terms that often recall Boethius. ' You say yesterday was as today [cp. 110/23f]. . . . What doth that argue, but that there is a constancie in the everlasting governour ? ' (p. 407). Chance offers no sufficient explanation. ' Chaunce could never make all thinges of nothing.' ' If nothing but Chaunce hath glewed those pieces of this All ', as if you were to say that things are so ' by nature ', it is ' as much as if you said it is so, because it is so '. And if you claim that all things have their own distinct natures, it is impossible to believe that they could ever make a harmony and perfection without a force and Wisedome above their powers (p. 408). But all the mingling of many separate natures which we call ' this All ' is only ' a conspired ' and excellent unity, in as much as ' a right heavenly Nature ' indeed, as it were unnaturing them, doth so bridle them (p. 409).

Each thing is directed to an end, even speaking and laughing, even beauty, even a purse or a poem. ' This worlde therefore cannot otherwise consist but by a minde of

Wisedome, which governes it ' (p. 410). The true character of nature lies not merely in the assembly which makes up ' this All ' (the natural order), but in another ' right heavenly Nature ' (the supernatural order), in the intelligence which gives the unity, goodness, and beauty to universal nature. At the centre of nature is an inherent rationality which controls and unifies all the multiplicity.

Here then we can discern the ground of Sidney's idea of the imitation of nature in art and how an idea of poetry thus built up could satisfy the demands made by a supreme discipline of virtuous action. Poetry is the representation in words of a process of reason as it works in human affairs. The imitation in poetry is a high realism, not a realism which requires faithful portrayal of trivial detail articulated by mechanical mental processes, but a realism which depends upon the operation of the unified reason in man which constitutes him in the image of God, the reason which is the candle of the Lord. Only thus ' the voice of Nature is the voice of Truth ' (*Works*, vol. iii. p. 259).

Certain consequences follow. Any work of art should pay ' the tribute of undeceyving skill to so high perfections of Nature '. Art observes decorum, respects the truth it adorns, but does not obscure or in any way ' shadow the principall woorke '. Accordingly there are methods used by artists that are to be condemned: in poetry, mere verbalism and fantastical writing (**137**), the attempt to reduce poetry to exhibitionism or entertainment (**139**), and, we may assume, the playful use of the supernatural and the sacred. Such methods ' infect the fancy with unworthy objects ' (**125/27**); they display ' a courtesan-like painted affectation ' (**138/9**). They use art to show art and not to hide art, and they fly from nature and indeed abuse art (**139/32ff**).

THE LANGUAGE OF IMITATION

Sidney does not provide an analysis of the symbolising process that must underlie any theory of poetry. But he must often have been concerned with the problem. After all, much of Renaissance thought and most of Reformation

theology hammered ferociously at these difficulties in estab-
lishing a satisfying relationship between a symbol and what
it symbolised. The Puritans no more smashed images for
fun than Roman Catholics defended trans-substantiation out
of pride and obstinacy. It was all a huge, tangled, contro-
versy continued for generations, but left unconcluded for
each new intellectual age to resume.

One aspect of the problem, the connection between words
and reality, can perhaps be isolated as a literary question. It
is possible to separate two approaches in the late sixteenth
century. One, which, as far as literature is concerned, was
inherited from medieval training in the arts, can be
counted vaguely Aristotelian and rhetorical. It tends to
think of poetry as the product of a distinct art which mediates
between what is known and the distractible mind of man,
prone to fantasies and stored with pictures, by using elabor-
ate, richly coloured language which serves to fix the attention
of the hearer and to recall the appropriate images. Thus a
highly ornamented structure of words represents (almost in
the sense of ' stands instead of ') a truth. In general this is
the elocutionary attitude which we commonly associate with
the late Elizabethan poets, when, as Puttenham put it (*Arte*,
p. 159), language was never ' so well appointed for all pur-
poses of the excellent poet, as when it is gallantly arrayed in
all its colours which figure can set vpon it '.

But there was another approach. Sidney sets the rival
theories alongside each other in Sonnet LVIII of *Astrophil
and Stella*:

> Doubt there hath bene, when with his golden chaine
> The Oratour so farre men's harts doth bind,
> That no pace else their guided steps can find,
> But as he them more short or slacke doth raine,
> Whether with words his soveraignty he gaine,
> Cloth'd with fine tropes with strongest reasons lin'd,
> Or else pronouncing grace, wherewith his mind
> Prints his owne lively forme in rudest braine.

Poems, ed. Ringler, pp. 193-4

According to the elocutionary ideal, the Orator (or poet)
gains his mastery over his hearers with words ' cloth'd with

fine tropes with strongest reasons lin'd '. But in the other theory, the poet works by ' pronouncing grace ', by transforming the meaning direct into word and voice and gesture. This approach is based on traditional teaching in rhetoric on the art of delivery, but in the sixteenth century it acquired a theological colouring, largely through the teaching of Augustine. When John Jewel, lecturing in the humanities at Oxford in the 1540s, delivered his *Oratio contra Rhetoricam*, he heartily decried contemporary rhetorical teaching, concerned as it was with fine tropes and colours. He proposed to abandon rhetoric and turn to poetry instead. What need of childish ornament? ' Truth indeed is clear and simple.' Jewel and Tyndale, Thomas Becon, the later scholars responsible for the Authorised Version of the Bible, and Herbert, govern their use of words as if they afforded a direct ' pronouncing of grace '. They were adopting an Augustinian approach to the use of symbols.[1]

Augustine thought of words in their ordinary use as conventional signs; that is, words are arbitrarily assigned to objects by men and in ordinary use they have no correspondence with things apart from this assignation. But in origin and in their best use, words have an internal, ' natural ' function. By words, ' a master within us ' teaches us the truth. And then words have a kind of permanent integrity and validity. Words used in this way can be audible and visible signs of a direct apprehension of invisible and inaudible truths. Here lay the logical basis of allegory as understood by the early theologians in relation to Scripture and by late-medieval and Renaissance writers in relation to secular literature.

With the Florentine neo-Platonists this notion was taken further. The philosopher or the poet or whosoever is rapt in a divine fury catches a sight of truth directly. It comes by intuition, by the sudden vision of truth. Thus an image, whether named by a word attached to it or apprehended simply as an image in the mind, could have a particular importance; it could disclose in a flash what the use of

[1] See E. Gilson, *Introduction à l'étude de saint Augustin* (Paris, 1929), chap. 5.

conventional words or even of richly coloured language could not provide. Problems concerning this sort of intuition haunted many painters and emblem-makers as well as many critics in the sixteenth century.[1] Leonardo da Vinci argued on this basis that painting is manifestly superior to poetry and all other arts because painting alone can present a series of valid immediate intuitions.

But the different approaches and the rival theories about the language of poetry were not kept distinct. If truth could be seen in a flash, as an image, the handling of the truth by the mind would still involve for an educated Elizabethan, as habitual heir to a rich medieval estate of abstract analysis, a good deal of conceptual thinking. If a picture of a little blind, armed, and naked boy stood as an image of Love, it might be argued (and it was) that simply by looking at the image you could grasp what love is. Countless artists in mineral, paint, and print exploit this assumption in the sixteenth and seventeenth centuries. But even as the artists elaborated their images, and even as their patrons gazed, all their habits of thought were constructing trains and groupings of concepts. In practice the images were dissipated. Thus the process that went on was probably much more like that described by Locke in the assembling of a ' complex Idea ', than the neo-Platonists' flashing recognition of a Platonic Idea. Though in theory this intuitional image is set against the didactic image few men kept them entirely separate. As often, the elocutionary and the Augustinian poetic melt and run into each other.

Sidney's hold on this question we can fairly gather from Sir John Hoskins' *Directions for Speech and Style . . . exemplified . . . out of Arcadia* (probably 1599) (ed. Hudson). Hoskins (born 1566) may never have known Sidney personally, but he knew his friends inside and outside the Inns of Courts, and he knew and admired Sidney's works and took them as standard. What Hoskins has to say about the nature of the language of imitation catches Sidney's own thought as we can piece it together from *Arcadia, Astrophil and*

[1] Cp. E. H. Gombrich, ' *Icones Symbolicae*: the visual image in neo-Platonic thought ', *JWCI*, **11** (1948), 163–92.

Stella, the *Apology*, and the translations. Hoskins begins his
treatise in terms that Ben Jonson borrowed. ' The conceits
of the mind are pictures of things and the tongue is interpreter
of those pictures. The order of God's creatures in them-
selves is not only admirable and glorious, but eloquent; then
he that could apprehend the consequence of things, in their
truth, and utter his apprehensions as truly were a right orator.
Therefore Cicero said much when he said, *dicere recte nemo
potest nisi qui prudenter intellegit* ' (p. 2).

This states exactly Sidney's mind. Hoskins presents the
idea of the double speech of man: the external is the audible
voice carrying the meaning; the internal derives directly
from illumination as Augustine had spoken of it; and this
internal speech corresponds exactly with an apprehension of
the reality of things. It deals in concepts, and the function
of the tongue is to turn these concepts into conventional
sounds. Words are secondary and in a sense not very im-
portant, the envelopes in which concepts are delivered (cp.
140/16). They become important or at least obtrusive when
they are inadequate. For, as Hoskins explains, the order of
God's creatures is beautiful and to the purified thought
directly persuasive, telling its own tale. The difficulty which
confronts a writer, orator, or poet, is to get his conceptual
apprehension of this splendour into words; for ' disordered
speech is not so much injury to the lips . . . or to the thoughts
. . . as to the right proportion and coherence of things in
themselves, so wrongfully expressed ' (p. 2). A failure to
communicate the splendour of creation is a diminution of
that splendour, and of the honour that we should show to
God. The moral responsibility of the poet is heavy.

And this Sidney acknowledges. The writing of poetry,
even considered as an art of words, is a moral activity. A
poet's prime motive force in composition is in response to a
' light of nature '—to a discovery made by reason. This,
kept pure and bright, has to be worked into words by the
exercise of ' an undeceyving skill ', as Pamela worked her
stitches into an embroidery. Writing poetry demands the
most vigorous use of reason. It is an active discovery, a
making of what is to be found. The poet is ' lifted up with

the vigour of his own invention ' to range freely ' within the zodiac of his own wit ' (**100**/21ff). The making is the active recognition of newly discovered patterns, but existing or at least existable patterns, not a making out of nothing. It is *eikastike*, making likenesses, not *phantastike*, fantastic imaginings (**125**/25ff), not the delivery from the brain of much matter which never was begotten by knowledge (**133**/7f). Sidney turns away from the elocutionary ideal as it was taught for instance in the medieval arts of poetry or as it was still being taught by Puttenham. Sidney rejects the notion of a poem as a bright and patterned self-supporting construction where the brightness and pattern are painted on with words, and turns towards the Augustinian ideal which would regard a poem as the setting out of a direct communication of a certain vision of truth—as exhibiting a special ' grace in pronouncing '.

The difficulty we have in re-stating Sidney's position can be considerably reduced if we refer to chronology. Sidney precedes Descartes (1596–1650) by little more than one generation. Sidney thinks as a literary man on the eve of Cartesianism. He is groping forwards to a position from which a man would be able to see all the interesting and important processes as taking place within the mind, where even dealings with external things must be with the mind, not the senses, where ultimately the only truly reliable ideas are those that are invented by the thinker himself.

Sidney draws near to this position. It is clear that he regards the basic process in poetic imitation as the conceptualising, in arriving at ' that Idea, or fore-conceit of the work ' (**101**/4). This mental process Hoskins (p. 42) refers to specifically as ' Sir Philip Sidney's course '. His Muse and Stella, if they were ever different personages, taught him the same lesson:

> . . . look in thy heart and write.

When the full-fledged Cartesian was to do this he found there a mental world in parallel with and independent of the outer world of matter, the world in which his body moved. Sidney could not have been expected to see this clearly with a metaphysician's clarity, but yet it is the system built by Descartes on his *Cogito ergo sum* which Sidney adumbrates in his treatment of the ' other nature ' created by the poet. (Perhaps we should recognise his distrust of history as also a shadow of comprehensive Cartesian doubt.) Yet he comes to these problems not by way of metaphysics but by following trains of thought to be found in contemporary rhetorical and artistic theory.

THE OTHER NATURE

The most famous and most eloquent passage of the *Apology* (**100**/21ff) is an exposition of a few lines in the first chapter of Scaliger's *Poetices*. Sidney makes of the borrowing something different from that which Scaliger intended. Sidney's account of the ' other nature ' created by the poet has resonant religious and transcendental overtones which Scaliger lacks. Sidney had heard these tones elsewhere. He could have heard them abroad in courts and studios and lecture theatres, on his grand tour, but he could also have heard them in London after his return. It is highly characteristic of his easy power of assimilation—though troublesome to an editor —that he should borrow from one obvious author material with which to expound a different type of theory which he must have known about from other theorists who are left unnamed.

We have seen how, in Sidney's eyes, the right use of a poet's reason can discern the inherent reason within universal nature. A poet even on this common Aristotelian basis can provide something, as Fracastorius expresses it in *Naugerius*, ' more perfect, dearer and more agreeable than anything in nature '. The imitation thus produced follows the ideal behind nature rather than the actual in nature which has been warped by fortune and circumstance. Zelmane in *Arcadia* gazes with admiration at Amphialus, ' being such a right manlike man, as Nature often erring, yet shewes she would faine make ' (*Works*, vol. i, p. 212). But if a poet can rise to a higher level of ideal imitation, if he can present this other ' right heavenly Nature ' of which Pamela spoke, which as it were ' unnatures Nature ', then his imitation certainly takes on something of the character of a new creation.

The whole idea of creation was still generally regarded as the prerogative of God. Whatever early sixteenth-century critics may appear to us to say, it is always best to assume that they are thinking of a poet's work as fiction-making, not as creation: their verb is *effingere*, not *creare*. And Sidney certainly does not think of poetry as a creation in any sixteenth-century sense of the word (see **100**/21ff note).

But the change was coming. This notion of poetry as a creation, a notion which was to have an influential course in European literature, was already in embryo in neo-Platonic speculation. We have already noticed that Bovelles at the beginning of the century took up the Augustinian thought of the medieval Franciscans on the two faces of the soul and how he spoke of the mind as the efficient cause of intellectual species. Ficino had elaborated similar doctrine from Plato and applied it to the arts of men; in this way the neo-Platonists accepted the illusionism condemned by Plato and used it as a means of getting at the Divine Idea. Human powers are comparable in mode of working with the divine power. What God creates in the world by His thought, man conceives in himself by intellectual act and expresses it in language, puts it into his books, and makes a copy of it by using earthly materials.[1]

Speculation of this sort fertilised artistic theory, and the times were propitious for development. During the Counter-Reformation towards the end of the sixteenth century the need for a comprehensive theory of art was felt to be compulsive. Sidney the eager Protestant politician and humanist was fully aware of this need to establish a relevant, consistent, and solid foundation for Protestant art. Hence his interest in the great Huguenot writers of France, where the problem was more urgent and had been faced earlier. During the 1580s also in Italy and somewhat later in Spain a conscious attempt was being made to provide a religious sanction to the artistic exploits of the humanists and the pictorial artists. The

[1] M. Ficino, *Theologia platonica*, xiii, 3; cp. Chastel, *op. cit.*, pp. 59ff.

demand for theory which should provide an ultimate justifi-
cation (or condemnation) of art was European, but it took
different forms in different countries according to their
different faiths and national policies and the social position
of their artists.[1] Inevitably such efforts in theorising meant
an increase in discipline and control. The belief that human
art, cauterised by the fiercest orthodoxy, can be an imitation
of the work of God was held most exuberantly in Spain.
Among the Jesuits on the other hand, as represented by
Jacobus Pontanus in his popular *Institutiones Poeticae* (Ingol-
stadt, 1594), any idea of creation on the poet's part is com-
pletely excluded: poetry is tolerated as a branch of moral
wisdom, and the charms of poetry are permitted as a conces-
sion to human weakness. The lyres, Muses, rivers, trees, a
poet talks about are acceptable just because they are, as
Sidney would say slightingly, 'wholly imaginative' (**101**/7).
Their use is fictitious, ' well-known to all, but believed in by
none '. This is the sort of trivialising, aesthetic approach to
poetry which we find Puttenham defending (*Arte*, pp. 111–
112), and Sidney throughout all his work rebutting.

But in many countries with many writers there are attempts
to work out less restricted theories than the Jesuit's, in which
the poet can be viewed as an imitator in some slight sense of
the divine processes of creation. Usually such views are care-
fully enfolded in classical mythology. To give some psycho-
logical substance to such bold theories, great play was made
by writers of different persuasions, by Ronsard most notably,
but also by du Bartas, Tasso, Chapman, with the old and
venerable notion of the ' divine fury ' (see note **130**/7ff), as
found in Plato's *Ion*. Possessed by this fury, a poet's spirit
was thought to rise to a direct awareness of the divine har-
mony and acquire a supernatural wisdom. This divine fury
was advanced to the status of a whole ethos in *De Gl' Heroici
Furori* (1585) which Giordano Bruno wrote in England and

---

[1] See C. Dejob, *De l'influence du Concile de Trente sur la littérature et
les beaux-arts* (Paris-Toulouse, 1884); G. Toffanin, *La Fine dell' Umane-
simo* (Turin, 1920), pp. 159–62, whence the quotations from J. Pontanus
are taken; E. R. Curtius, *op. cit.*, pp. 547–72, with particular reference
to Spain.

dedicated to Sidney. In this book Bruno has something to
say about poetry and many examples to demonstrate what
poetry is like. But it is not what Sidney thinks poetry is. No
Englishman in the 1580s was less of a ' poor layman ' as far
as heroic furies were concerned than Sidney, as with mock
humility he pretended to be in Sonnet LXXIV of *Astrophil
and Stella*; yet his view is fairly summed up by an ironical
dismissal:

> Some do I heare of Poets' furie tell
> But (God wot) wot not what they meane by it.

Sidney's idea of the ' other nature ' does not depend on a
' divine fury ' for its motive force. It is the product of what
we have seen was a much more controllable, if no less vigor-
ous activity, the exercise of judgment and right reason.

Sidney's belief that the poet can deliver a second and a
golden world is related to his belief in the importance of the
conceptualising process. It is the corollary to the answer he
returned to a basic question posed by several critics of art at
the end of the sixteenth century: how are sense-impressions
related to the mental processes of the artist? This problem
in art was worked out most carefully at this time by Federico
Zuccaro and Giovanno Paolo Lommazo. Lommazo (born
at Milan in 1538), a painter of some ability, becoming blind,
turned to theory and literary work instead, and published
Trattato dell' arte della pittura, scultura et architettura (1584–
1585) and *Idea del tempio della pittura* (1590). The *Trattato*
was translated in part into English before the end of the
century at the instigation of the miniaturist Nicholas Hilliard,
with whom Sidney on occasion, as we know, discussed techni-
calities of painting. Federico Zuccaro (born in Rome in
1543), a more notable artist than Lommazo, painted in Eng-
land for a short period though his book *L'Idea de' pittori,
scultori et architetti* was not published till 1607. But the ideas
of both men were representative of some advanced thinking
about the pictorial arts in the last years of the sixteenth and
first years of the seventeenth centuries and were familiar to
some intellectual circles in England.

Minor differences there are said to be between Lommazo's

and Zuccaro's theories, but they are closely at one in their assertion that the Idea in the artist's mind is the regulating principle in all he fashions, and that he is independent of sense-impressions save in as much as his senses can help him to body forth his Idea. In Sidney's terms the artist is freed from the limiting dependence on nature if he can apprehend the 'right heavenly Nature' through his 'fore-conceit' or Idea.

But it is worth quoting from Zuccaro at some length to show how close is the correspondence in thought with Sidney (**100f**). Zuccaro thus describes the origin of the Idea in God and the rôle of the Idea in the work of the artist:

Almighty God, the great and supreme cause of all things, in his manner of working which is uncompelled by necessity, contemplates within Himself the Idea through which He comprehends in a single glance everything that has been, is, will be and can be. This Idea which He has within His mind is consubstantial with Him, since in Him it is not and cannot be *accidenter*, as it is pure act. Thus, in His goodness and in order to show in miniature the high excellence of the divine art, He created man in His image and likeness, incorruptible in soul because of its immaterial substance, endowed with the power of intellect and will, so that he might be the superior and lord over all creation in the world, except the angels, and become as it were a second God. He wished still to give him the faculty of forming within himself an intellectual Idea so that he might know all created forms and fashion (*formasse*) within himself a new world, and thus internally possess and enjoy in having spiritually what externally in nature he rejoices over and rules. Furthermore with this Idea, imitating God as it were, and rivalling nature, He gave him the ability to produce an infinite number of artefacts resembling nature's, and in pictures and carvings make a New Paradise appear on earth. Man nevertheless in forming this internal Idea acts very differently from God, for God has a single Idea which comprehends all substances and includes everything inalienably, because all that is in God is God. But man forms many Ideas in himself because the things of which he forms the Ideas are distinct from himself, and thus his Ideas exist *accidenter*. Moreover, man's Ideas have low origins in the senses.[1]

This is obviously a psychological account of the artistic process which has been fitted into a theological, indeed with Zuccaro a Thomistic, background. Lommazo presents a very similar account, but with more Platonic colouring.

The doctrine is esoteric, as Sidney admits (**101**/24). But he sets it out quite faithfully and clearly. His own exposition plainly indicates the theological foundations of the theory (**101**/14ff): the use of the terms ' Idea or fore-conceit ' (**101**/4), and ' another nature ' (**100**/23) suggest the doctrine directly; and Sidney's golden world with its ' pleasant rivers, fruitful trees, sweet-smelling flowers ' is undeniably that New Paradise on earth that Zuccaro's artist designs. We must believe that Sidney is writing with a direct knowledge of advanced contemporary theorising on art, acquired, probably even formulated in part, by Sidney himself in eager discussion in courts and chambers rather than drawn from books.

In the history of the pictorial arts, Lommazo and Zuccaro are spoken of as theorists of a phase of late mannerism, and the particular phase that they represent is usually considered as but an episode in the development of European art.[2] If we require a label for Sidney's theory of poetry, the epithet ' mannerist ' may perhaps be borrowed.

UTILE ET DULCE

Sidney's theory of poetry implies a doctrine of man. Feigning together with ' delightful teaching ' is the mark of the true poet (**103**/30). The end of poetry is ' to teach and de-

---

[1] Translated from F. Zuccaro, *L'Idea de' pittori, scultori et architetti* (Turin, 1607), vol. i, 7, p. 50 as quoted in E. Panofsky, *Idea* (Leipzig, 1924), p. 108.

[2] See Anthony Blunt, *Artistic Theory in Italy, 1450–1600* (Oxford, 1940), chap. 9; Rensselaer W. Lee, ' *Ut Pictura Poesis* : the humanistic theory of painting ', *Art Bulletin* (College Art Association of America, N.Y.), **22** (1940), 197–269, particularly 207ff.

light ' (**101**/36). These famous words belong to Horatian criticism.

> Aut prodesse volunt, aut delectare poetae,
> Aut simul et jucunda et idonea dicere vitae.
>
> *Art*, 333-4
>
> Poets would either profit or delight;
> Or mixing sweet and fit, teach life the right.
>
> B. Jonson's trans.

Wherever we look into medieval and Renaissance literary history, profit and delight we shall see engaged in an interminable see-saw, now one up, now the other; occasionally we may find them in equipoise. But in the late sixteenth century the pedagogical character given to the verbal arts, and the rising prestige of poetry among these arts, weight the balance heavily in favour of didacticism. Nevertheless, there were some who in theory as well as many who in practice set the pleasures of poetry very high: Minturno and J. Pontanus in their different ways, but particularly Castelvetro: ' Poetry was fashioned principally for delight and not for utility, as Aristotle has shown '; but other critics read Aristotle differently.

There is no doubt at all that Sidney considers the didactic element more important. His whole treatise and argument hang on the usefulness he finds in poetry. The delight we have in poetry is real and substantial, but it is instrumental to the major end. Poetry has a supreme advantage as a teaching discipline because it can make the discipline a pleasure. This is suggested again and again in the *Apology*. And Sidney thinks of the delight as good in itself not simply as palatable; thinking thus he agrees with the thought of his age.

Most of the humanists rejected the fierce physical asceticism which in the Middle Ages had edified even the most exalted spiritual lives. The issue had been first raised most forcibly by Lorenzo Valla in *De Voluptate* (1440), an impetuous justification of human nature, expressing an optimistic belief that nature itself provides in man a scale of values which man scorns at his peril. The desire for *voluptas* is a datum of human existence. Pleasure whencesoever it comes concerns both mind and body. ' We cannot live without taste, hearing, smell and touch; so that a man who dares to fly against nature, ignores his own good.'

We need not argue Valla's libertinage or his orthodoxy. The importance of his *De Voluptate* is that it is daringly articulate. It became one of the most widely read encouragements to a belief that the natural desires of men are legitimate. Eventually new attitudes of behaviour arising from this belief were to penetrate everywhere and to afford the moral bases for the modern sense of ' humanism '. Already in the sixteenth century they signal the decline of rigorism. They are accompaniments of the assertion of the superiority of the active and secular over the contemplative and monastic life. They reflect the intellectual interpretation of existence according to which the natural is absorbed into the supernatural. The characteristically medieval sense of the banishment of man as an exile from heaven onto an unreal earth faded. For the first time in England it was possible instead to have a sense that an innocent and unshadowed joy in the things of this world was proper and lawful.[1]

Sidney agreed that in man there is a pleasure-seeking principle which is to be respected. It has to be used as the trigger of knowledge and virtue. ' Who will be taught, if he be not moved with desire to be taught ? ' (**112/32**). Until men ' find a pleasure in the exercise of the mind, great promises of much knowledge will little persuade them that know not the fruits of knowledge ' (**98/6**). And virtue is seen to have a delightful and attractive grace (**119/20ff**).

In distinguishing delight from laughter, which he considers in the main a reaction to a sense of incongruity, Sidney emphasises that we delight in things ' that have a conveniency to ourselves, or to the general nature ' (**136/16**). Delight is made up of a recognition of harmony, perfection, goodness, success. It makes an appeal to the understanding and judgment, for astonishment or admiration is a part of it. So too is a certain dilation of spirit. Delight is active, or to speak

[1] See Don Cameron Allen, *SP* 41 (1944), 1–15; Edward Surtz, *The Praise of Pleasure in More's Utopia* (Cambridge, Mass., 1957), chaps. 1–7.

more accurately, the accompaniment or mode of certain intellectual and moral activities.

Delight has historically a prime place in theories of imitation. ' It is natural for all to delight in works of imitation ', Aristotle observed. We can see this from experience. ' Though the objects themselves may be painful to see, we delight to view the most realistic representations of them in art, the forms for example of the lowest animals and of dead bodies. The explanation is to be found in a further fact: to be learning something is the greatest of pleasures not only to the philosopher but also to the rest of mankind, however small their capacity for it; the reason of the delight in seeing the picture is that one is at the same time learning—gathering the meaning of things ' (*Poetics*, 4). And Sidney would go further. Poetry by using words which mediate truth directly can supply an adequate mental substitute for sense-experience and so catch something of the delight of the senses itself. The imitation in poetry can thus satisfy the appetite of the whole mind which seeks for relationships, correspondences, and patterns, as well as for images of experience, and the mind itself comes to experience an excited contentment when it finds these satisfactions.

THE POWER TO MOVE

Delight gives to instruction the power to move. Being moved does not simply imply the display or discharge of emotion or perturbation of the mind. It is the mental stimulation to action that is produced by emotional agitation. By being moved men are persuaded to do something, or to believe something that can serve as a ground for future action. According to Sidney's explanation, tragedy ' with stirring the affects of admiration and commiseration teacheth the uncertainty of this world ' (**118/1**): so it can modify the actual policies of rulers. Heroic poetry moves similarly. By stirring the passions, poetry exercises a control upon the will and in this way initiates courses of action. ' Moving is of a higher degree than teaching, it may by this appear, that it is well nigh the cause and the effect of teaching ' (**112/30**ff). By delighting, poetry can move a man to perform what it teaches. Poetry thus has a threefold aim: to teach, to delight, and to move. The notion has a long history (see **112**/30ff note).

A threefold aim was commonly admitted for oratory in the system of ancient rhetoric. Cicero spoke of the accomplished orator as one who speaks to prove or demonstrate, to delight, and to move. To prove a case is the basic task, to delight is part of the necessary charm the orator must exercise in order to ingratiate himself with his audience, to move is to sway minds in order to ensure the triumph of the case. Since rhetorical theory and poetic practice ran so closely together throughout the Middle Ages and the Renaissance, it was inevitable that the threefold aim of ancient rhetoric should be extended to poetry. The three aims had been usually associated with three styles: demonstration with the ' low ', plain style, delighting with an easy ' middle ' style, moving with a powerful ' high ' style. These three styles of oratory were likewise transferred to poetry in the Middle Ages and continued to occupy a place in practice and in theory until Wordsworth's time. All Renaissance critics are aware of these distinctions.

The three aims of oratory and the three appropriate styles were often discussed in connection with the three kinds of oratory which the ancients distinguished: judicial oratory, the most inclusive kind, which was concerned with proving guilt or innocence; the epideictic, concerned with expressing praise or blame; the deliberative, which sought to arrive at a decision which should guide action. Outside the law courts and public assemblies these three kinds could not be strictly kept apart, and the usefulness of the distinction was almost completely lost when practical rhetoric (actual speech-making for political or civic purposes) largely disappeared towards the end of the Roman Empire. For the next thousand years and more, European discourse was dominated not by the demands of forum or senate but by the needs of the Christian pulpit. *On Christian Doctrine* by St Augustine, the professor of rhetoric converted to the faith, enables us to see the process by which the old system of rhetoric is adapted to its new purpose. A sermon is not designed primarily to prove, or to praise or to deliberate. The sermon is a discourse which shows how a passage of Scripture directs us to live a good and faithful life. The threefold aim is collapsed into one: a preacher preaches to move men to holiness. The three different styles become tactical instruments to be employed as they are found appropriate.

Augustine's dissolving and reforming of the old rhetorical programme is of lasting importance. He laid a masterful hand on the traditional theory of discourse and moulded it to fit his single-minded but comprehensive purpose. Through the Renaissance, modern European literary theory develops by secularising these Christian re-formulations of the ancient doctrine of rhetoric. Augustine's summary in the last book of *On Christian Doctrine* contains the germ of a whole theory of literature which many Renaissance writers, including Sidney, made their own: ' to speak eloquently, is to speak wisely as well, and is simply to express truths which it is expedient to teach, in fit and proper words ' (*PL* 34, col. 119). Augustine has already synthesised the Horatian, the Ciceronian, and the Platonic principles.

Of course Sidney is not modelling his theory on Augustine directly. Nor for that matter was Minturno, who repeated Augustine's statement of the triple aim ' to teach, to please, and to move ' in place of Cicero's ' to prove, to please, and to move '. Nevertheless, the influence of Augustine on Petrarch and many other humanists, on the Florentine neo-Platonists, and of course on most of the Reformers, we know to have been profound and multiplex.[1] We should perhaps recognise that the typical Renaissance idea of the Christian poet as a mover to virtuous action is in direct line of descent through a thousand years of ecclesiastical culture from Augustine's ideal of the Christian preacher.

THE QUESTION OF TRUTH

Sidney's earnestness obliges us to ask what he conceived to be the relation between poetry and the truth. He gives a

[1] See P. O. Kristeller, ' Augustine and the early Renaissance ', in *Studies in Renaissance Thought and Letters*, pp. 355–72.

brief, formal answer when he replies to the charge that poets are liars. The poet is no liar, because he does not affirm. The poet makes no claim that his propositions are true. Yet this rebuttal, sufficient for the exposition of his theme, does not face the question that is implicitly raised by many other passages of the *Apology*. Sidney asserts for instance that poetry makes truth shine through the fog of sense (**119**/19), that it is an art of true doctrine (**130**/33). And of course the whole treatment of imitation and the ' other nature ' would be a superfluity, all moonshine and self-deception, if no logical relation at all were to be established between the fiction and reality.

Where Sidney dilates on the ' other nature ' he is borrowing from Scaliger. Scaliger, denying that poetry is to be thought of as good writing *simpliciter*, shows that the end of all discourse is to establish faith or belief; all discourse is then persuasive and for that reason is open to rhetorical assessment. Scaliger goes on to show that all the issues with which rhetoric deals (the demonstrative, the judicial, and the deliberative) are included within the scope of poetry, and that all the relationships involved between speaker and audience in communication are also exploited by the poet. Scaliger shows, in short, that poetry is a kind of consolidated art of persuasion which at all points goes beyond the frontiers of traditional rhetoric. Just as the ordinary life of man offers a field in which rhetoric picks out its relevant material, poetry concerns another composite and ordered field, a manufactured world, another nature made of words.

Sidney certainly does not stress the rhetorical character of Scaliger's second nature, yet he can scarcely have failed to observe it, or to have realised its importance. For he was, we know, interested in these theoretical aspects of rhetoric. Sir John Hoskins regarded Aristotle's *Rhetoric* ' as the directest means of skill to describe, to move, to appease, or to prevent any motion whatsoever; whereunto whosoever can fit his speech shall be truly eloquent. This was my opinion ever; and Sir Philip Sidney betrayed his knowledge in this book of Aristotle to me before ever I knew that he had translated any part of it. For I found the two first books Englished

by him in the hands of the noble studious Henry Wotton '
(95/1 note) (*Directions*, p. 41). Aristotle treated his material in
the first two Books of *Rhetoric* not as a practical art but as
offering the underlying theory of an art which deals with the
presentation of probable knowledge.

This is the way in which Sidney views the logical status of
poetry. If knowledge could be full and perfect, if all things
could be known, then the historian's bare ' was ' (110/20ff)
might give us ground enough for action; or again, if the
light of reason were unhindered and undarkened, then we
could find and trust the philosopher's generalisations abso-
lutely. But knowledge is uncertain, conditional, and partial,
and reason is bounded. Hence truth is accessible only in
terms of ' probabilities '—or to use Sidney's excellent phrase,
as ' conjectured likelihood ' (110/25).

Antiquity had recognised that there are degrees of cer-
tainty in knowledge, and had related different logical arts to
the degrees that were to be distinguished. It had devised a
method of dealing with knowledge which aimed at the cer-
tainty of scientific demonstration; this was logic proper. But
it envisaged also an art to deal with knowledge lacking this
certainty, with matters of opinion in ethics, politics, and the
arts; and this it knew as dialectic, ' the logic of probabilities '.

In the sixteenth century, as we have seen, the ambition of
Ramus was to formulate a keen exact instrument for deal-
ing with this same uncircumscribed range of thought and
its uncertain status as truth, to devise a verbal calculus of
probability. Ramus, following Rudolph Agricola, denied
the distinction which the ancients and the scholastics had
made between a logic concerned with certainty and a logic
of opinion—dialectic. There is for Ramus only one, viz.
dialectic. All human knowledge is uncertain and rests on
fragile particulars. As a result Ramists usually tend to stress
the importance of specials or particular examples in order to
prove universal propositions.

Although man may be ignorant of all things, this is not
in any sense to declare that he should not seek or that he
cannot invent, in view of the fact that he has naturally in

himself the power to understand all things; and when he
shall have before his eyes the art of invention by its univer-
sal kinds, as a sort of mirror reflecting for him the universal
and general images of all things, it will be much easier for
him by means of these images to recognise each single
species, and therefore to invent that which he is seeking.[1]

Thus all specials or individuals are identified and located
by the generalising power of the art of invention.

Aristotle had dealt with proof of this sort in *Rhetoric*, I, 11,
19; it depends upon ' the relation of part to part, of like to
like when both come under the same genus, but one of them
is better known than the other. For example, to prove that
Dionysius is aiming at a tyranny, because he asks for a body-
guard, one might say that Pisistratus before him and Thea-
genes of Megara did the same, and when they obtained what
they asked for, made themselves tyrants. . . . All these ex-
amples are contained under the same universal proposition,
that one who is aiming at a tyranny asks for a bodyguard.'
The proof is from a particular to a particular, from Pisistratus
to Dionysius. Of course such an argument is from analogy;
it assumes the validity of the inductive process and provides
no demonstration, but simply a probability.

But this is exactly what Sidney's understanding of poetry
requires. A poem is an example, the paradigm of Aristotle's
Rhetoric. It does not seek to give demonstrative certainty;
it cannot, and the affairs of human life are not the sort of
material which can be brought to certain demonstration.
But a poem does provide an example dealing with one human
situation which implies a reference to another human situa-
tion. It can intend this transfer because all life, all nature is
coherent, organised, pervaded by general reason. That the
ground of ' this All ' is reason guarantees the validity of an
argument from example.

To recapitulate then. In poetry by reference to the univer-
sals the poet creates another nature. This is the material
which he uses for his persuasion to virtue. Each poem con-

---

[1] *La dialectique de M. Pierre de la Ramée . . . en deux livres* (Paris,
1576), Pt. i, p. 37.

sidered as a form of argument is a paradigm or example. It is a construction controlled by reason in its conception, and working by reasonableness in its argument, and achieving its establishing faith by relying on the rationality of its hearer. As a verbal statement it is not an affirmation but a ' conjectured likelihood '. On the other hand, the truthfulness of the relationship between the poem and the ' fore-conceit ' is worked out by the exercise of an undeceiving skill in art. The poet in his poem presents us with a working small-scale model of a part of reality and thereby discloses the true order and motion of the finite world in which we live.

That Sidney believes that poetry considered in respect of its logical status is essentially example is made plain throughout the *Apology*, most explicitly when he instances the fable of Menenius and the parables of Nathan and of Christ. By treating poetry as example he has surmounted all the inadequacies that are attached to the earlier Renaissance view of poetry as allegory, as veiled theology or moral philosophy. Implicit is also a denial that verse is an essential of poetry. The truth of poetry is not to be discovered by stripping off the poetic ornaments. It is enunciated directly on the level of ' conjectured likelihood '. It is visible as a total reflection which stands beside the reality and has a sort of independence, and is produced by viewing the reality in the divine mirror of general reason of which Ramus speaks.

THE POET

When Coleridge started to write about poetry in a famous chapter in the *Biographia Litteraria*, he continued and ended by writing about the poet. In the *Apology* the poet has a character only as an embodiment of the art: ' yet say I and say again, I speak of the art and not of the artificer ' (111/20). A striking example of Sidney's tendency to merge, even in his syntax, the poet into the art is seen in 115/27ff; and in 110/19f, where the poet is compared with history, and 115/32-4, where poetry becomes itself the ' workman '. This lack of distinction between the art and the artist is a sure sign that Sidney in general is not much concerned with the mental state of a man writing poetry, that aspect of literary composition over which most modern criticism lingers.

Yet the poet is named often enough in the *Apology*. He is presented as the composite of the great poets of the past. He has an inherited dignity: poets were the first light-givers, the deliverers of knowledge, the fathers of learning (**96**/12ff), the first bringers-in of civility (**114**/34), the right popular philosophers, the monarchs of all learning (**113**/19). And as the end of knowledge is virtuous action, so the poet is a teacher of virtue (**103**/5), the kindler of courage (**127**/5ff). In times past, Sidney remembers, the poet had a rôle in the religious life of a nation (**98**/20ff, **141**/33).

This is an ideal of the poet drawn from antiquity, and most readily to be compared with the ideal of the orator as set out by Cicero and Quintilian. The *Apology* seeks to show that this is the permanent ideal. Poets should still be grave and wise men able to give national counsel, men such as other lands knew in Sidney's time: George Buchanan, whom Sidney mentions with profound respect (**131**/20, **137**/17), or Pierre Ronsard, the greatest of the practising poets of contemporary Europe, whom Sidney does not mention at all. Sidney believes that the poet should still teach moral virtue to governors and always work to the greatest good of his country. In beautifying his mother-tongue, the poet fashions it as an instrument of national power and glory and, as a devoted patriot, rightly earns the laurels which victorious captains wear.

The poet is given no private character. His worth is publicly displayed, and the high status which he should hold is the recognition of his usefulness to his national society. He is the conscience and the mouthpiece of those who guide the state. His sympathies are aristocratic; better still if his origins are. Sidney significantly finds ' in the Earl of Surrey's lyrics many things tasting of a noble birth, and worthy of a noble mind ' (**133**/23). Surrey's nobility is part of his poetic achievement. In origin and in destination, poetry relates to kings and emperors, cardinals and chancellors, great warriors and great men of church and state.

In transferring the ideal poet of antiquity into his own time and society, Sidney makes him a courtier—a courtier after Castiglione's model, or one of Elyot's governors, a man skilled in all the arts of social control through words which a prince may need, a man who clearly envisages the highest good of his prince and people and is able by the force and attractiveness of his utterance to recommend these highest goods. If our democratic heritage leads us to assume too readily nowadays that courtiers must be gilded butterflies, we could recall the lives, works, interests, and also the frustrated ambitions of the ' happy, blessed trinity ' of poets, Sidney himself, Sir Edward Dyer, and Fulke Greville. Or better still remember Sidney's own example of Nathan the prophet (115/16). For the courtier-poet should be able to play Nathan's rôle also, as Sidney himself played it, in a less sublime situation, when he addressed his bold letter to Queen Elizabeth exhorting her not to marry the Frenchman, Alençon.

A poet should write for the instruction of his prince; but he is not apparently thereby committed to publication. If the work was read and marked in the governing circles to which it was directed, that apparently was enough. In fact, as we know, Sidney himself published nothing during his lifetime; and the *Apology* under its mock self-depreciation conceals a certain disdain for the whole business of publication through the booksellers. The subtle mind theorising freely on the nobility of discourse seems still to have retained something of the ancient prejudice ' as if it were ', as Puttenham puts it (*Arte*, p. 21), ' a discredit for a Gentleman, to seeme learned, and to shew himselfe amorous of any good Art '. And perhaps Sidney shows something of the apprehension of an amateur moving in the professional world of European men of letters, as well as a self-interested mockery which seeks to dissociate itself from what pedants, sycophants, and hackwriters can be represented as having made their own. Time brought its revenge on Sidney. All too often he has been regarded as a poet of easy sentiment; and the light tone, the deliberate gentlemanly carelessness, the allusiveness of the *Apology* may have promoted a solid argument for the original audience, but they have persuaded many later readers that the whole is a gifted amateur's rhapsody. Sir Philip

Sidney, like Sir Peter Blakeney, another sweet enemy of
France, was decidedly serious, well informed, and com-
petent; but it irked them both to appear so.

Sidney is anxious to set before his contemporaries what
they could make of poetry. The charges that can be made
against the worth of poetry are prompted by the conduct of
writers who do not clearly envisage the ideal. So he speaks
for others as well as for himself when he deprecates his own
' unelected vocation ' (95/32). All of them must ' look them-
selves in an unflattering glass of reason ' (132/28). They
have still not got their sights high enough and their aim
straight. They are still ' poor poets ' (123/2), objects for
sympathetic contempt, half-hearted writers, paper-blurrers
who need to take the business of poetry more seriously, but
not necessarily more solemnly, who require, above all, more
self-discipline. As a result of the carelessness of these poet-
apes (141/25), only base men are attracted by the rewards of
the printers (132/3), and poetry altogether is dishonoured.

Sidney briefly examines what is required of the new poet.
He repeats the old tag that the poet is born not made (132/
36). The character of this inborn ability is not clearly set
out. He thinks of it as an inclination of talent rather than as
an absolute, innate faculty. ' And like as in beholding a
paynted Table, or in reading the verses of a Poet, we imagine
not therefore that there was a peculiar and immediate abilitie
of paynting or versifying in the mynd or sovereyne part of
their soule; but we referre those skilles and al other like, unto
Wit and Will ' (*Works*, vol. iii, p. 334). For, although Sidney
speaks of poetry as the work of a ' divine force ', he does not
conceive of this as daemonic possession nor does he hold any
literal belief in inspiration except in relation to the Scriptures.
Though he is willing to use Plato's theory of the divine char-
acter of the poetic gift to reject Plato's charge of liar against
the poet, he states plainly that Plato ' attributeth unto poesy
more than myself do, namely to be a very inspiring of a divine
force, far above man's wit ' (130/7). And Sidney's reason
for refusing to believe that there is a ' peculiar and immediate
abilitie . . . of versifying ' is not far to seek. To do so
would be to cherish immodestly inflated notions of human

ability. Sidney takes the Christian faith seriously. Only in the Scriptures can the Christian recognise this ' very inspiring of a divine force '. Poetry is, as he maintains throughout the *Apology*, a human, non-divine art. ' Plato found fault that the poets of his time filled the world with wrong opinions of the gods, making light tales of that unspotted essence ' (**129**/13); ' they had not the light of Christ ' (**129**/26). The Scriptures repel Plato's charge; human poetry written by faithful Christians escapes it.

Sidney's indirect treatment of the motive power of poetic composition shows that he thinks of it as operating at a much slacker intensity than that of a ' divine fury '. If a man's talent is ' inclinable ' to poetry (and this is surely a sober enough way of referring to a divine gift), then let him look into the ' unflattering glass of reason '. There he will find that the art of poetry consists in imitating the mode of working of the rationality inherent in universal nature. Art, invention, and exercise, these are three things that make a poet (**133**/1), as Ben Jonson sets out at greater length in *Discoveries*. Here again Sidney returns poetry to the medieval discipline of rhetoric. But so overriding is the principle of idealised realism towards which his theory tends that he concludes his discussion on the nature of the poet with the old notion that the highest art is the art which conceals art. So, just as in what he has to say the poet produces an ' other nature ', so in the method of saying it the poet should appear to reproduce another ' natural ' process, and use as it were a ' second natural voice '. Here again we may feel Sidney's sympathy with the Ramist programme (cp. **33–4**). Art and the ' method of nature ' converge. By the use of art, invention, and exercise a man with a talent ' inclinable ' to poetry makes himself what he is by nature, a poet.

THE POEM

The poem is rarely treated in direct fashion. The approach proper enough in the *Apology* is the reverse of Sidney's or any other poet's experience. Sidney came to think about poetry after he had taken to writing poems. But in the *Apology* the

poem is thought of primarily in terms of the general theory.
It is for this reason that the *Apology* often perplexes the modern
reader if he looks first for criticism of individual pieces in the
Dryden style—criticism which gives open judgments and
appraisals without declaring the prejudices on which judg-
ments are made or the conventions of taste which control the
responses. But in the *Apology* the few judgments expressed,
for example, of the ballad of Percy and Douglas, or of the
Shepherd's Calendar, are incidental to the argument.

The individual poem is thought of as an exemplification
of a kind of poetry. Sidney adapts the two-fold analysis of
the poet's activity inherited from the Middle Ages, according
to which a poem was examined first as to its fable and second
according to its metrical form.

Sidney is obliged to modify this scheme. He cannot of
course allow an essential character to a poem merely from a
consideration of fable and metre. His classification of poems
must relate to his comprehensive definition of poetry and also
to his claim that poetry is the supreme art. He could not
show that poetry excels all other disciplines if any poem
could be presented as Castelvetro would treat it, as a versified
history, or as the allegorists would, as a piece of versified
divinity. There are, Sidney admits (101/37), divine and
philosophical poets, and there are historians who use poetic
methods (97/26; 110/32). But he is contending that it is the
poetry that gives power to the poet-philosophers and to the
historians, not the other disciplines which give substance to
poetry. A poem whatever its subject matter or its form gives
an idealised imitation with a persuasive intent. All poems
with this character are the work of ' right poets ' (102/24).
' Right poets ' are not makers of ' pure ' poetry, in Thomas
Gray's or in Verlaine's sense, of exquisite, non-utility expres-
sions appealing only to the aesthetic sensibility, nor are they
' mere ' poets, high-class verbal decorators of recognisably
useful maxims, as J. Pontanus regarded them. Any poet
can be a ' right poet ' if he achieves the right sort of imitation.
But writers who take up available information or established
theories and put them directly into verse, these are mere
copyists.

Since imitation as Sidney conceives it is the essence of poetry, verse form can be only an ancillary. Unlike his chief authority, Scaliger, but like several other critics of the sixteenth century, including Minturno, Sidney does not consider verse an essential of poetry. It is obvious that he treats the prose *Cyropaedia* of Xenophon, much of the Scripture, and many of the prose romances as essentially poetic. No doubt he rewrote the *Arcadia* as a heroic poem. But the supreme usefulness of verse is often justified on rational grounds. There should be no rhyme without reason (**133**/36). Verse confers the splendour that splendid subjects demand. By its harmony it possesses a sort of congruence with the ideal quality of successful imitation. It makes the imitation clearer and more conspicuous, and fastens it more solidly in the mind (**122**/22). In using verse a writer declares the rationality of poetry, ' not speaking (table talk fashion, or like men in a dream) words as they chanceably fall from the mouth, but peizing each syllable of each word by just proportion according to the dignity of the subject ' (**103**/34).

This last phrase ' according to the dignity of the subject ' indicates Sidney's sense of the principle of decorum, the principle which dominates Horace's notions about poetry. In this context it is of course primarily a literary and not a moral term and embodies the insistence that for an imitation to satisfy it must be made in adequate, relevant, and appropriate words: yet of course the principle overruns into morality, for the imitation is directed towards moral ends. Sidney is deeply committed to this principle of propriety. He has nothing to say in favour of those who ' please an ill-pleased eye with wanton shows of better hidden matters ' (**125**/32).

The great objection to ' our tragedies and comedies ' is that they fail to observe the rules of decorum in respect ' of honest civility ' and ' of skilful poetry ' (**133**/37). All the ridiculous huddlings of place and sprawlings of time (**134**), the matchings of hornpipes and funerals (**136**/2), are condemned by decorum. So are the swelling but nerveless phrases of many love-poets (**137**/32ff), and the tasteless exuberance of those who ' cast sugar and spice ' upon every poetic dish (**138**/24) or throw thunderbolts of eloquence into familiar epistles (**138**/34). In all such cases as these Sidney is applying an old principle, but one inherent in his own doctrine of imitation.

The belief that there was a particularly appropriate way of presenting a particular theme stresses in all Horatian criticism the division into genres. Sidney reproduces this type of theorising, but rather unsystematically, as he admits paying attention to those kinds in which he is interested. He distinguishes the different kinds according to the different imitative and didactic ends to which they are directed. The end of each is the inculcation of a stimulus to some specific moral activity by men at a certain social level. So tragedy is the sort of writing which warns great men and aspirants to greatness of the need to behave with discretion. It uses a style suited to the converse of the great. It gives its warning by arousing horrified astonishment and a degree of sympathy. These sentiments Sidney believes can both appal and teach; thus presumably he would understand the Aristotelian *catharsis*. Comedy is writing of a kind which teaches ordinary men not to make fools of themselves in public; it teaches by representing the shame and contempt which men incur who do make fools of themselves in this way.

The ingredients of these formulas go back through the Middle Ages, although they gained a new relevance in the sixteenth century by the revival of intellectual interest in dramatic representation. Sidney applies a keener analysis than any of his predecessors writing in the vernacular. The *Apology* affords the earliest English discussion, and one of the earliest European discussions in detail with an eye to actual presentation, of the famous three unities, of action, time, and place. A requirement that the action of a story should be coherent and unified was entailed in Aristotle's insistence on the supreme importance of plot. In Horace's summary words (*Art*, 23),

> In short, I bid, let what thou work'st upon,
> Be simple quite throughout and wholly one.
> B. Jonson's trans.

The Italian commentators of the late sixteenth century elaborate these suggestions into a theory. Sidney argues for observance of the principle without sharply identifying it (135/13ff). 'This needs no further to be enlarged; the dullest wit may conceive it' (135/28).

The unities of time and place which hang together have slighter foundations in antiquity. Aristotle simply observes, however, that tragic dramatists seek as far as possible to restrict the action 'within a single circuit of the sun' (*Poetics*, 5). Robortello applies this observation to all drama, and Scaliger requires a correspondence between the time taken in representation and the time of the action represented (*Poetices*, III, xcvi, pp. 334–5). The theory of the need for observing the unity of place appears to germinate in the *Poetics*, 24, where Aristotle observes that a play, as distinct from a narrative poem, consists in what can take place on one stage and be connected with one set of actors. It is well known that it was Castelvetro who first enunciated on this slight basis the need to confine the action to a particular locality.

Sidney does not suggest that the unities constitute inviolable precepts. As he presents them they are sensible recommendations arrived at by applying reason to the problems inherent in dramatic presentation. They are products of a sense of artistic economy and of concentration of effort, and of his bias towards his own type of realism. There is no convincing evidence that Sidney took anything directly from Castelvetro, in whose writings (which otherwise we cannot show that he had read) the early neo-classical doctrine of the drama is formulated much more clearly than in Scaliger, whom we know Sidney had read. Once again, it is likely that his recommendations are his own, in the sense that they are the outcome of some current reading, and some reports of others' reading, of much literary conversation, and of personal thought and argument. Ideas such as Sidney had about the drama must have circulated freely at the court, in the great households and Inns of Court (see notes on 133f).

In a *milieu* of such lively discussion it is likely that Sidney with his strongly realistic sense saw, even as we do now looking back upon the early drama, that most critical formulas elaborated from authority and tradition left a wide area quite unexploited between the high tragedy of princes and the low comedy of humble life. Although Sidney heartily disapproves of the clumsy and purposeless mixing of styles and subject matters (**135**/30ff), he does seem to suggest that an acceptable design for tragi-comedy can be invented (**136**/1; cp. **116**/4). What he has to say on ' the teaching delightfulness ' (**137**/16) implies a middle mode of dramatic composition, directed neither to princes nor to clowns, but fitted to an intelligent, educated, thoughtful audience—in fact, plays which should provide satisfying imitations of the tragi-comical glories and servitudes of courtiers' lives. The theory of such unified decorous tragi-comedy was worked out after Sidney's time by Guarini. Sidney provides no more than hints. But his interest in tragi-comedy and other mixed modes (**116**/1ff), surprising in so summary a treatment of the genres, indicates again the experimental and scrupulously sensible approach which he makes to contemporary literature. He is not seeking to disinter and impose old rules but to ensure that in the present situation poets shall try to write as intelligently and efficiently as possible. Artificial rules and imitative patterns (**133**/3) would be useless unless writers held this rational ideal before them. ' We should exercise to know '; too often poets work ' very fore-backwardly . . . and exercise as having known ' (**133**/6).

Sidney's sharp eye for the contemporary situation is apparent in the other genres he discusses. In the 1580s it was topical to discourse on ' pastoral, pastoral-comical, historical-pastoral, tragi-comical-historical-pastoral ' with an enthusiasm which had grown tedious by the time of Polonius, who, it must be admitted, in his literary preferences as well as in his methods of deliberation shows how musty disillusionment disintegrated Sidney's bright ideal of the wise and literary courtier. For more than a score of years after the publication of Barnabe Googe's *Eglogs* (1563), pastoral poetry had remained in fashion and developed. As with the other genres, Sidney characterises it both by its form—it is written in ' low style ', with ' the poor pipe ' (**116**/15)—and by its fables.

In its application he sees its usefulness, in lamenting the misery of the oppressed, in teaching the contentment of the quiet life, or in anatomising private questions of conscience.

Sidney's treatment of the lyric is altogether traditional. It would have been understood perfectly by Bede or Chaucer, but not immediately by any modern reader who thinks like Ruskin that the lyric is ' the expression of emotion '. In the old belief, the lyric was poetry of praise or dispraise, written to inculcate attitudes of approval or disapproval, formally controlled by its origin in song. This legacy of music is to be observed in the extreme ornamentation required: lacking this, the ballad of Percy and Douglas—a lyric in Sidney's classification—is, though moving, a barbarous composition. An accomplished lyric, whether a hymn of valour or a song of love, should aim at the gorgeousness of Pindar, at an eloquence taught by art. But its association with music gives also to lyric a claim on moral attention. This attitude towards the lyric common to sixteenth-century poets is illuminated by recalling those efforts of the French academies in the middle of the century to transfer to French lyric verse the dignity and moral splendour of the Psalms. More than once in the *Apology* Sidney asserts the pre-eminence of the Psalms as lyric verse, and he acknowledged it in practice by producing with his sister that version of the Psalter which won Donne's praise.

But for Sidney, as for every Renaissance writer, the heroic poem is the noblest work of man (cp. **119/26**). The belief follows naturally enough on the theory that it is ' the poet's task to imitate to admiration and to portray the Idea itself, clothed in all its beauty—which Aristotle calls the universal ' (see note on **102/25ff**). For heroic poetry is the imitation in perfection of human action. Nearly all that Sidney has to say in celebration of poetry assumes that heroic poetry is the palmary kind. To this kind he has recourse in all the turns of his argument. It is this kind which fulfils most completely his notions of poetry as example and as an instrument of virtue. Virgil's *Aeneid* above all other compositions showed to Renaissance men what art as an imitation of life implied.

In Aeneas a man may see all that he ought to be. But for Sidney, unlike Scaliger, the *Aeneid* does not stand absolutely alone. Xenophon's Cyrus, too, figures forth the ideal.

Sidney's special admiration for Cyrus shows the political cast of his didacticism; moreover, he anticipates the creed which was to sustain Spenser in the *Faery Queen*. In his prefatory letter written to Sir Walter Raleigh, Spenser explains: ' For this cause is Xenophon preferred before Plato, for that the one, in the exquisite depth of his judgement, formed a Commune welth, such as it should be; but the other in the person of Cyrus, and the Persians, fashioned a government such as might best be: So much more profitable and gratious is doctrine by ensample, then by rule.' The *Faery Queen* was designed within the benevolent circuit of Sidney's ideas about the heroic poem; so too of course was the revised *Arcadia*.

If we relate Spenser's achievement, particularly in the *Faery Queen*, with Sidney's promise, we should perhaps develop hints in the *Apology* which indicate his concern with religious poetry (cp. **137**/25ff). If, too, we recall the religious character of much of the neo-Platonism of the Florentines, and the theological emphasis given to mannerist theories of art during the 1580s, and remember the interest Sidney and many Puritans in the late sixteenth century were to exhibit in the cosmopoesy of du Bartas, we can discern already as one of the consequences of the theories embodied in the *Apology* an interest which was to become dominant in the seventeenth century in the composition of religious epic. From the time he wrote the *Apology* Sidney was working, and we can scarcely say unconsciously working, to promote a Protestant poetry in England. Undoubtedly the crown of such a work he would have considered a religious epic.

In this respect literary history written during the present century has largely ignored or obscured the seventeenth-century achievement in poetry which is initiated in the *Apology*.[1] Sidney intimates a purpose in poetry, a method of

[1] See, however, Lily B. Campbell, *Divine Poetry and Drama in Sixteenth Century England* (Cambridge, 1959).

using words, and a function of theme which were to sustain the new religious and moral poetry. Spenser develops these suggestions. So do Spenser's successors, the Fletchers and George Wither. Ben Jonson, George Herbert, and the New England poets follow Sidney with their individual modifications. But it is Milton who inherits the doctrine of the *Apology* most unreservedly. In Milton's literary theory and practice, in his range, even in the order of his works, particularly perhaps in *Paradise Regained* with its fastidious dialogues of conscience in an Arcadian wilderness, Sidney would have rejoiced to see his own literary aspirations realised with compelling magniloquence.

PROSODY AND DICTION

What Sidney has to say on these topics may be left in the main to speak for itself (**138**ff). Verse is not essential to poetry but is highly appropriate. The physical basis of verse is musical. The harmony, symmetry, and proportion of verse symbolises, as music symbolises, the order which reason perceives in the universe and which reason seeks to portray in poetic imitation. Throughout the Middle Ages music was approached theoretically as the science of proportions. It was believed on ancient authority, directly from Boethius and indirectly from Plato and Pythagoras, that music, heard or unheard, could effect a link between the divine proportion of the heavens and the microcosm of man. ' What passions cannot music raise and quell? ' Music could be the instructor of the soul and passions—it is ' the most divine striker of the senses ' (**122**/7).

This belief in the moral power of music is one of the chief reasons for sixteenth-century poets' experimentation in classical measures of verse; among these Sidney himself was prominent, as we learn from the Harvey-Spenser correspondence and can see for ourselves in many of the verses in *Arcadia*. But from the testimony of the *Apology* we have no justification for exaggerating Sidney's interest in classical metres into a critical waywardness on his part. He finds the classical ' more fit for music . . . and more fit lively to express divers passions ' (140/28); but the native rhythms have their beauties too (140/30ff): the English language gives them resources that other languages lack.

Rarely has any attempt been made to appreciate what this experimentation was assuming and intending. No English writer of ability and intelligence intended to write verses which would conform with the ideal schemes of Latin versification which modern classical scholarship has devised. Virgil himself often faltered by this standard, Horace was always stumbling. We can easily go wrong if we fail to recognise that Sidney and many of his contemporaries inherited habits of reading Latin verse, and these habits were medieval and English. In such readings we can be sure that English rhythms of speech were more important than ideal quantitative schemes. Right through medieval times Latin measures had been naturalised: for example, the Latin septenary produced the Common Metre of English hymns. The achievements of accurate classical scholarship, which often represents a desiccation of the humanist impulse in the seventeenth and eighteenth centuries, hinder us from realising the basically medieval handling by the Elizabethans of the Latin language.

Sidney in experimenting with and in recommending classical measures is not seeking to denature English. He is promoting experiments whereby the effects which a poet sought could be brought more completely under his control. He is willing to seek everywhere for means whereby poetry can be given dignity and power. Many of the metrical triumphs, many of the astonishing verbal effects achieved carefully and consciously by the lyric poets of the late sixteenth century, by Thomas Campion, Dowland, or Shakespeare, much of the sinewy sequaciousness of the narrative poets (particularly of course Spenser), with their harmoniously sustained syntax, spring from the experimentation in Latin measures. The release from rhyme encouraged poets to pay attention to positioning and relating words otherwise, to a stricter consideration of devices for emphasis and coordination. The easy convenience and self-propulsion of rhyming, Sidney saw (**133**/29ff) could beguile a poet into inconsequential nonsense. He wants the English poet to exploit to the full the persuasive and expressive potentialities of the language with regard to both ' forcible quality ' and ' best-measured quantity ' (**122**/3); to formalise by conscious art the rhythms inherent in English speech.[1]

Similar concerns are apparent in Sidney's recommendations about diction. On diction as on verse he has thought more than he writes, so that his treatment can afford to be magisterially perfunctory.

Again we can remark his swift appreciation of the situation by the end of the 1570s. He is not troubled by the lack of resources the language can command, as Elyot or Ascham had been, nor by the indiscriminate introduction of aureate, inkhorn, obsolete, translated, or new-coined words. He does not seem to find the early-Elizabethan argument about the sources of vocabulary still relevant. Poets should give careful attention to the selection and use of words and make a scrupulous use of ornamentation. Then the rough English virtues, the vigour, the honest attractiveness of the old poetry can blossom into eloquence. There are resources enough (**140**/5). What is more necessary now is to learn how to use them properly. Sidney's perceptiveness here is all the more impressive when it is compared for instance with Webbe's or Puttenham's reiteration of old arguments on diction, or when we reflect on what would have counted more with Sidney, how much of the work of the French Pléiade, whose general achievement Sidney was certainly emulating, had been devoted to this problem of the enrichment of the vernacular.

We who have had taste fixed, probably for too long now, by Wordsworth's re-formulation of the anti-rhetorical rhetoric which had developed at the end of the seventeenth century, and as a result reject almost by instinct the conscious use of verbal ornamentation, may find Sidney's ideal over-elaborate and over-adorned, may even indeed find some

[1] See John Thompson, *The Founding of English Metre* (London, 1961), who shows that Sidney is to be considered the first fully equipped and accomplished metrist in modern English poetry.

difficulty in distinguishing his ideal, as exemplified in prac-
tice, from Puttenham's or Lyly's. They were in fact opposed
and known to be. Michael Drayton, in his *Elegy: to Henry
Reynolds*, remembered that it was Sidney that

> did first reduce
> Our tongue from Lillies writing then in use.

Sidney was thought to have used and to have recommended
for others' use a strong, masculine, and fully expressive style.
But of course in attempting this style, which is valued not
for its own sake, but for its effectiveness, he is consciously
relying upon a whole traditional art of rhetorical devices. He
accepts as completely as Cicero, or Augustine, or Chaucer,
or Ramus, or Shakespeare, that the traditional figures of
speech are the means which a writer must use if he wants to
make his utterance effective. No writer could avoid them,
except for restricted experimental purposes, any more than a
modern writer can escape full stops and commas. But from
what Sidney has to say about the function of similes (**139**/10),
or the use of repetition of phrase or cadence (**138**/36), we can
conclude that he tends to conceive of figures rather as figures
of thought than figures of speech. We have seen that he be-
lieves a poet morally obliged to be fully eloquent: his words
should transmit the full splendour and complexity of what he
is representing. But they should remain transparent. Decora-
tion on the verbal surface of the expression itself, ' seeming
fineness ' (**139**/4), is to be avoided. Sidney requires in style
what he looks for in the fable, conformity to the rationality
which sustains nature. Once again we detect the sympathy
with Ramism in its demand for a plain and ' natural ' style.
Yet at the same time it is a re-adoption of Augustine's pro-
gramme for the preacher: to speak eloquently is to speak
wisely as well, to teach in fit and proper words which pay a
proper respect to the matter, but which do not deform or
obscure it. Just as he believes that the aim of poetry in the
last resort is to teach political self-responsibility, and that the
type of the poet is the learned and judicious courtier, so
Sidney finds that the style which in use most clearly indicates

the ideal is a courtier's (**139**/27ff) who follows ' by practice he findeth fittest to nature ' and ' therein (though he know it not) doth according to art ' (**139**/30). Poetry is written for courtiers, by courtiers, in courtly speech. We must acknowledge that it was no restricted, ignoble, or unproductive ideal.

AN
APOLOGIE
for Poetrie.

Written by the right noble, vertu-
ous, and learned, *Sir* Phillip
Sidney, *Knight.*

Odi profanum vulgus, et arceo.

AT LONDON,
Printed for *Henry Olney*, and are to be fold at
his fhop in Paules Church-yard, at the figne
of the George, neere to Cheap-gate.
Anno. 1595.

AN APOLOGY FOR POETRY

WHEN the right virtuous Edward Wotton and I were at the Emperor's court together, we gave ourselves to learn horsemanship of John Pietro Pugliano, one that with great commendation had the place of an esquire in his stable. And he, according to the fertileness of the Italian 5 wit, did not only afford us the demonstration of his practice, but sought to enrich our minds with the contemplations therein which he thought most precious. But with none I remember mine ears were at any time more loaden, than when (either angered with slow payment, or moved with our 10 learner-like admiration) he exercised his speech in the praise of his faculty. He said soldiers were the noblest estate of mankind, and horsemen the noblest of soldiers. He said they were the masters of war and ornaments of peace, speedy goers and strong abiders, triumphers both in camps and courts. 15 Nay, to so unbelieved a point he proceeded, as that no earthly thing bred such wonder to a prince as to be a good horseman. Skill of government was but a *pedanteria* in comparison. Then would he add certain praises, by telling what a peerless beast a horse was, the only serviceable courtier without flattery, the 20 beast of most beauty, faithfulness, courage, and such more, that if I had not been a piece of a logician before I came to him, I think he would have persuaded me to have wished myself a horse. But thus much at least with his no few words he drave into me, that self-love is better than any gilding to 25 make that seem gorgeous wherein ourselves are parties.

Wherein, if Pugliano's strong affection and weak arguments will not satisfy you, I will give you a nearer example of myself, who (I know not by what mischance) in these my not old years and idlest times having slipped into the title of a poet, 30 am provoked to say something unto you in the defence of that my unelected vocation, which if I handle with more good will than good reasons, bear with me, since the scholar is to be pardoned that followeth the steps of his master. And yet

I must say that, as I have just cause to make a pitiful defence of poor Poetry, which from almost the highest estimation of learning is fallen to be the laughing-stock of children, so have I need to bring some more available proofs, since the former 5 is by no man barred of his deserved credit, the silly latter hath had even the names of philosophers used to the defacing of it, with great danger of civil war among the Muses.

And first, truly, to all them that, professing learning, inveigh against Poetry, may justly be objected that they go 10 very near to ungratefulness, to seek to deface that which, in the noblest nations and languages that are known, hath been the first light-giver to ignorance, and first nurse, whose milk by little and little enabled them to feed afterwards of tougher knowledges. And will they now play the hedgehog that, 15 being received into the den, drave out his host? Or rather the vipers, that with their birth kill their parents? Let learned Greece in any of her manifold sciences be able to show me one book before Musaeus, Homer, and Hesiod, all three nothing else but poets. Nay, let any history be brought 20 that can say any writers were there before them, if they were not men of the same skill, as Orpheus, Linus, and some other are named, who, having been the first of that country that made pens deliverers of their knowledge to their posterity, may justly challenge to be called their fathers in learning: for 25 not only in time they had this priority (although in itself antiquity be venerable) but went before them, as causes to draw with their charming sweetness the wild untamed wits to an admiration of knowledge. So, as Amphion was said to move stones with his poetry to build Thebes, and Orpheus 30 to be listened to by beasts—indeed stony and beastly people— so among the Romans were Livius Andronicus, and Ennius. So in the Italian language the first that made it aspire to be a treasure-house of science were the poets Dante, Boccaccio, and Petrarch. So in our English were Gower and Chaucer, 35 after whom, encouraged and delighted with their excellent fore-going, others have followed, to beautify our mother tongue, as well in the same kind as in other arts.

This did so notably show itself, that the philosophers of Greece durst not a long time appear to the world but under the masks of poets. So Thales, Empedocles, and Parmenides sang their natural philosophy in verses; so did Pythagoras and Phocylides their moral counsels; so did Tyrtaeus in war matters, and Solon in matters of policy: or rather they, being poets, did exercise their delightful vein in those points of highest knowledge, which before them lay hid to the world. For that wise Solon was directly a poet it is manifest, having written in verse the notable fable of the Atlantic Island, which was continued by Plato.

And truly even Plato whosoever well considereth shall find that in the body of his work, though the inside and strength were Philosophy, the skin as it were and beauty depended most of Poetry: for all standeth upon dialogues wherein he feigneth many honest burgesses of Athens to speak of such matters, that, if they had been set on the rack, they would never have confessed them; besides his poetical describing the circumstances of their meetings, as the well ordering of a banquet, the delicacy of a walk, with interlacing mere tales, as Gyges' Ring, and others, which who knoweth not to be flowers of poetry did never walk into Apollo's garden.

And even historiographers (although their lips sound of things done, and verity be written in their foreheads) have been glad to borrow both fashion and perchance weight of poets. So Herodotus entitled his History by the name of the nine Muses; and both he and all the rest that followed him either stole or usurped of Poetry their passionate describing of passions, the many particularities of battles, which no man could affirm, or, if that be denied me, long orations put in the mouths of great kings and captains, which it is certain they never pronounced.

So that truly neither philosopher nor historiographer could at the first have entered into the gates of popular judgments, if they had not taken a great passport of Poetry, which in all nations at this day, where learning flourisheth not, is plain to be seen; in all which they have some feeling of Poetry.

In Turkey, besides their law-giving divines, they have no other writers but poets. In our neighbour country Ireland, where truly learning goeth very bare, yet are their poets held in a devout reverence. Even among the most barbarous and

simple Indians where no writing is, yet have they their poets who make· and sing songs, which they call *areytos*, both of their ancestors' deeds and praises of their gods—a sufficient probability that, if ever learning come among them, it must
5 be by having their hard dull wits softened and sharpened with the sweet delights of Poetry; for until they find a pleasure in the exercises of the mind, great promises of much knowledge will little persuade them that know not the fruits of knowledge. In Wales, the true remnant of the ancient Britons,
10 as there are good authorities to show the long time they had poets, which they called *bards*, so through all the conquests of Romans, Saxons, Danes, and Normans, some of whom did seek to ruin all memory of learning from among them, yet do their poets even to this day last; so as it is not more notable
15 in soon beginning than in long continuing.

But since the authors of most of our sciences were the Romans, and before them the Greeks, let us a little stand upon their authorities, but even so far as to see what names they have given unto this now scorned skill.
20   Among the Romans a poet was called *vates*, which is as much as a diviner, foreseer, or prophet, as by his conjoined words *vaticinium* and *vaticinari* is manifest: so heavenly a title did that excellent people bestow upon this heart-ravishing knowledge. And so far were they carried into the admiration
25 thereof, that they thought in the chanceable hitting upon any such verses great foretokens of their following fortunes were placed. Whereupon grew the word of *Sortes Virgilianae*, when by sudden opening Virgil's book they lighted upon any verse of his making as it is reported by many: whereof
30 the Histories of the Emperors' Lives are full, as of Albinus, the governor of our island, who in his childhood met with this verse,

Arma amens capio nec sat rationis in armis;

and in his age performed it: which, although it were a very
35 vain and godless superstition, as also it was to think that spirits were commanded by such verses—whereupon this word charms, derived of *carmina*, cometh—so yet serveth it to show the great reverence those wits were held in. And

altogether not without ground, since both the oracles of
Delphos and Sibylla's prophecies were wholly delivered in
verses. For that same exquisite observing of number and
measure in words, and that high flying liberty of conceit
proper to the poet, did seem to have some divine force in it. 5

And may not I presume a little further, to show the reason-
ableness of this word *vates*, and say that the holy David's
Psalms are a divine poem? If I do, I shall not do it without
the testimony of great learned men, both ancient and modern.
But even the name psalms will speak for me, which being 10
interpreted, is nothing but songs; then, that it is fully written
in metre, as all learned hebricians agree, although the rules
be not yet fully found; lastly and principally, his handling
his prophecy, which is merely poetical. For what else is the
awaking his musical instruments, the often and free changing 15
of persons, his notable *prosopopeias*, when he maketh you, as
it were, see God coming in His majesty, his telling of the
beasts' joyfulness, and hills leaping, but a heavenly poesy,
wherein almost he showeth himself a passionate lover of that
unspeakable and everlasting beauty to be seen by the eyes of 20
the mind, only cleared by faith? But truly now having
named him, I fear me I seem to profane that holy name,
applying it to Poetry, which is among us thrown down to so
ridiculous an estimation. But they that with quiet judgments
will look a little deeper into it, shall find the end and working 25
of it such as, being rightly applied, deserveth not to be
scourged out of the Church of God.

But now let us see how the Greeks named it, and how
they deemed of it. The Greeks called him ' a poet ', which
name hath, as the most excellent, gone through other lang- 30
uages. It cometh of this word *poiein*, which is ' to make ':
wherein I know not whether by luck or wisdom, we English-
men have met with the Greeks in calling him ' a maker ':
which name, how high and incomparable a title it is, I had
rather were known by marking the scope of other sciences 35
than by my partial allegation.

There is no art delivered to mankind that hath not the works
of Nature for his principal object, without which they could
not consist, and on which they so depend, as they become

actors and players, as it were, of what Nature will have set
forth. So doth the astronomer look upon the stars, and, by
that he seeth, setteth down what order Nature hath taken
therein. So do the geometrician and arithmetician in their
5 diverse sorts of quantities. So doth the musician in times
tell you which by nature agree, which not. The natural
philosopher thereon hath his name, and the moral philosopher
standeth upon the natural virtues, vices, and passions of man;
and ' follow Nature ' (saith he) ' therein, and thou shalt not
10 err '. The lawyer saith what men have determined; the
historian what men have done. The grammarian speaketh
only of the rules of speech; and the rhetorician and logician,
considering what in Nature will soonest prove and persuade,
thereon give artificial rules, which still are compassed within
15 the circle of a question according to the proposed matter.
The physician weigheth the nature of a man's body, and the
nature of things helpful or hurtful unto it. And the meta-
physic, though it be in the second and abstract notions, and
therefore be counted supernatural, yet doth he indeed build
20 upon the depth of Nature.

Only the poet, disdaining to be tied to any such subjection,
lifted up with the vigour of his own invention, doth grow in
effect into another nature, in making things either better
than Nature bringeth forth, or, quite anew, forms such as
25 never were in Nature, as the Heroes, Demigods, Cyclops,
Chimeras, Furies, and such like: so as he goeth hand in hand
with Nature, not enclosed within the narrow warrant of her
gifts, but freely ranging only within the zodiac of his own wit.

Nature never set forth the earth in so rich tapestry as divers
30 poets have done; neither with pleasant rivers, fruitful trees,
sweet-smelling flowers, nor whatsoever else may make the
too much loved earth more lovely. Her world is brazen, the
poets only deliver a golden.

But let those things alone, and go to man—for whom as the
35 other things are, so it seemeth in him her uttermost cunning
is employed—and know whether she have brought forth so
true a lover as Theagenes, so constant a friend as Pylades, so
valiant a man as Orlando, so right a prince as Xenophon's
Cyrus, so excellent a man every way as Virgil's Aeneas.

Neither let this be jestingly conceived, because the works of the one be essential, the other in imitation or fiction; for any understanding knoweth the skill of the artificer standeth in that *Idea* or fore-conceit of the work, and not in the work itself. And that the poet hath that *Idea* is manifest, by de- 5 livering them forth in such excellency as he hath imagined them. Which delivering forth also is not wholly imaginative, as we are wont to say by them that build castles in the air; but so far substantially it worketh, not only to make a Cyrus, which had been but a particular excellency as Nature might 10 have done, but to bestow a Cyrus upon the world to make many Cyruses, if they will learn aright why and how that maker made him.

Neither let it be deemed too saucy a comparison to balance the highest point of man's wit with the efficacy of Nature; 15 but rather give right honour to the heavenly Maker of that maker, who having made man to His own likeness, set him beyond and over all the works of that second nature: which in nothing he showeth so much as in Poetry, when with the force of a divine breath he bringeth things forth far surpassing 20 her doings, with no small argument to the incredulous of that first accursed fall of Adam: since our erected wit maketh us know what perfection is, and yet our infected will keepeth us from reaching unto it. But these arguments will by few be understood, and by fewer granted. Thus much (I hope) 25 will be given me, that the Greeks with some probability of reason gave him the name above all names of learning.

Now let us go to a more ordinary opening of him, that the truth may be more palpable: and so I hope, though we get not so unmatched a praise as the etymology of his names will 30 grant, yet his very description, which no man will deny, shall not justly be barred from a principal commendation.

Poesy therefore is an art of imitation, for so Aristotle termeth it in his word *mimesis*, that is to say, a representing, counterfeiting, or figuring forth—to speak metaphorically, a 35 speaking picture—with this end, to teach and delight.

Of this have been three several kinds. The chief, both in antiquity and excellency, were they that did imitate the inconceivable excellencies of God. Such were David in his

Psalms; Solomon in his Song of Songs, in his Ecclesiastes,
and Proverbs; Moses and Deborah in their Hymns; and
the writer of Job: which, beside other, the learned Emanuel
Tremellius and Franciscus Junius do entitle the poetical part
5 of the Scripture. Against these none will speak that hath the
Holy Ghost in due holy reverence. In this kind, though in a
full wrong divinity, were Orpheus, Amphion, Homer in his
Hymns, and many other, both Greeks and Romans. And
this poesy must be used by whosoever will follow St James's
10 counsel in singing psalms when they are merry, and I know
is used with the fruit of comfort by some, when, in sorrowful
pangs of their death-bringing sins, they find the consolation
of the never-leaving goodness.

The second kind is of them that deal with matters philo-
15 sophical: either moral, as Tyrtaeus, Phocylides, and Cato;
or natural, as Lucretius and Virgil's Georgics; or astro-
nomical, as Manilius and Pontanus; or historical, as Lucan:
which who mislike, the fault is in their judgements quite
out of taste, and not in the sweet food of sweetly uttered
20 knowledge.

But because this second sort is wrapped within the fold of
the proposed subject, and takes not the course of his own
invention, whether they properly be poets or no let gram-
marians dispute, and go to the third, indeed right poets, of
25 whom chiefly this question ariseth. Betwixt whom and these
second is such a kind of difference as betwixt the meaner sort
of painters, who counterfeit only such faces as are set before
them, and the more excellent, who having no law but wit,
bestow that in colours upon you which is fittest for the eye
30 to see: as the constant though lamenting look of Lucretia,
when she punished in herself another's fault; wherein he
painteth not Lucretia whom he never saw, but painteth the
outward beauty of such a virtue. For these third be they
which most properly do imitate to teach and delight, and to
35 imitate borrow nothing of what is, hath been, or shall be;
but range, only reined with learned discretion, into the divine
consideration of what may be and should be. These be they
that, as the first and most noble sort may justly be termed
vates, so these are waited on in the excellentest languages and

best understandings, with the foredescribed name of poets; for these indeed do merely make to imitate, and imitate both to delight and teach: and delight to move men to take that goodness in hand, which without delight they would fly as from a stranger, and teach, to make them know that goodness 5 whereunto they are moved: which being the noblest scope to which ever any learning was directed, yet want there not idle tongues to bark at them.

These be subdivided into sundry more special denominations. The most notable be the Heroic, Lyric, Tragic, 10 Comic, Satiric, Iambic, Elegiac, Pastoral, and certain others, some of these being termed according to the matter they deal with, some by the sorts of verses they liked best to write in; for indeed the greatest part of poets have apparelled their poetical inventions in that numbrous kind of writing which is 15 called verse—indeed but apparelled, verse being but an ornament and no cause to Poetry, since there have been many most excellent poets that never versified, and now swarm many versifiers that need never answer to the name of poets. For Xenophon, who did imitate so excellently as to give us 20 *effigiem justi imperii*, ' the portraiture of a just empire,' under the name of Cyrus (as Cicero saith of him), made therein an absolute heroical poem. So did Heliodorus in his sugared invention of that picture of love in Theagenes and Chariclea; and yet both these writ in prose: which I speak to show that 25 it is not rhyming and versing that maketh a poet—no more than a long gown maketh an advocate, who though he pleaded in armour should be an advocate and no soldier. But it is that feigning notable images of virtues, vices, or what else, with that delightful teaching, which must be the right de- 30 scribing note to know a poet by, although indeed the senate of poets hath chosen verse as their fittest raiment, meaning, as in matter they passed all in all, so in manner to go beyond them: not speaking (table talk fashion or like men in a dream) words as they chanceably fall from the mouth, but peizing 35 each syllable of each word by just proportion according to the dignity of the subject.

Now therefore it shall not be amiss first to weigh this latter sort of Poetry by his works, and then by his parts, and if in neither of these anatomies he be condemnable, I hope we shall obtain a more favourable sentence. This purifying of wit, this enriching of memory, enabling of judgment, and enlarging of conceit, which commonly we call learning, under 5 what name soever it come forth, or to what immediate end soever it be directed, the final end is to lead and draw us to as high a perfection as our degenerate souls, made worse by their clayey lodgings, can be capable of. This, according to the inclination of the man, bred many formed impressions. 10 For some that thought this felicity principally to be gotten by knowledge, and no knowledge to be so high and heavenly as acquaintance with the stars, gave themselves to Astronomy; others, persuading themselves to be demi-gods if they knew the causes of things, became natural and supernatural philos- 15 ophers; some an admirable delight drew to Music; and some the certainty of demonstration to the Mathematics. But all, one and other, having this scope—to know, and by knowledge to lift up the mind from the dungeon of the body to the enjoying his own divine essence. But when by the 20 balance of experience it was found that the astronomer look- ing to the stars might fall into a ditch, that the inquiring philosopher might be blind in himself, and the mathematician might draw forth a straight line with a crooked heart, then lo, did proof, the overruler of opinions, make manifest that 25 all these are but serving sciences, which, as they have each a private end in themselves, so yet are they all directed to the highest end of the mistress-knowledge, by the Greeks called *architectonike*, which stands (as I think) in the knowledge of a man's self, in the ethic and politic consideration, with the 30 end of well-doing and not of well-knowing only: even as the saddler's next end is to make a good saddle, but his farther end to serve a nobler faculty, which is horsemanship; so the horseman's to soldiery, and the soldier not only to have the skill, but to perform the practice of a soldier. So that, the 35 ending end of all earthly learning being virtuous action, those skills, that most serve to bring forth that, have a most just title to be princes over all the rest.

Wherein if we can, show we the poet's nobleness, by setting him before his other competitors, among whom as principal challengers step forth the moral philosophers, whom, me thinketh, I see coming towards me with a sullen gravity, as though they could not abide vice by daylight, rudely clothed for to witness outwardly their contempt of outward things, with books in their hands against glory, whereto they set 5 their names, sophistically speaking against subtlety, and angry with any man in whom they see the foul fault of anger. These men casting largesse as they go of definitions, divisions, and distinctions, with a scornful interrogative do soberly ask whether it be possible to find any path so ready to lead a man 10 to virtue as that which teacheth what virtue is—and teacheth it not only by delivering forth his very being, his causes, and effects, but also by making known his enemy, vice, which must be destroyed, and his cumbersome servant, passion, which must be mastered, by showing the generalities that 15 containeth it, and the specialities that are derived from it; lastly, by plain setting down, how it extendeth itself out of the limits of a man's own little world to the government of families, and maintaining of public societies.

The historian scarcely giveth leisure to the moralist to say 20 so much, but that he, loaden with old mouse-eaten records, authorising himself (for the most part) upon other histories, whose greatest authorities are built upon the notable foundation of hearsay; having much ado to accord differing writers and to pick truth out of partiality; better acquainted with a 25 thousand years ago than with the present age, and yet better knowing how this world goeth than how his own wit runneth; curious for antiquities and inquisitive of novelties; a wonder to young folks and a tyrant in table talk, denieth, in a great chafe, that any man for teaching of virtue, and virtuous actions 30 is comparable to him. ' I am *testis temporum, lux veritatis, vita memoriæ, magistra vitæ, nuncia vetustatis.* The philosopher ', saith he, ' teacheth a disputative virtue, but I do an active. His virtue is excellent in the dangerless Academy of Plato, but mine showeth forth her honourable face in 35 the battles of Marathon, Pharsalia, Poitiers, and Agincourt. He teacheth virtue by certain abstract considerations, but I only bid you follow the footing of them that have gone before you. Old-aged experience goeth beyond the fine-witted philosopher, but I give the experience of many ages. Lastly, if he make the song-book, I put the learner's hand to the lute; and if he be the guide, I am the light.'

Then would he allege you innumerable examples, confer-
5 ring story by story, how much the wisest senators and princes have been directed by the credit of history, as Brutus, Alphonsus of Aragon, and who not, if need be? At length the long line of their disputation maketh a point in this, that the one giveth the precept, and the other the example.

10   Now whom shall we find (since the question standeth for the highest form in the school of learning) to be moderator? Truly, as me seemeth, the poet; and if not a moderator, even the man that ought to carry the title from them both, and much more from all other serving sciences. Therefore com-
15 pare we the poet with the historian and with the moral philosopher; and if he go beyond them both, no other human skill can match him. For as for the divine, with all reverence it is ever to be excepted, not only for having his scope as far beyond any of these as eternity exceedeth a moment, but even
20 for passing each of these in themselves. And for the lawyer, though *jus* be the daughter of justice, and justice the chief of virtues, yet because he seeketh to make men good rather *formidine poenae* than *virtutis amore*; or, to say righter, doth not endeavour to make men good, but that their evil hurt
25 not others; having no care, so he be a good citizen, how bad a man he be: therefore as our wickedness maketh him necessary, and necessity maketh him honourable, so is he not in the deepest truth to stand in rank with these who all endeavour to take naughtiness away and plant goodness even in the
30 secretest cabinet of our souls. And these four are all that any way deal in that consideration of men's manners, which being the supreme knowledge, they that best breed it deserve the best commendation.

The philosopher therefore and the historian are they which
35 would win the goal, the one by precept, the other by example. But both, not having both, do both halt. For the philosopher, setting down with thorny argument the bare rule, is so hard of utterance and so misty to be conceived, that one that hath no other guide but him shall wade in him till he be old before

he shall find sufficient cause to be honest. For his knowledge standeth so upon the abstract and general, that happy is that man who may understand him, and more happy that can apply what he doth understand. On the other side, the historian, wanting the precept, is so tied, not to what should be but to what is, to the particular truth of things and not to the general reason of things, that his example draweth no necessary consequence, and therefore a less fruitful doctrine.

Now doth the peerless poet perform both: for whatsoever the philosopher saith should be done, he giveth a perfect picture of it in some one by whom he presupposeth it was done, so as he coupleth the general notion with the particular example. A perfect picture I say, for he yieldeth to the powers of the mind an image of that whereof the philosopher bestoweth but a wordish description, which doth neither strike, pierce, nor possess the sight of the soul so much as that other doth.

For as in outward things, to a man that had never seen an elephant or a rhinoceros, who should tell him most exquisitely all their shapes, colour, bigness, and particular marks; or of a gorgeous palace, the architecture, with declaring the full beauties might well make the hearer able to repeat, as it were by rote, all he had heard, yet should never satisfy his inward conceits with being witness to itself of a true lively knowledge; but the same man, as soon as he might see those beasts well painted, or the house well in model, should straightways grow, without need of any description, to a judicial comprehending of them: so no doubt the philosopher with his learned definition—be it of virtue, vices, matters of public policy or private government—replenisheth the memory with many infallible grounds of wisdom, which, notwithstanding, lie dark before the imaginative and judging power, if they be not illuminated or figured forth by the speaking picture of poesy.

Tully taketh much pains, and many times not without poetical helps, to make us know the force love of our country hath in us. Let us but hear old Anchises speaking in the midst of Troy's flames, or see Ulysses in the fulness of all Calypso's delights bewail his absence from barren and

beggarly Ithaca. Anger, the Stoics say, was a short madness:
let but Sophocles bring you Ajax on a stage, killing and
whipping sheep and oxen, thinking them the army of Greeks,
with their chieftains Agamemnon and Menelaus, and tell me
5 if you have not a more familiar insight into anger than finding
in the schoolmen his genus and difference. See whether
wisdom and temperance in Ulysses and Diomedes, valour in
Achilles, friendship in Nisus and Euryalus, even to an ignorant
man carry not an apparent shining; and, contrarily, the re-
10 morse of conscience in Oedipus, the soon repenting pride of
Agamemnon, the self-devouring cruelty in his father Atreus,
the violence of ambition in the two Theban brothers, the
sour-sweetness of revenge in Medea; and, to fall lower, the
Terentian Gnatho and our Chaucer's Pandar so expressed
15 that we now use their names to signify their trades; and
finally, all virtues, vices, and passions so in their own natural
seats laid to the view, that we seem not to hear of them, but
clearly to see through them.

But even in the most excellent determination of goodness,
20 what philosopher's counsel can so readily direct a prince, as
the feigned Cyrus in Xenophon; or a virtuous man in all
fortunes, as Aeneas in Virgil; or a whole commonwealth, as
the way of Sir Thomas More's *Utopia*? I say the way, be-
cause where Sir Thomas More erred, it was the fault of the
25 man and not of the poet, for that way of patterning a common-
wealth was most absolute, though he perchance hath not so
absolutely performed it. For the question is, whether the
feigned image of poesy or the regular instruction of philosophy
hath the more force in teaching: wherein if the philosophers
30 have more rightly showed themselves philosophers than the
poets have attained to the high top of their profession, as in
truth,

Mediocribus esse poetis,
Non dii, non homines, non concessere columnae;

35 it is, I say again, not the fault of the art, but that by few men
that art can be accomplished.

Certainly, even our Saviour Christ could as well have
given the moral commonplaces of uncharitableness and

humbleness as the divine narration of Dives and Lazarus; or of disobedience and mercy, as that heavenly discourse of the lost child and the gracious father; but that His through-searching wisdom knew the estate of Dives burning in hell, and of Lazarus being in Abraham's bosom, would more 5 constantly (as it were) inhabit both the memory and judgment. Truly, for myself, me seems I see before my eyes the lost child's disdainful prodigality, turned to envy a swine's dinner: which by the learned divines are thought not historical acts, but instructing parables.   10

For conclusion, I say the philosopher teacheth, but he teacheth obscurely, so as the learned only can understand him; that is to say, he teacheth them that are already taught. But the poet is the food for the tenderest stomachs, the poet is indeed the right popular philosopher, whereof Aesop's tales 15 give good proof; whose pretty allegories, stealing under the formal tales of beasts, make many, more beastly than beasts, begin to hear the sound of virtue from these dumb speakers.

But now may it be alleged that if this imagining of matters be so fit for the imagination, then must the historian needs 20 surpass, who bringeth you images of true matters, such as indeed were done, and not such as fantastically or falsely may be suggested to have been done. Truly, Aristotle himself, in his discourse of poesy, plainly determineth this question, saying that Poetry is *philosophoteron* and *spoudaioteron*, 25 that is to say, it is more philosophical and more studiously serious than history. His reason is, because poesy dealeth with *katholou*, that is to say, with the universal consideration, and the history with *kathekaston*, the particular: ' now ', saith he, ' the universal weighs what is fit to be said or done, 30 either in likelihood or necessity (which the poesy considereth in his imposed names), and the particular only marks whether Alcibiades did, or suffered, this or that.' Thus far Aristotle: which reason of his (as all his) is most full of reason.

For indeed, if the question were whether it were better to 35 have a particular act truly or falsely set down, there is no doubt which is to be chosen, no more than whether you had rather have Vespasian's picture right as he was, or, at the painter's pleasure, nothing resembling. But if the question

be for your own use and learning, whether it be better to
have it set down as it should be, or as it was, then certainly
is more doctrinable the feigned Cyrus of Xenophon than the
true Cyrus in Justin, and the feigned Aeneas in Virgil than
5 the right Aeneas in Dares Phrygius: as to a lady that desired
to fashion her countenance to the best grace, a painter should
more benefit her to portray a most sweet face, writing Canidia
upon it, than to paint Canidia as she was, who, Horace
sweareth, was foul and ill favoured.

10   If the poet do his part aright, he will show you in Tantalus,
Atreus, and such like, nothing that is not to be shunned; in
Cyrus, Aeneas, Ulysses, each thing to be followed; where
the historian, bound to tell things as things were, cannot be
liberal (without he will be poetical) of a perfect pattern, but,
15 as in Alexander or Scipio himself, show doings, some to be
liked, some to be misliked. And then how will you discern
what to follow but by your own discretion, which you had
without reading Quintus Curtius? And whereas a man may
say, though in universal consideration of doctrine the poet
20 prevaileth, yet that the history, in his saying such a thing was
done, doth warrant a man more in that he shall follow—the
answer is manifest: that if he stand upon that *was*—as if he
should argue, because it rained yesterday, therefore it should
rain to-day—then indeed it hath some advantage to a gross
25 conceit; but if he know an example only informs a conjec-
tured likelihood, and so go by reason, the poet doth so far
exceed him as he is to frame his example to that which is most
reasonable, be it in warlike, politic, or private matters; where
the historian in his bare *was* hath many times that which we
30 call fortune to overrule the best wisdom. Many times he
must tell events whereof he can yield no cause; or, if he do,
it must be poetical.

For that a feigned example hath as much force to teach as
a true example (for as for to move, it is clear, since the feigned
35 may be tuned to the highest key of passion), let us take one
example wherein a poet and a historian do concur. Herodotus
and Justin do both testify that Zopyrus, King Darius' faithful
servant, seeing his master long resisted by the rebellious
Babylonians, feigned himself in extreme disgrace of his king:

for verifying of which, he caused his own nose and ears to be cut off, and so flying to the Babylonians, was received, and for his known valour so far credited, that he did find means to deliver them over to Darius. Much like matter doth Livy record of Tarquinius and his son. Xenophon excellently feigneth such another stratagem performed by Abradatas in Cyrus' behalf. Now would I fain know, if occasion be presented unto you to serve your prince by such an honest dissimulation, why you do not as well learn it of Xenophon's fiction as of the other's verity? And truly so much the better, as you shall save your nose by the bargain; for Abradatas did not counterfeit so far. So then the best of the historian is subject to the poet; for whatsoever action, or faction, whatsoever counsel, policy, or war stratagem the historian is bound to recite, that may the poet (if he list) with his imitation make his own, beautifying it both for further teaching, and more delighting, as it pleaseth him: having all, from Dante's heaven to his hell, under the authority of his pen. Which if I be asked what poets have done so, as I might well name some, yet say I and say again, I speak of the art, and not of the artificer.

Now, to that which commonly is attributed to the praise of histories, in respect of the notable learning is gotten by marking the success, as though therein a man should see virtue exalted and vice punished—truly that commendation is peculiar to Poetry, and far off from history. For indeed Poetry ever setteth virtue so out in her best colours, making Fortune her well-waiting handmaid, that one must needs be enamoured of her. Well may you see Ulysses in a storm, and in other hard plights; but they are but exercises of patience and magnanimity, to make them shine the more in the near-following prosperity. And of the contrary part, if evil men come to the stage, they ever go out (as the tragedy writer answered to one that misliked the show of such persons) so manacled as they little animate folks to follow them. But the historian, being captived to the truth of a foolish world, is many times a terror from well-doing, and an encouragement to unbridled wickedness.

For see we not valiant Miltiades rot in his fetters? the

just Phocion and the accomplished Socrates put to death like traitors? the cruel Severus live prosperously? the excellent Severus miserably murdered? Sylla and Marius dying in their beds? Pompey and Cicero slain then when they would
5 have thought exile a happiness? See we not virtuous Cato driven to kill himself, and rebel Caesar so advanced that his name yet, after 1600 years, lasteth in the highest honour? And mark but even Caesar's own words of the forenamed Sylla (who in that only did honestly, to put down his dishonest
10 tyranny), *literas nescivit*, as if want of learning caused him to do well. He meant it not by Poetry, which, not content with earthly plagues, deviseth new punishments in hell for tyrants, nor yet by Philosophy, which teacheth *occidendos esse*; but no doubt by skill in History, for that indeed can afford your
15 Cypselus, Periander, Phalaris, Dionysius, and I know not how many more of the same kennel, that speed well enough in their abominable injustice or usurpation. I conclude therefore, that he excelleth History, not only in furnishing the mind with knowledge, but in setting it forward to that
20 which deserveth to be called and accounted good: which setting forward, and moving to well-doing, indeed setteth the laurel crown upon the poet as victorious, not only of the historian, but over the philosopher, howsoever in teaching it may be questionable.

25 For suppose it be granted (that which I suppose with great reason may be denied) that the philosopher, in respect of his methodical proceeding, doth teach more perfectly than the poet, yet do I think that no man is so much *philophilosophos* as to compare the philosopher in moving with the poet.

30 And that moving is of a higher degree than teaching, it may by this appear, that it is well nigh the cause and the effect of teaching. For who will be taught, if he be not moved with desire to be taught? and what so much good doth that teaching bring forth (I speak still of moral doctrine) as that
35 it moveth one to do that which it doth teach? For, as Aristotle saith, it is not *gnosis* but *praxis* must be the fruit. And how *praxis* cannot be, without being moved to practise, it is no hard matter to consider.

The philosopher showeth you the way, he informeth you

of the particularities, as well of the tediousness of the way,
as of the pleasant lodging you shall have when your journey
is ended, as of the many by-turnings that may divert you
from your way. But this is to no man but to him that will
read him, and read him with attentive studious painfulness; 5
which constant desire whosoever hath in him, hath already
passed half the hardness of the way, and therefore is beholding
to the philosopher but for the other half. Nay truly, learned
men have learnedly thought that where once reason hath so
much overmastered passion as that the mind hath a free desire 10
to do well, the inward light each mind hath in itself is as good
as a philosopher's book; seeing in Nature we know it is well
to do well, and what is well and what is evil, although not in
the words of art which philosophers bestow upon us; for
out of natural conceit the philosophers drew it. But to be 15
moved to do that which we know, or to be moved with desire
to know, *hoc opus, hic labor est.*

Now therein of all sciences (I speak still of human, and
according to the human conceits) is our poet the monarch.
For he doth not only show the way, but giveth so sweet a 20
prospect into the way, as will entice any man to enter into it.
Nay, he doth, as if your journey should lie through a fair
vineyard, at the first give you a cluster of grapes, that full of
that taste, you may long to pass further. He beginneth not
with obscure definitions, which must blur the margent with 25
interpretations, and load the memory with doubtfulness;
but he cometh to you with words set in delightful proportion,
either accompanied with, or prepared for, the well enchanting
skill of music; and with a tale forsooth he cometh unto you,
with a tale which holdeth children from play, and old men 30
from the chimney corner. And, pretending no more, doth
intend the winning of the mind from wickedness to virtue:
even as the child is often brought to take most wholesome
things by hiding them in such other as have a pleasant taste:
which, if one should begin to tell them the nature of aloes or 35
rhubarb they should receive, would sooner take their physic
at their ears than at their mouth. So is it in men (most of
which are childish in the best things, till they be cradled in
their graves): glad they will be to hear the tales of Hercules,

Achilles, Cyrus, and Aeneas; and, hearing them, mus
hear the right description of wisdom, valour, and
which, if they had been barely, that is to say philosop
set out, they would swear they be brought to school
5   That imitation whereof Poetry is, hath the most conv
to Nature of all other, insomuch that, as Aristotle saith, those
things which in themselves are horrible, as cruel battles, un-
natural monsters, are made in poetical imitation delightful.
Truly, I have known men, that even with reading *Amadis de*
10 *Gaule* (which God knoweth wanteth much of a perfect poesy)
have found their hearts moved to the exercise of courtesy,
liberality, and especially courage. Who readeth Aeneas
carrying old Anchises on his back, that wisheth not it were
his fortune to perform so excellent an act? Whom do not
15 the words of Turnus move, the tale of Turnus having planted
his image in the imagination?

> *Fugientem haec terra videbit?*
> *Usque adeone mori miserum est?*

Where the philosophers, as they scorn to delight, so must
20 they be content little to move—saving wrangling whether
virtue be the chief or the only good, whether the contempla-
tive or the active life do excel—which Plato and Boethius well
knew, and therefore made mistress Philosophy very often
borrow the masking raiment of Poesy. For even those hard-
25 hearted evil men who think virtue a school name, and know
no other good but *indulgere genio*, and therefore despise
the austere admonitions of the philosopher, and feel not
the inward reason they stand upon, yet will be content to
be delighted—which is all the good-fellow poet seemeth to
30 promise—and so steal to see the form of goodness (which
seen they cannot but love) ere themselves be aware, as if they
took a medicine of cherries.
   Infinite proofs of the strange effects of this poetical inven-
tion might be alleged; only two shall serve, which are so
35 often remembered as I think all men know them. The one
of Menenius Agrippa, who, when the whole people of Rome
had resolutely divided themselves from the senate, with ap-
parent show of utter ruin, though he were (for that time) an

excellent orator, came not among them upon trust of figura-
tive speeches or cunning insinuations, and much less with
farfetched maxims of Philosophy, which (especially if they
were Platonic) they must have learned geometry before they
could well have conceived; but forsooth he behaves himself 5
like a homely and familiar poet. He telleth them a tale, that
there was a time when all the parts of the body made a
mutinous conspiracy against the belly, which they thought
devoured the fruits of each other's labour: they concluded
they would let so unprofitable a spender starve. In the end, 10
to be short (for the tale is notorious, and as notorious that it
was a tale), with punishing the belly they plagued themselves.
This applied by him wrought such effect in the people, as I
never read that ever words brought forth but then so sudden
and so good an alteration; for upon reasonable conditions a 15
perfect reconcilement ensued. The other is of Nathan the
prophet, who, when the holy David had so far forsaken God
as to confirm adultery with murder, when he was to do the
tenderest office of a friend, in laying his own shame before
his eyes, sent by God to call again so chosen a servant, how 20
doth he it but by telling of a man whose beloved lamb was
ungratefully taken from his bosom?—the application most
divinely true, but the discourse itself feigned; which made
David (I speak of the second and instrumental cause) as in
a glass to see his own filthiness, as that heavenly psalm of 25
mercy well testifieth.

By these, therefore, examples and reasons, I think it may
be manifest that the poet, with that same hand of delight,
doth draw the mind more effectually than any other art doth.
And so a conclusion not unfitly ensueth: that, as virtue is the 30
most excellent resting place for all worldly learning to make
his end of, so Poetry, being the most familiar to teach it, and
most princely to move towards it, in the most excellent work
is the most excellent workman.

But I am content not only to decipher him by his works 35
(although works in commendation or dispraise must ever
hold an high authority), but more narrowly will examine his
parts; so that, as in a man, though all together may carry a
presence full of majesty and beauty, perchance in some one

defectious piece we may find a blemish. Now in his parts, kinds, or species (as you list to term them), it is to be noted that some poesies have coupled together two or three kinds, as tragical and comical, whereupon is risen the tragi-comical.
5 Some, in the like manner, have mingled prose and verse, as Sannazzaro and Boethius. Some have mingled matters heroical and pastoral. But that cometh all to one in this question, for, if severed they be good, the conjunction cannot be hurtful. Therefore, perchance forgetting some and
10 leaving some as needless to be remembered, it shall not be amiss in a word to cite the special kinds, to see what faults may be found in the right use of them.

Is it then the Pastoral poem which is misliked? For perchance where the hedge is lowest they will soonest leap over.
15 Is the poor pipe disdained, which sometime out of Meliboeus' mouth can show the misery of people under hard lords or ravening soldiers? And again, by Tityrus, what blessedness is derived to them that lie lowest from the goodness of them that sit highest; sometimes, under the pretty tales of wolves
20 and sheep, can include the whole considerations of wrong-doing and patience; sometimes show that contention for trifles can get but a trifling victory: where perchance a man may see that even Alexander and Darius, when they strave who should be cock of this world's dunghill, the benefit they
25 got was that the afterlivers may say,

> *Haec memini et victum frustra contendere Thirsin:*
> *Ex illo Corydon, Corydon est tempore nobis.*

Or is it the lamenting Elegiac? which in a kind heart would move rather pity than blame, who bewails with the great
30 philosopher Heraclitus the weakness of mankind and the wretchedness of the world; who surely is to be praised, either for compassionate accompanying just causes of lamentation, or for rightly painting out how weak be the passions of woefulness. Is it the bitter but wholesome Iambic? which rubs
35 the galled mind, in making shame the trumpet of villainy with bold and open crying out against naughtiness. Or the Satiric? who

> *Omne vafer vitium ridenti tangit amico;*

who sportingly never leaveth until he make a man laugh at
folly, and at length ashamed to laugh at himself, which he
cannot avoid, without avoiding the folly; who, while

circum praecordia ludit,

giveth us to feel how many headaches a passionate life 5
bringeth us to; how, when all is done,

Est Ulubris, animus si nos non deficit aequus.

No, perchance it is the Comic, whom naughty play-makers
and stage-keepers have justly made odious. To the argument
of abuse I will answer after. Only thus much now is to be 10
said, that the Comedy is an imitation of the common errors
of our life, which he representeth in the most ridiculous and
scornful sort that may be, so as it is impossible that any be-
holder can be content to be such a one.

Now, as in geometry the oblique must be known as well as 15
the right, and in arithmetic the odd as well as the even, so in
the actions of our life who seeth not the filthiness of evil
wanteth a great foil to perceive the beauty of virtue. This
doth the Comedy handle so in our private and domestical
matters, as with hearing it we get as it were an experience, 20
what is to be looked for of a niggardly Demea, of a crafty
Davus, of a flattering Gnatho, of a vainglorious Thraso; and
not only to know what effects are to be expected, but to know
who be such, by the signifying badge given them by the
comedian. And little reason hath any man to say that men 25
learn evil by seeing it so set out; since, as I said before, there
is no man living but, by the force truth hath in Nature, no
sooner seeth these men play their parts, but wisheth them *in
pistrinum*; although perchance the sack of his own faults lie
so behind his back that he seeth not himself dance the same 30
measure; whereto yet nothing can more open his eyes than
to find his own actions contemptibly set forth.

So that the right use of Comedy will (I think) by nobody
be blamed, and much less of the high and excellent Tragedy,
that openeth the greatest wounds, and showeth forth the 35
ulcers that are covered with tissue; that maketh kings fear
to be tyrants, and tyrants manifest their tyrannical humours;

that, with stirring the affects of admiration and commisera-
tion, teacheth the uncertainty of this world, and upon how
weak foundations gilden roofs are builded; that maketh us
know,

5   *Qui sceptra saevus duro imperio regit,*
          Timet timentes, metus in auctorem redit.

But how much it can move, Plutarch yieldeth a notable
testimony of the abominable tyrant Alexander Pheraeus,
from whose eyes a tragedy, well made and represented, drew
10 abundance of tears, who without all pity had murdered
infinite numbers, and some of his own blood; so as he that
was not ashamed to make matters for tragedies, yet could not
resist the sweet violence of a tragedy. And if it wrought no
further good in him, it was that he, in despite of himself,
15 withdrew himself from hearkening to that which might
mollify his hardened heart. But it is not the Tragedy they
do mislike; for it were too absurd to cast out so excellent a
representation of whatsoever is most worthy to be learned.

Is it the Lyric that most displeaseth? who with his tuned
20 lyre and well-accorded voice, giveth praise, the reward of
virtue, to virtuous acts; who gives moral precepts, and
natural problems; who sometimes raiseth up his voice to the
height of the heavens, in singing the lauds of the immortal
God. Certainly, I must confess my own barbarousness, I
25 never heard the old song of Percy and Douglas that I found
not my heart moved more than with a trumpet; and yet is it
sung but by some blind crowder, with no rougher voice than
rude style; which, being so evil apparelled in the dust and
cobwebs of that uncivil age, what would it work, trimmed in
30 the gorgeous eloquence of Pindar? In Hungary I have seen
it the manner at all feasts, and other such meetings, to have
songs of their ancestors' valour, which that right soldierlike
nation think the chiefest kindlers of brave courage. The
incomparable Lacedemonians did not only carry that kind of
35 music ever with them to the field, but even at home, as such
songs were made, so were they all content to be the singers
of them; when the lusty men were to tell what they did, the
old men what they had done, and the young men what they

would do. And where a man may say that Pindar many times praiseth highly victories of small moment, matters rather of sport than virtue; as it may be answered, it was the fault of the poet, and not of the poetry, so indeed the chief fault was in the time and custom of the Greeks, who set those toys at so high a price that Philip of Macedon reckoned a horserace won at Olympus among his three fearful felicities. But as the unimitable Pindar often did, so is that kind most capable and most fit to awake the thoughts from the sleep of idleness, to embrace honourable enter- prises.

There rests the Heroical, whose very name (I think) should daunt all backbiters; for by what conceit can a tongue be directed to speak evil of that which draweth with it no less champions than Achilles, Cyrus, Aeneas, Turnus, Tydeus, and Rinaldo? who doth not only teach and move to a truth, but teacheth and moveth to the most high and excellent truth; who maketh magnanimity and justice shine through- out all misty fearfulness and foggy desires; who, if the saying of Plato and Tully be true, that who could see virtue would be wonderfully ravished with the love of her beauty—this man sets her out to make her more lovely in her holiday apparel, to the eye of any that will deign not to disdain until they understand. But if anything be already said in the de- fence of sweet Poetry, all concurreth to the maintaining the Heroical, which is not only a kind, but the best and most accomplished kind of Poetry. For as the image of each action stirreth and instructeth the mind, so the lofty image of such worthies most inflameth the mind with desire to be worthy, and informs with counsel how to be worthy. Only let Aeneas be worn in the tablet of your memory, how he governeth himself in the ruin of his country; in the preserving his old father, and carrying away his religious ceremonies; in obey- ing the god's commandment to leave Dido, though not only all passionate kindness, but even the human consideration of virtuous gratefulness, would have craved other of him; how in storms, how in sports, how in war, how in peace, how a fugitive, how victorious, how besieged, how besieging, how to strangers, how to allies, how to enemies, how to his own;

lastly, how in his inward self, and how in his outward govern-
ment; and I think, in a mind not prejudiced with a prejudica-
ting humour, he will be found in excellency fruitful, yea,
even as Horace saith,

5   *melius Chrysippo et Crantore.*

But truly I imagine it falleth out with these poet-whippers,
as with some good women, who often are sick, but in faith
they cannot tell where. So the name of Poetry is odious to
them, but neither his cause nor effects, neither the sum that
10 contains him, nor the particularities descending from him,
give any fast handle to their carping dispraise.

Since then Poetry is of all human learning the most ancient
and of most fatherly antiquity, as from whence other learnings
have taken their beginnings; since it is so universal that no
15 learned nation doth despise it, nor no barbarous nation is
without it; since both Roman and Greek gave divine names
unto it, the one of ' prophesying ', the other of ' making ',
and that indeed that name of ' making ' is fit for him, con-
sidering that whereas other arts retain themselves within
20 their subject, and receive, as it were, their being from it, the
poet only bringeth his own stuff, and doth not learn a conceit
out of a matter, but maketh matter for a conceit; since
neither his description nor his end containeth any evil, the
thing described cannot be evil; since his effects be so good as
25 to teach goodness and to delight the learners; since therein
(namely in moral doctrine, the chief of all knowledges) he
doth not only far pass the historian, but, for instructing, is
well nigh comparable to the philosopher, and, for moving,
leaves him behind him; since the Holy Scripture (wherein
30 there is no uncleanness) hath whole parts in it poetical, and
that even our Saviour Christ vouchsafed to use the flowers
of it; since all his kinds are not only in their united forms
but in their severed dissections fully commendable; I think
(and think I think rightly) the laurel crown appointed for
35 triumphing captains doth worthily (of all other learnings)
honour the poet's triumph.

But because we have ears as well as tongues, and that the
lightest reasons that may be will seem to weigh greatly, if

nothing be put in the counterbalance, let us hear, and, as well as we can, ponder, what objections may be made against this art, which may be worthy either of yielding or answering.

First, truly I note not only in these *mysomousoi*, poet-haters, but in all that kind of people who seek a praise by dispraising others, that they do prodigally spend a great many wandering words in quips and scoffs, carping and taunting at each thing which, by stirring the spleen, may stay the brain from a through-beholding the worthiness of the subject. Those kind of objections, as they are full of very idle easiness, since there is nothing of so sacred a majesty but that an itching tongue may rub itself upon it, so deserve they no other answer, but, instead of laughing at the jest, to laugh at the jester. We know a playing wit can praise the discretion of an ass, the comfortableness of being in debt, and the jolly commodity of being sick of the plague. So of the contrary side, if we will turn Ovid's verse,

Ut lateat virtus proximitate mali,

that ' good lie hid in nearness of the evil ', Agrippa will be as merry in showing the vanity of science as Erasmus was in commending of folly. Neither shall any man or matter escape some touch of these smiling railers. But for Erasmus and Agrippa, they had another foundation, than the superficial part would promise. Marry, these other pleasant faultfinders, who will correct the verb before they understand the noun, and confute others' knowledge before they confirm their own, I would have them only remember that scoffing cometh not of wisdom; so as the best title in true English they get with their merriments is to be called good fools, for so have our grave forefathers ever termed that humorous kind of jesters.

But that which giveth greatest scope to their scorning humours is rhyming and versing. It is already said (and, as I think, truly said) it is not rhyming and versing that maketh poesy. One may be a poet without versing, and a versifier without poetry. But yet presuppose it were inseparable (as indeed it seemeth Scaliger judgeth) truly it were an inseparable commendation. For if *oratio* next to *ratio*, speech next to reason, be the greatest gift bestowed upon mortality, that

cannot be praiseless which doth most polish that blessing of
speech; which considers each word, not only (as a man may
say) by his forcible quality, but by his best measured quan-
tity, carrying even in themselves a harmony—without, per-
5 chance, number, measure, order, proportion be in our time
grown odious. But lay aside the just praise it hath, by being
the only fit speech for Music (Music, I say, the most divine
striker of the senses), thus much is undoubtedly true, that if
reading be foolish without remembering, memory being the
10 only treasurer of knowledge, those words which are fittest
for memory are likewise most convenient for knowledge.

Now, that verse far exceedeth prose in the knitting up of
the memory, the reason is manifest: the words (besides their
delight, which hath a great affinity to memory) being so set
15 as one word cannot be lost but the whole work fails; which
accuseth itself, calleth the remembrance back to itself, and
so most strongly confirmeth it. Besides, one word so, as it
were, begetting another, as, be it in rhyme or measured verse,
by the former a man shall have a near guess to the follower.
20 Lastly, even they that have taught the art of memory have
showed nothing so apt for it as a certain room divided into
many places well and thoroughly known. Now, that hath the
verse in effect perfectly, every word having his natural seat,
which seat must needs make the words remembered. But
25 what needeth more in a thing so known to all men? Who
is it that ever was a scholar that doth not carry away some
verses of Virgil, Horace, or Cato, which in his youth he
learned, and even to his old age serve him for hourly lessons?:
as

30   *Percontatorem fugito, nam garrulus idem est.*

        Dum sibi quisque placet, credula turba sumus.

But the fitness it hath for memory is notably proved by all
delivery of arts: wherein for the most part, from Grammar
to Logic, Mathematic, Physic, and the rest, the rules chiefly
35 necessary to be borne away are compiled in verses. So that
verse being in itself sweet and orderly, and being best for
memory, the only handle of knowledge, it must be in jest
that any man can speak against it.

Now then go we to the most important imputations laid to the poor poets. For aught I can yet learn, they are these. First, that there being many other more fruitful knowledges, a man might better spend his time in them than in this. Secondly, that it is the mother of lies. Thirdly, that it is the 5 nurse of abuse, infecting us with many pestilent desires, with a siren's sweetness drawing the mind to the serpent's tale of sinful fancy—and herein, especially, comedies give the largest field to ear (as Chaucer saith); how both in other nations and in ours, before poets did soften us, we were full of courage, 10 given to martial exercises, the pillars of manlike liberty, and not lulled asleep in shady idleness with poets' pastimes. And lastly, and chiefly, they cry out with an open mouth as if they outshot Robin Hood, that Plato banished them out of his commonwealth. Truly, this is much, if there be much 15 truth in it.

First, to the first, that a man might better spend his time is a reason indeed; but it doth (as they say) but *petere principium*: for if it be, as I affirm, that no learning is so good as that which teacheth and moveth to virtue, and that none can 20 both teach and move thereto so much as Poetry, then is the conclusion manifest that ink and paper cannot be to a more profitable purpose employed. And certainly, though a man should grant their first assumption, it should follow (methinks) very unwillingly, that good is not good because better 25 is better. But I still and utterly deny that there is sprung out of earth a more fruitful knowledge.

To the second therefore, that they should be the principal liars, I answer paradoxically, but truly, I think truly, that of all writers under the sun the poet is the least liar, and, though 30 he would, as a poet can scarcely be a liar. The astronomer, with his cousin the geometrician, can hardly escape, when they take upon them to measure the height of the stars. How often, think you, do the physicians lie, when they aver things good for sicknesses, which afterwards send Charon a great 35 number of souls drowned in a potion before they come to his ferry? And no less of the rest, which take upon them to affirm. Now for the poet, he nothing affirms, and therefore never lieth. For, as I take it, to lie is to affirm that to be true

which is false; so as the other artists, and especially the his-
torian, affirming many things, can, in the cloudy knowledge
of mankind, hardly escape from many lies. But the poet (as
I said before) never affirmeth. The poet never maketh any
5 circles about your imagination, to conjure you to believe for
true what he writes. He citeth not authorities of other his-
tories, but even for his entry calleth the sweet Muses to in-
spire into him a good invention; in truth, not labouring to
tell you what is or is not, but what should or should not be.
10 And therefore, though he recount things not true, yet because
he telleth them not for true, he lieth not—without we will
say that Nathan lied in his speech before-alleged to David;
which as a wicked man durst scarce say, so think I none so
simple would say that Aesop lied in the tales of his beasts;
15 for who thinks that Aesop writ it for actually true were well
worthy to have his name chronicled among the beasts he
writeth of. What child is there that, coming to a play, and
seeing *Thebes* written in great letters upon an old door, doth
believe that it is Thebes? If then a man can arrive, at that
20 child's age, to know that the poets' persons and doings are
but pictures what should be, and not stories what have been,
they will never give the lie to things not affirmatively but
allegorically and figuratively written. And therefore, as in
History looking for truth, they go away full fraught with false-
25 hood, so in Poesy looking but for fiction, they shall use the
narration but as an imaginative ground-plot of a profitable
invention.

But hereto is replied, that the poets give names to men they
write of, which argueth a conceit of an actual truth, and so,
30 not being true, proves a falsehood. And doth the lawyer lie
then, when under the names of ' John a Stile ' and ' John a
Noakes ' he puts his case? But that is easily answered. Their
naming of men is but to make their picture the more lively,
and not to build any history: painting men, they cannot
35 leave men nameless. We see we cannot play at chess but
that we must give names to our chessmen; and yet, methinks,
he were a very partial champion of truth that would say we
lied for giving a piece of wood the reverend title of a bishop.
The poet nameth Cyrus or Aeneas no other way than to show

what men of their fames, fortunes, and estates should do.

Their third is, how much it abuseth men's wit, training it
to wanton sinfulness and lustful love: for indeed that is the
principal, if not the only, abuse I can hear alleged. They say
the Comedies rather teach than reprehend amorous conceits. 5
They say the Lyric is larded with passionate sonnets, the
Elegiac weeps the want of his mistress, and that even to the
Heroical Cupid hath ambitiously climbed. Alas, Love, I
would thou couldst as well defend thyself as thou canst offend
others. I would those on whom thou dost attend could either 10
put thee away, or yield good reason why they keep thee. But
grant love of beauty to be a beastly fault (although it be very
hard, since only man, and no beast, hath that gift to discern
beauty); grant that lovely name of Love to deserve all hateful
reproaches (although even some of my masters the philos- 15
ophers spent a good deal of their lamp-oil in setting forth
the excellency of it); grant, I say, whatsoever they will have
granted, that not only love, but lust, but vanity, but (if they
list) scurrility, possesseth many leaves of the poets' books;
yet think I, when this is granted, they will find their sentence 20
may with good manners put the last words foremost, and not
say that Poetry abuseth man's wit, but that man's wit abuseth
Poetry.

For I will not deny but that man's wit may make Poesy,
which should be *eikastike*, which some learned have defined, 25
' figuring forth good things ', to be *phantastike*, which doth
contrariwise infect the fancy with unworthy objects; as the
painter, that should give to the eye either some excellent
perspective, or some fine picture, fit for building or fortifica-
tion, or containing in it some notable example, as Abraham 30
sacrificing his son Isaac, Judith killing Holofernes, David
fighting with Goliath, may leave those, and please an ill-
pleased eye with wanton shows of better hidden matters.
But what, shall the abuse of a thing make the right use odious ?
Nay truly, though I yield that Poesy may not only be abused, 35
but that being abused, by the reason of his sweet charming
force, it can do more hurt than any other army of words, yet
shall it be so far from concluding that the abuse should give
reproach to the abused, that contrariwise it is a good reason,

that whatsoever, being abused, doth most harm, being rightly used (and upon the right use each thing conceiveth his title), doth most good.

Do we not see the skill of Physic (the best rampire to our often-assaulted bodies), being abused, teach poison, the most violent destroyer? Doth not knowledge of Law, whose end is to even and right all things, being abused, grow the crooked fosterer of horrible injuries? Doth not (to go to the highest) God's word abused breed heresy, and His name abused become blasphemy? Truly a needle cannot do much hurt, and as truly (with leave of ladies be it spoken) it cannot do much good. With a sword thou mayest kill thy father, and with a sword thou mayest defend thy prince and country. So that, as in their calling poets the fathers of lies they say nothing, so in this their argument of abuse they prove the commendation.

They allege herewith, that before poets began to be in price our nation hath set their hearts' delight upon action, and not upon imagination, rather doing things worthy to be written, than writing things fit to be done. What that before-time was, I think scarcely Sphinx can tell, since no memory is so ancient that hath the precedence of Poetry. And certain it is that, in our plainest homeliness, yet never was the Albion nation without poetry. Marry, this argument, though it be levelled against poetry, yet is it indeed a chainshot against all learning, or bookishness, as they commonly term it. Of such mind were certain Goths, of whom it is written that, having in the spoil of a famous city taken a fair library, one hangman (belike fit to execute the fruits of their wits who had murdered a great number of bodies), would have set fire on it. 'No,' said another very gravely, 'take heed what you do, for while they are busy about these toys, we shall with more leisure conquer their countries.'

This indeed is the ordinary doctrine of ignorance, and many words sometimes I have heard spent in it; but because this reason is generally against all learning, as well as Poetry, or rather, all learning but Poetry; because it were too large a digression to handle, or at least too superfluous (since it is manifest that all government of action is to be gotten by

knowledge, and knowledge best by gathering many know-
ledges, which is reading), I only, with Horace, to him that is
of that opinion,

jubeo stultum esse libenter;

for as for Poetry itself, it is the freest from this objection. 5
   For Poetry is the companion of the camps. I dare under-
take, Orlando Furioso, or honest King Arthur, will never
displease a soldier: but the quiddity of *ens* and *prima materia*
will hardly agree with a corslet. And therefore, as I said in
the beginning, even Turks and Tartars are delighted with 10
poets. Homer, a Greek, flourished before Greece flourished.
And if to a slight conjecture a conjecture may be opposed,
truly it may seem, that as by him their learned men took
almost their first light of knowledge, so their active men
received their first motions of courage. Only Alexander's 15
example may serve, who by Plutarch is accounted of such
virtue, that Fortune was not his guide but his footstool;
whose acts speak for him, though Plutarch did not,—indeed
the phoenix of warlike princes. This Alexander left his
schoolmaster, living Aristotle, behind him, but took dead 20
Homer with him. He put the philosopher Callisthenes to
death for his seeming philosophical, indeed mutinous, stub-
bornness, but the chief thing he ever was heard to wish for
was that Homer had been alive. He well found he received
more bravery of mind by the pattern of Achilles than by 25
hearing the definition of fortitude. And therefore, if Cato
misliked Fulvius for carrying Ennius with him to the field,
it may be answered that, if Cato misliked it, the noble Fulvius
liked it, or else he had not done it: for it was not the excellent
Cato Uticensis (whose authority I would much more have 30
reverenced), but it was the former, in truth a bitter punisher
of faults, but else a man that had never well sacrificed to the
graces. He misliked and cried out upon all Greek learning,
and yet, being four score years old, began to learn it, belike
fearing that Pluto understood not Latin. Indeed, the Roman 35
laws allowed no person to be carried to the wars but he that
was in the soldiers' roll, and therefore, though Cato misliked
his unmustered person, he misliked not his work. And if

he had, Scipio Nasica, judged by common consent the best Roman, loved him. Both the other Scipio brothers, who had by their virtues no less surnames than of Asia and Afric, so loved him that they caused his body to be buried in their 5 sepulchre. So as Cato's authority being but against his person, and that answered with so far greater than himself, is herein of no validity.

But now indeed my burden is great; now Plato's name is laid upon me, whom, I must confess, of all philosophers I 10 have ever esteemed most worthy of reverence, and with great reason: since of all philosophers he is the most poetical. Yet if he will defile the fountain out of which his flowing streams have proceeded, let us boldly examine with what reasons he did it. First, truly a man might maliciously object that 15 Plato, being a philosopher, was a natural enemy of poets. For indeed, after the philosophers had picked out of the sweet mysteries of Poetry the right discerning true points of knowledge, they forthwith, putting it in method, and making a school-art of that which the poets did only teach by a divine 20 delightfulness, beginning to spurn at their guides, like ungrateful prentices, were not content to set up shops for themselves, but sought by all means to discredit their masters; which by the force of delight being barred them, the less they could overthrow them, the more they hated them. For in- 25 deed, they found for Homer seven cities strave who should have him for their citizen; where many cities banished philosophers as not fit members to live among them. For only repeating certain of Euripides' verses, many Athenians had their lives saved of the Syracusans, when the Athenians 30 themselves thought many philosophers unworthy to live. Certain poets, as Simonides and Pindar, had so prevailed with Hiero the First, that of a tyrant they made him a just king; where Plato could do so little with Dionysius, that he himself of a philosopher was made a slave. But who should 35 do thus, I confess, should requite the objections made against poets with like cavillation against philosophers; as likewise one should do that should bid one read *Phaedrus* or *Symposium* in Plato, or the discourse of love in Plutarch, and see whether any poet do authorize abominable filthiness, as they

do.   Again, a man might ask out of what commonwealth
Plato did banish them.   In sooth, thence where he himself
alloweth community of women.   So as belike this banishment
grew not for effeminate wantonness, since little should poeti-
cal sonnets be hurtful when a man might have what woman 5
he listed.   But I honour philosophical instructions, and bless
the wits which bred them: so as they be not abused, which
is likewise stretched to Poetry.

   St Paul himself (who yet, for the credit of poets, allegeth
twice two poets, and one of them by the name of a prophet), 10
setteth a watchword upon Philosophy,—indeed upon the
abuse.   So doth Plato upon the abuse, not upon Poetry.
Plato found fault that the poets of his time filled the world
with wrong opinions of the gods, making light tales of that
unspotted essence, and therefore would not have the youth 15
depraved with such opinions.   Herein may much be said;
let this suffice: the poets did not induce such opinions, but
did imitate those opinions already induced.   For all the Greek
stories can well testify that the very religion of that time stood
upon many and many-fashioned gods, not taught so by the 20
poets, but followed according to their nature of imitation.
Who list may read in Plutarch the discourses of Isis and
Osiris, of the cause why oracles ceased, of the divine provi-
dence, and see whether the theology of that nation stood not
upon such dreams which the poets indeed superstitiously 25
observed and truly (since they had not the light of Christ)
did much better in it than the philosophers, who, shaking off
superstition, brought in atheism.   Plato therefore (whose
authority I had much rather justly construe than unjustly
resist) meant not in general of poets, in those words of which 30
Julius Scaliger saith, *Qua authoritate barbari quidam atque
hispidi abuti velint ad poetas e republica exigendos*; but only
meant to drive out those wrong opinions of the Deity (whereof
now, without further law, Christianity hath taken away all
the hurtful belief), perchance (as he thought) nourished by 35
the then esteemed poets.   And a man need go no further
than to Plato himself to know his meaning: who, in his
dialogue called *Ion*, giveth high and rightly divine commenda-
tion to Poetry.   So as Plato, banishing the abuse, not the

thing—not banishing it, but giving due honour unto it—shall
be our patron and not our adversary. For indeed I had much
rather (since truly I may do it) show their mistaking of Plato
(under whose lion's skin they would make an ass-like braying
against Poesy) than go about to overthrow his authority;
whom, the wiser a man is, the more just cause he shall find
to have in admiration; especially since he attributeth unto
Poesy more than myself do, namely, to be a very inspiring of
a divine force, far above man's wit, as in the afore-named
dialogue is apparent.

Of the other side, who would show the honours have been
by the best sort of judgments granted them, a whole sea of
examples would present themselves: Alexanders, Caesars,
Scipios, all favourers of poets; Laelius, called the Roman
Socrates, himself a poet, so as part of *Heautontimorumenos* in
Terence was supposed to be made by him; and even the
Greek Socrates, whom Apollo confirmed to be the only wise
man, is said to have spent part of his old time in putting
Aesop's fables into verses. And therefore, full evil should it
become his scholar Plato to put such words in his master's
mouth against poets. But what need more ? Aristotle writes
the Art of Poesy: and why, if it should not be written ?
Plutarch teacheth the use to be gathered of them, and how,
if they should not be read? And who reads Plutarch's either
history or philosophy, shall find he trimmeth both their
garments with guards of Poesy. But I list not to defend
Poesy with the help of her underling Historiography. Let it
suffice that it is a fit soil for praise to dwell upon; and what
dispraise may set upon it, is either easily overcome, or trans-
formed into just commendation.

So that, since the excellencies of it may be so easily and so
justly confirmed, and the low-creeping objections so soon
trodden down: it not being an art of lies, but of true doctrine;
not of effeminateness, but of notable stirring of courage; not
of abusing man's wit, but of strengthening man's wit; not
banished, but honoured by Plato; let us rather plant more
laurels for to engarland our poets' heads (which honour of
being laureate, as besides them only triumphant captains
wear, is a sufficient authority to show the price they ought to

be had in) than suffer the ill-favouring breath of such wrong-speakers once to blow upon the clear springs of Poesy.

But since I have run so long a career in this matter, methinks, before I give my pen a full stop, it shall be but a little more lost time to inquire why England (the mother of excellent minds) should be grown so hard a stepmother to poets, who certainly in wit ought to pass all other, since all only proceedeth from their wit, being indeed makers of themselves, not takers of others. How can I but exclaim,

Musa, mihi causas memora, quo numine laeso? 10

Sweet Poesy, that hath anciently had kings, emperors, senators, great captains, such as, besides a thousand others, David, Adrian, Sophocles, Germanicus, not only to favour poets, but to be poets; and of our nearer times can present for her patrons a Robert, king of Sicily, the great King Francis 15 of France, King James of Scotland; such cardinals as Bembus and Bibbiena: such famous preachers and teachers as Beza and Melanchthon; so learned philosophers as Fracastorius and Scaliger; so great orators as Pontanus and Muretus; so piercing wits as George Buchanan; so grave counsellors as, 20 besides many, but before all, that Hospital of France, than whom (I think) that realm never brought forth a more accomplished judgment, more firmly builded upon virtue— I say these, with numbers of others, not only to read others' poesies, but to poetise for others' reading—that Poesy, thus 25 embraced in all other places, should only find in our time a hard welcome in England, I think the very earth lamenteth it, and therefore decketh our soil with fewer laurels than it was accustomed. For heretofore poets have in England also flourished, and, which is to be noted, even in those times 30 when the trumpet of Mars did sound loudest. And now that an overfaint quietness should seem to strew the house for poets, they are almost in as good reputation as the mountebanks at Venice. Truly even that, as of the one side it giveth great praise to Poesy, which like Venus (but to better pur- 35 pose) hath rather be troubled in the net with Mars than enjoy the homely quiet of Vulcan; so serves it for a piece of a reason why they are less grateful to idle England, which now can scarce endure the pain of a pen. Upon this necessarily followeth, that base men with servile wits undertake it, who think it enough if they can be rewarded of the printer. And so as Epaminondas is said, with the honour of his virtue to have made an office, by his exercising it, which before was contemptible, to become highly respected, so these, no more but setting their names to it, by their own disgracefulness disgrace the most graceful Poesy. For now, as if all the Muses were got with child to bring forth bastard poets, without any commission they do post over the banks of Helicon, till they make the readers more weary than post-horses; while, in the meantime, they,

Queis meliore luto finxit praecordia Titan,

are better content to suppress the outflowing of their wit, than, by publishing them, to be accounted knights of the same order.

But I that, before ever I durst aspire unto the dignity, am admitted into the company of the paper-blurrers, do find the very true cause of our wanting estimation is want of desert, taking upon us to be poets in despite of Pallas. Now wherein we want desert were a thankworthy labour to express; but if I knew, I should have mended myself. But I, as I never desired the title, so have I neglected the means to come by it. Only, overmastered by some thoughts, I yielded an inky tribute unto them. Marry, they that delight in Poesy itself should seek to know what they do, and how they do; and especially look themselves in an unflattering glass of reason, if they be inclinable unto it. For Poesy must not be drawn by the ears; it must be gently led, or rather it must lead; which was partly the cause that made the ancient-learned affirm it was a divine gift, and no human skill: since all other knowledges lie ready for any that hath strength of wit; a poet no industry can make, if his own genius be not carried unto it; and therefore is it an old proverb, *orator fit, poeta nascitur.* Yet confess I always that as the fertilest ground must be manured, so must the highest-flying wit have a Daedalus to guide him. That Daedalus, they say, both in this and in other, hath three wings to bear itself up into the air of due commendation: that is, Art, Imitation, and Exercise. But these, neither artificial rules nor imitative patterns, we much cumber ourselves withal. Exercise indeed we do, but that very fore-backwardly: for where we should exercise to know, we exercise as having known; and so is our brain delivered of much matter which never was begotten by knowledge. For there being two principal parts—matter to be expressed by words and words to express the matter—in neither we use Art or Imitation rightly. Our matter is *quodlibet* indeed, though wrongly performing Ovid's verse,

> *Quicquid conabor dicere, versus erit:*

never marshalling it into an assured rank, that almost the readers cannot tell where to find themselves.

Chaucer, undoubtedly, did excellently in his *Troilus and Criseyde*; of whom, truly, I know not whether to marvel more, either that he in that misty time could see so clearly, or that we in this clear age walk so stumblingly after him. Yet had he great wants, fit to be forgiven in so reverent antiquity. I account the *Mirror of Magistrates* meetly furnished of beautiful parts, and in the Earl of Surrey's lyrics many things tasting of a noble birth, and worthy of a noble mind. The *Shepherd's Calendar* hath much poetry in his eclogues, indeed worthy the reading, if I be not deceived. That same framing of his style to an old rustic language I dare not allow, since neither Theocritus in Greek, Virgil in Latin, nor Sannazzaro in Italian did affect it. Besides these, do I not remember to have seen but few (to speak boldly) printed, that have poetical sinews in them: for proof whereof, let but most of the verses be put in prose, and then ask the meaning, and it will be found that one verse did but beget another, without ordering at the first what should be at the last; which becomes a confused mass of words, with a tingling sound of rhyme, barely accompanied with reason.

Our Tragedies and Comedies (not without cause cried out against), observing rules neither of honest civility nor of skilful Poetry, excepting *Gorboduc* (again, I say, of those that

I have seen), which notwithstanding, as it is full of stately
speeches and well-sounding phrases, climbing to the height
of Seneca's style, and as full of notable morality, which it
doth most delightfully teach, and so obtain the very end of
5 Poesy, yet in truth it is very defectious in the circumstances,
which grieveth me, because it might not remain as an exact
model of all tragedies. For it is faulty both in place and time,
the two necessary companions of all corporal actions. For
where the stage should always represent but one place, and
10 the uttermost time presupposed in it should be, both by
Aristotle's precept and common reason, but one day, there
is both many days, and many places, inartificially imagined.

But if it be so in *Gorboduc*, how much more in all the rest?
where you shall have Asia of the one side, and Afric of the
15 other, and so many other under-kingdoms, that the player,
when he cometh in, must ever begin with telling where he is,
or else the tale will not be conceived. Now ye shall have
three ladies walk to gather flowers and then we must believe
the stage to be a garden. By and by we hear news of ship-
20 wreck in the same place, and then we are to blame if we accept
it not for a rock. Upon the back of that comes out a hideous
monster with fire and smoke, and then the miserable beholders
are bound to take it for a cave. While in the meantime two
armies fly in, represented with four swords and bucklers, and
25 then what hard heart will not receive it for a pitched field?

Now of time they are much more liberal, for ordinary it is
that two young princes fall in love. After many traverses,
she is got with child, delivered of a fair boy, he is lost, groweth
a man, falls in love, and is ready to get another child, and all
30 this in two hours' space: which, how absurd it is in sense,
even sense may imagine, and Art hath taught, and all ancient
examples justified, and at this day, the ordinary players in
Italy will not err in. Yet will some bring in an example of
Eunuchus in Terence, that containeth matter of two days,
35 yet far short of twenty years. True it is, and so was it to be
played in two days, and so fitted to the time it set forth. And
though Plautus hath in one place done amiss, let us hit with
him, and not miss with him. But they will say, How then
shall we set forth a story, which containeth both many places

and many times? And do they not know that a tragedy is tied to the laws of Poesy, and not of History; not bound to follow the story, but, having liberty, either to feign a quite new matter, or to frame the history to the most tragical conveniency? Again, many things may be told which cannot be 5 showed, if they know the difference betwixt reporting and representing. As, for example, I may speak (though I am here) of Peru, and in speech digress from that to the description of Calicut; but in action I cannot represent it without Pacolet's horse. And so was the manner the ancients took, 10 by some *nuncius* to recount things done in former time or other place.

Lastly, if they will represent an history, they must not (as Horace saith) begin *ab ovo*, but they must come to the principal point of that one action which they will represent. By 15 example this will be best expressed. I have a story of young Polydorus, delivered for safety's sake, with great riches, by his father Priam to Polymnestor, king of Thrace, in the Trojan war time. He, after some years, hearing the overthrow of Priam, for to make the treasure his own, murdereth the 20 child. The body of the child is taken up by Hecuba. She, the same day, findeth a sleight to be revenged most cruelly of the tyrant. Where now would one of our tragedy writers begin, but with the delivery of the child? Then should he sail over into Thrace, and so spend I know not how many 25 years, and travel numbers of places. But where doth Euripides? Even with the finding of the body, leaving the rest to be told by the spirit of Polydorus. This need no further to be enlarged; the dullest wit may conceive it.

But besides these gross absurdities, how all their plays be 30 neither right tragedies, nor right comedies, mingling kings and clowns, not because the matter so carrieth it, but thrust in clowns by head and shoulders, to play a part in majestical matters, with neither decency nor discretion, so as neither the admiration and commiseration, nor the right sportfulness, 35 is by their mongrel tragi-comedy obtained. I know Apuleius did somewhat so, but that is a thing recounted with space of time, not represented in one moment; and I know the ancients have one or two examples of tragi-comedies, as Plautus hath

Amphitrio. But, if we mark them well, we shall find, that
they never, or very daintily, match hornpipes and funerals.
So falleth it out that, having indeed no right comedy, in that
comical part of our tragedy, we have nothing but scurrility,
5 unworthy of any chaste ears, or some extreme show of dolt-
ishness, indeed fit to lift up a loud laughter, and nothing else:
where the whole tract of a comedy should be full of delight,
as the tragedy should be still maintained in a well-raised
admiration.

10   But our comedians think there is no delight without
laughter; which is very wrong, for though laughter may
come with delight, yet cometh it not of delight, as though
delight should be the cause of laughter; but well may one
thing breed both together. Nay, rather in themselves they
15 have, as it were, a kind of contrariety: for delight we scarcely
do but in things that have a conveniency to ourselves or to the
general nature; laughter almost ever cometh of things most
disproportioned to ourselves and nature. Delight hath a joy
in it, either permanent or present. Laughter hath only a
20 scornful tickling. For example, we are ravished with delight
to see a fair woman, and yet are far from being moved to
laughter. We laugh at deformed creatures, wherein certainly
we cannot delight. We delight in good chances, we laugh
at mischances; we delight to hear the happiness of our friends,
25 or country, at which he were worthy to be laughed at that
would laugh. We shall, contrarily, laugh sometimes to find
a matter quite mistaken and go down the hill against the
bias, in the mouth of some such men, as for the respect of
them one shall be heartily sorry, yet he cannot choose but
30 laugh; and so is rather pained than delighted with laughter.
Yet deny I not but that they may go well together: for as in
Alexander's picture well set out we delight without laughter,
and in twenty mad antics we laugh without delight; so in
Hercules, painted with his great beard and furious coun-
35 tenance, in woman's attire, spinning at Omphale's com-
mandment, it breedeth both delight and laughter. For the
representing of so strange a power in love procureth delight:
and the scornfulness of the action stirreth laughter.

    But I speak to this purpose, that all the end of the comical part be not upon such scornful matters as stirreth laughter only, but, mixed with it, that delightful teaching which is the end of Poesy. And the great fault even in that point of laughter, and forbidden plainly by Aristotle, is that they stir laughter in sinful things, which are rather execrable than 5 ridiculous; or in miserable, which are rather to be pitied than scorned. For what is it to make folks gape at a wretched beggar, or a beggarly clown; or, against law of hospitality, to jest at strangers, because they speak not English so well as we do? What do we learn? since it is certain 10

> Nil habet infelix paupertas durius in se,
> Quam quod ridiculos homines facit.

But rather a busy loving courtier; a heartless threatening Thraso; a self-wise-seeming schoolmaster; an awry-trans-formed traveller: these if we saw walk in stage names, which 15 we play naturally, therein were delightful laughter, and teaching delightfulness: as in the other, the tragedies of Buchanan do justly bring forth a divine admiration. But I have lavished out too many words of this play matter. I do it because, as they are excelling parts of Poesy, so is there none so much 20 used in England, and none can be more pitifully abused; which, like an unmannerly daughter showing a bad education, causeth her mother Poesy's honesty to be called in question.

Other sorts of Poetry almost have we none, but that lyrical kind of songs and sonnets: which, Lord, if He gave us so 25 good minds, how well it might be employed, and with how heavenly fruit, both private and public, in singing the praises of the immortal beauty, the immortal goodness of that God who giveth us hands to write and wits to conceive; of which we might well want words, but never matter; of which we 30 could turn our eyes to nothing, but we should ever have new-budding occasions. But truly many of such writings as come under the banner of unresistible love; if I were a mistress, would never persuade me they were in love; so coldly they apply fiery speeches, as men that had rather read lovers' 35 writings (and so caught up certain swelling phrases which hang together like a man which once told me the wind was at north-west and by south, because he would be sure to name winds enough), than that in truth they feel those passions, which easily (as I think) may be betrayed by that same forcibleness or *energia* (as the Greeks cáll it) of the writer. But let this be a sufficient though short note, that we miss the right use of the material point of Poesy.

Now, for the outside of it, which is words, or (as I may term it) diction, it is even well worse. So is that honey-flowing matron eloquence apparelled, or rather disguised, in a courtesan-like painted affectation: one time with so far-fetched words, they may seem monsters, but must seem strangers, to any poor Englishman; another time with coursing of a letter, as if they were bound to follow the method of a dictionary; another time with figures and flowers extremely winter-starved. But I would this fault were only peculiar to versifiers, and had not as large possession among prose-printers, and (which is to be marvelled) among many scholars, and (which is to be pitied) among some preachers. Truly I could wish, if at least I might be so bold to wish in a thing beyond the reach of my capacity, the diligent imitators of Tully and Demosthenes (most worthy to be imitated) did not so much keep Nizolian paper-books of their figures and phrases, as by attentive translation (as it were) devour them whole, and make them wholly theirs. For now they cast sugar and spice upon every dish that is served to the table, like those Indians, not content to wear earrings at the fit and natural place of the ears, but they will thrust jewels through their nose and lips, because they will be sure to be fine.

Tully, when he was to drive out Catiline, as it were with a thunderbolt of eloquence, often used that figure of repetition, *Vivit. Vivit? Imo vero etiam in senatum venit*, &c. Indeed, inflamed with a well-grounded rage, he would have his words (as it were) double out of his mouth, and so do that artificially which we see men do in choler naturally. And we, having noted the grace of those words, hale them in sometime to a familiar epistle, when it were too too much collar to be choleric. How well store of *similiter cadences* doth sound with the gravity of the pulpit, I would but invoke Demosthenes' soul to tell, who with a rare daintiness useth them. Truly they have made me think of the sophister that with too much sublety would prove two eggs three, and though he might be counted a sophister, had none for his labour. So these men bringing in such a kind of eloquence, well may they obtain an opinion of a seeming fineness, but persuade few—which should be the end of their fineness.　　　5

Now for similitudes in certain printed discourses, I think all herbarists, all stories of beasts, fowls, and fishes are rifled up, that they come in multitudes to wait upon any of our conceits; which certainly is as absurd a surfeit to the ears as is possible: for the force of a similitude not being to prove 10 anything to a contrary disputer, but only to explain to a willing hearer; when that is done, the rest is a most tedious prattling, rather over-swaying the memory from the purpose whereto they were applied, than any whit informing the judgment, already either satisfied, or by similitudes not to be 15 satisfied. For my part, I do not doubt, when Antonius and Crassus, the great forefathers of Cicero in eloquence, the one (as Cicero testifieth of them) pretended not to know art, the other not to set by it, because with a plain sensibleness they might win credit of popular ears; which credit is the nearest 20 step to persuasion; which persuasion is the chief mark of Oratory—I do not doubt (I say) but that they used these tracks very sparingly; which, who doth generally use, any man may see doth dance to his own music, and so be noted by the audience more careful to speak curiously than to speak 25 truly.

Undoubtedly (at least to my opinion undoubtedly) I have found in divers smally learned courtiers a more sound style than in some professors of learning; of which I can guess no other cause, but that the courtier, following that which by 30 practise he findeth fittest to nature, therein (though he know it not) doth according to art, though not by art: where the other, using art to show art, and not to hide art (as in these cases he should do), flieth from nature, and indeed abuseth art.

But what? methinks I deserve to be pounded for straying 35 from Poetry to Oratory: but both have such an affinity in this wordish consideration, that I think this digression will make my meaning receive the fuller understanding—which is not to take upon me to teach poets how they should do,

but only, finding myself sick among the rest, to show some
one or two spots of the common infection grown among the
most part of writers; that, acknowledging ourselves some-
what awry, we may bend to the right use both of matter and
5 manner: whereto our language giveth us great occasion,
being indeed capable of any excellent exercising of it.   I
know some will say it is a mingled language.   And why not
so much the better, taking the best of both the other?
Another will say it wanteth grammar.   Nay truly, it hath
10 that praise, that it wanteth not grammar: for grammar it
might have, but it needs it not; being so easy of itself, and
so void of those cumbersome differences of cases, genders,
moods, and tenses, which I think was a piece of the Tower
of Babylon's curse, that a man should be put to school to
15 learn his mother-tongue.   But for the uttering sweetly and
properly the conceits of the mind, which is the end of speech,
that hath it equally with any other tongue in the world; and
is particularly happy in compositions of two or three words
together, near the Greek, far beyond the Latin: which is
20 one of the greatest beauties can be in a language.

Now of versifying there are two sorts, the one ancient, the
other modern: the ancient marked the quantity of each
syllable, and according to that framed his verse; the modern
observing only number (with some regard of the accent),
25 the chief life of it standeth in that like sounding of the words,
which we call rhyme.   Whether of these be the most excel-
lent, would bear many speeches: the ancient (no doubt)
more fit for music, both words and time observing quantity,
and more fit lively to express divers passions, by the low or
30 lofty sound of the well-weighed syllable.   The latter likewise,
with his rhyme, striketh a certain music to the ear; and, in
fine, since it doth delight, though by another way, it obtains
the same purpose: there being in either sweetness, and want-
ing in neither majesty.   Truly the English, before any other
35 vulgar language I know, is fit for both sorts: for, for the
ancient, the Italian is so full of vowels that it must ever be
cumbered with elisions; the Dutch so, of the other side,
with consonants, that they cannot yield the sweet sliding fit
for a verse; the French in his whole language hath not one

word that hath his accent in the last syllable saving two,
called *antepenultima*; and little more hath the Spanish, and
therefore very gracelessly may they use dactyls. The English
is subject to none of these defects.

Now for the rhyme, though we do not observe quantity, 5
yet we observe the accent very precisely, which other lan-
guages either cannot do, or will not do so absolutely. That
caesura, or breathing place in the midst of the verse, neither
Italian nor Spanish have, the French and we never almost
fail of. Lastly, even the very rhyme itself the Italian cannot 10
put in the last syllable, by the French named the masculine
rhyme, but still in the next to the last, which the French call
the female, or the next before that, which the Italians term
sdrucciola. The example of the former is *buono : suono*, of the
sdrucciola, *femina : semina*. The French, of. the other side, 15
hath both the male, as *bon : son*, and the female, as *plaise :
taise*, but the *sdrucciola* he hath not: where the English hath
all three, as *due : true*, *father : rather*, *motion : potion*; with
much more which might be said, but that I find already the
triflingness of this discourse is much too much enlarged. 20

So that since the ever-praiseworthy Poesy is full of virtue-
breeding delightfulness, and void of no gift that ought to be
in the noble name of learning; since the blames laid against
it are either false or feeble; since the cause why it is not es-
teemed in England is the fault of poet-apes, not poets; since, 25
lastly, our tongue is most fit to honour Poesy, and to be
honoured by Poesy; I conjure you all that have had the evil
luck to read this ink-wasting toy of mine, even in the name
of the Nine Muses, no more to scorn the sacred mysteries of
Poesy, no more to laugh at the name of poets, as though they 30
were next inheritors to fools, no more to jest at the reverent
title of a rhymer; but to believe, with Aristotle, that they
were the ancient treasurers of the Grecians' divinity; to
believe, with Bembus, that they were first bringers-in of all
civility; to believe, with Scaliger, that no philosopher's pre- 35
cepts can sooner make you an honest man than the reading
of Virgil; to believe, with Clauserus, the translator of Cor-
nutus, that it pleased the heavenly Deity, by Hesiod and

Homer, under the veil of fables, to give us all knowledge, Logic, Rhetoric, Philosophy natural and moral, and *quid non ?*; to believe, with me, that there are many mysteries contained in Poetry, which of purpose were written darkly, lest by 5 profane wits it should be abused; to believe, with Landino, that they are so beloved of the gods that whatsoever they write proceeds of a divine fury; lastly, to believe themselves, when they tell you they will make you immortal by their verses.

10   Thus doing, your name shall flourish in the printers' shops; thus doing, you shall be of kin to many a poetical preface; thus doing, you shall be most fair, most rich, most wise, most all; you shall dwell upon superlatives. Thus doing, though you be *libertino patre natus*, you shall suddenly grow *Herculea* 15 *proles*,

Si quid mea carmina possunt.

Thus doing, your soul shall be placed with Dante's Beatrix, or Virgil's Anchises. But if (fie of such a but) you be born so near the dull-making cataract of Nilus that you cannot 20 hear the planet-like music of Poetry, if you have so earth-creeping a mind that it cannot lift itself up to look to the sky of Poetry, or rather, by a certain rustical disdain, will become such a mome as to be a Momus of Poetry; then, though I will not wish unto you the ass's ears of Midas, nor to be 25 driven by a poet's verses (as Bubonax was) to hang himself, nor to be rhymed to death, as is said to be done in Ireland; yet thus much curse I must send you, in the behalf of all poets, that while you live, you live in love, and never get favour for lacking skill of a sonnet, and, when you die, your 30 memory die from the earth for want of an epitaph.

NOTES

The text of the *Apology* in Olney's edition is prefaced by an address *To the Reader*, and by *Foure Sonnets written by Henrie Constable to Sir Phillip Sidneys soule*.

To the Reader

The stormie Winter (deere Chyldren of the Muses) which hath so long held backe the glorious Sunshine of diuine Poesie, is heere by the sacred pen-breathing words of diuine Sir *Philip Sidney*, not onely chased from our fame-inuiting Clyme, but vtterly for euer banisht eternitie : then graciously regreet the perpetuall spring of euer-growing inuention, and like kinde Babes, either enabled by wit or power, to help to support me poore Midwife, whose daring aduenture, hath deliuered from Obliuions wombe, this euer-to-be-admired wits miracle. Those great ones, who in themselues haue interr'd this blessed innocent, wil with *Aesculapius* condemne me as a detractor from their Deities : those who Prophet-like haue but heard presage of his coming, wil (if they wil doe wel) not onely defend, but praise mee, as the first publique bewrayer of Poesies *Messias*. Those who neither haue seene, thereby to interre, nor heard, by which they might be inflamed with desire to see, let them (of duty) plead to be my Champions, sith both theyr sight and hearing, by mine incurring blame is seasoned. Excellent Poesie, (so created by this Apologie), be thou my Defendresse ; and if any wound mee, let thy beautie (my soules Adamant) recure mee : if anie commend mine endeuored hardiment, to thee commend thy most diuinest fury as a winged incouragement : so shalt thou haue deuoted to thee, and to them obliged   *Henry Olney*.

Then follow the sonnets. (For texts of these poems see *The Poems of Henry Constable*, ed. Joan Grundy (Liverpool University Press, 1960), pp. 167–9 ; and for notes pp. 241–2).

    (i) *Giue pardon (blessed Soule) to my bold cries* . . .

    (ii) *Sweet Soule which now with heau'nly songs doost tel* . . .

(originally, according to Joan Grundy, *ed. cit.*, p. 241, inscribed to the Marquess of Piscat's soul)

    (iii) *Even as when great mens heires cannot agree* . . .

    (iv) *Great* Alexander *then did well declare* . . .

p. 95

1. **Edward Wotton** (1548–1626), first Baron Wotton of Marley, 1603 ; courtier and diplomatist, half-brother of the Stuart diplomatist and poet, Sir Henry Wotton (1568–1639). Sidney and Edward Wotton

spent the winter 1574–5 at the court of the Emperor Maximilian II at Vienna. Wotton was a beneficiary under Sidney's will and a pall-bearer at his funeral. George Chapman (*Poems*, ed. P. B. Bartlett (New York and London, 1941), pp. 404, 485), in the address of a sonnet dedicatory to Lord Wotton, recalls Sidney's eulogy of his friend here.

4. In the courts of the 16th c. the Esquire (or Equerry) of the Stable was a personage of importance and dignity ; see *NED s.* equerry, 2 and esquire, 1.c.

5. Sidney explained to his brother Robert : ' although some [Italians] indeede be excellentlie lerned, yett are they all given to soe counterfeit lerning, as a man shall learne of them more false groundes of thinges, then in anie place ells that I doe knowe ; for from a tapster upwardes they are all discoursers. In fine, certain qualities, as Horsmanshipp, Weapons, Vauting, and such like, they are better there then in those other countries ; for others more sounde they do little excell neerer places ' (*Works*, vol. iii, 127). With Sidney's amused account of Pugliano's horsemanship, cp. Montaigne, *Essays*, I, li, on an Italian steward's ' long, formall and eloquent discourse of the science or skill of epicurisme and gluttonie '.

7. **contemplations,** 'theorisings' : as opposed to *his practice* (6). Sidney, himself a notable horseman (and cp. his description of Dorus on horseback in *Arcadia* (*Works*, vol. i, 178–9)), counselled his brother : ' At horsemanshipp when you exercise it, reade Grison Claudio, and a book that is called *La gloria del cavallo* withall, that you may joyne the through contemplation of it with the exercise . . .' (*Works*, vol. iii, 133). Thomas Blundeville (see **10**) had already popularised Grisone's work in *The Art of rydyng and breaking great Horses* (1560 ?).

11. **admiration,** normally in Elizabethan English meaning ' wonderment ', here approaches its modern sense of ' extreme approval '.

12. **faculty,** a branch of art or science.

15. **strong abiders,** ' good stayers '. Praise of the horse as a school exercise was recommended by Priscian, *Praexercitamina* (ed. Halm, *Rhetores Minores*, p. 556) ; see T. W. Baldwin, *William Shakspere's Small Latine and lesse Greeke* (Urbana, Ill., 1944), ii, 187. Compare Plutarch, *How to tell a flatterer from a friend*, 6 (in particular for 20) ; G. Buchanan, *Silva*, vi, *Opera* (ed. Ruddiman, 1725), II, 340 ; Shakespeare, *Venus and Adonis*, 259ff., *Henry V*, III, vi ; B. Jonson, *Discoveries*, *Works* (ed. Herford and Simpson), vol. vii, 601.

18. **pedanteria.** From Italian ; cp. *pedante*, *Poems*, ed. Ringler, p. 124.

22. **a piece of a logician,** a bit of a logician ; cp. **131**/37 ; **140**/13. Sidney's well-known interest in Ramism (see **33**ff.) must have given point to the phrase. Moreover, Sidney may have heard at Padua in 1574 the lectures of Zabarelli (teaching there 1564–89), who followed the system of Averroes and treated poetry as part of logic. Earlier, at Oxford, he would have become familiar with Aristotelian logic ; see M. H. Curtius, *Studies in the Renaissance*, **5** (1958), 111–20. Many words and phrases in the *Apology* shew his interest in logic ; see notes on 23 ; **100**/11, 15 ; **105**/8 ; **108**/6 ; **110**/21ff. ; **115**/24 ; **118**/22 ; **123**/18 ; **127**/8 ; **133**/5ff., 11 ; **138**/39ff. ; **139**/6.

23. **wished myself a horse.** Cp. the similar wish expressed by one of Crato's pupils in logic in *De disciplina scholarium*, *PL* 64, col. 1230 (a favourite medieval text long ascribed to Boethius but probably of 13th

c. composition). *Homo* and *equus* were used as fixed terms in the syllogisms of medieval logic.

25. **self-love**, ' whereunto we versifiers are ever wont to be especially subject ', according to Daniel (Smith, ii, 383), who deplored it as ' the greatest hinderer to . . . the reformation of our errours '.

27. **Wherein,** *viz.* in persuading us of the power of self-love.
    affection, ' prejudice '.
    strong . . . weak. The antithesis is characteristic of Sidney's style in the *Apology* ; cp. **103**/33 ; **108**/13 ; **109**/18 ; **137**/20–1 ; etc.

33f. **scholar . . . his master.** That is, Sidney following the example of Pugliano.

p. 96

2ff. In lamenting the status of poetry Sidney is reproducing a humanist commonplace which contrasted contemporary disrespect for letters with the position of poetry in an idealised past : cp. Boccaccio, *De genealogia deorum*, V, vi (Osgood, p. 117) ; Salutati, *De laboribus Herculis*, ed. Ullman (Turin, 1951), I, i ; G. Fracastorius, *Naugerius*, trans. R. Kelso, *University of Illinois Studies in Language and Literature* **9** (1924), p. 54 ; Spenser, *Shepherd's Calendar*, October Eclogue ; and Sir Thomas Elyot, *Governour*, I, xiii, in a passage with which Sidney appears to have been familiar : ' For the name of a poete, wherat nowe (specially in this realme), men haue suche indignation, that they use onely poetes and poetry in the contempte of eloquence, was in auncient tyme in hygh estimation : in so moche that all wysdome was supposed to be therein included, and poetry was the first philosophy that euer was knowen : wherby men from their childhode were brought to the raison howe to lyue weil, lernynge therby nat onely maners and naturall affections, but also the wonderfull werkes of nature, mixting serious mater with thynges that were pleasaunt : as it shall be manifest to them that shall be so fortunate to rede the noble warkes of Plato and Aristotle, wherin he shall fynde the autoritie of poetes frequently alleged : ye and that more is, in poetes was supposed to be science misticall and inspired, and therfore in latine they were called *Vates*, which worde signifyeth as moche as prophetes' (ed. Croft, i, 120–2). Cp. Puttenham, *Arte*, Chap. viii, pp. 16–23. In France the Pléiade (and cp. Chapman in England later) worked their judgment that the world grossly undervalued poetry into their poetic theory in order to justify the esoteric character of their writing (see R. J. Clements, *Critical Theory and Practice of the Pléiade* (Cambridge, Mass., 1942), pp. 51–77) ; there are traces of this theory in the *Apology* ; see **142**/3f. note, and Olney's title-page motto.

4. **available,** ' powerful '.
    the former, *viz.* horsemanship.

5. **silly.** With a comic compassionate sense.

12. Cp. Harrington (Smith, ii, 194) : ' the verie first nurse and ancient grandmother of all learning '. The idea that the first poets were the earliest philosophers comes to the Renaissance from antiquity. Cicero, *Tusculan Disputations*, I, 3, was taken up by John Rainolds, *Oratio in laudem artis poeticae*, ed. W. Ringler (Princeton, 1940), p. 42, and by Thomas Lodge (Smith, i, 77). Cp. Cornelius Agrippa, *The Vanitie of the Arts and Sciences*, trans. J[ames] San[dford] (1569), cap. 49, ff. 63v–64, on natural philosophy, of which ' they say that Prometheus, Linus, Musaeus, Orpheus and Homer were the first inventors '. Sidney's

formulation, which is commonplace, derives from the Greek Strabo (*c.* 64 B.C.—*c.* A.D. 25), who in *Geographica*, I, 1 and 2, rebutted Eratosthenes' prejudice against the learning of the ancient poets. Cp. F. Robortello, *In librum Aristotelis de arte poetica explicationes* (Florence, 1548), p. 4 : ' [Strabo] makes it clear that poetry was formerly a kind of philosophy which through its fables gradually suckled and nurtured men until the time they would be more capable of understanding matters in philosophy which are most difficult '. On Strabo's importance in 16th c. critical thinking, see J. E. Spingarn, *A History of Literary Criticism in the Renaissance* (2nd ed., New York, 1908), p. 24 ; for further references, Weinberg, Index *s.n.*, ii, 1180 ; and cp. Richard Wills, *De Re Poetica*, ed. A. D. S. Fowler (Luttrell Reprints No. 17 ; Oxford, 1958), p. 76.

14. A fable of the snake and the hedgehog seems to have appeared first in the fable collection of Lorenzo Astemio, *Hecatomythium* (1495), and was incorporated into later Aesopic collections such as the popular schoolbook by J. Camerarius, *Fabellae Aesopicae* (Leipzig, 1564) : cp. **109**/15 note.

16. Cp. Pliny, *Natural History*, X, lxxxii, 2 : ' On the third day the viper hatches its young . . . and then pushes them out, one a day to the number of twenty. The last ones become so impatient of their confinement that they force a way through the sides of the mother and so kill her ' ; so also Aristotle, *History of Animals*, V, 34, Plutarch, *Concerning talkativeness*, 12, pseudo-Bede, *PL* 94, col. 540, etc. This birth of vipers affords a common Elizabethan simile : Thomas Wilson, *Arte of Rhetorique*, ed. G. H. Mair (Oxford, 1909), p. 125 ; John Lyly, *Euphues*, ed. M. Croll and H. Clemons (London, 1916), pp. 94, 401 ; Stephen Gosson, *Schoole of Abuse*, ed. E. Arber (1868), p. 46 ; Daniel (Smith, ii, 373) ; Fulke Greville, *Poems*, ed. G. Bullough (London, 1939), i, 179 ; and see note, Smith, i, 383.

17ff. Cp. Josephus, *Against Apion*, I, 2 : ' There is not any writing which the Greeks agree to be genuine among them ancienter than Homer's poems'. **Musaeus**, a legendary figure of pre-Homeric times, the type of the poet inspired by the Muses : in the Renaissance the late Greek poem *Hero and Leander* was ascribed to him ; in Greek tradition, his name was associated with the Athenian religious mysteries and a body of gnomic and mythological verse. **Hesiod** of Ascra in Boeotia flourished in the 8th c. B.C., author of the *Theogony* and *Works and Days*. It is now usually held that **Orpheus** was a pre-Homeric figure, but that the so-called Orphic writings are of a much later date. In classical times Orpheus was regarded as the son of a Muse, the servant of Apollo, a teacher of the religion of Dionysus, a revealer of sacred mysteries. He became a potent figure in Renaissance thought ; see D. P. Walker, *JWCI* **16** (1953), 100–20. **Linus** according to Homer (*Iliad*, xviii, 570) was the master of Orpheus ; other legend makes him the son of a Muse by Apollo. A full account of these ancient poets was given by Luis Vives in his notes to St Augustine, *Of the Citie of God* (trans. J. H., London, 1610), pp. 687f. The belief that poetry preceded all other forms of writing was handed down from classical antiquity (by e.g. Strabo, see above 12 note ; Plutarch, *The Oracles at Delphi no longer given in verse*), through the Middle Ages (by e.g. Isidore of Seville, *Etymologies*, VIII, 308, 317–18) to the Renaissance, when eulogists of poetry frequently supply lists of the ancient poets comparable with this given by Sidney : A. S. Minturno, *De poeta libri sex* (Venice, 1559), pp. 13ff. ; J. C. Scaliger, *Poetices libri septem* (1561) (cited from 5th ed. of 1617), I, ii,

p. 10 (see **97**/1ff. note) ; Rainolds, *Oratio*, pp. 42ff. ; and following Scaliger, Wills, *De re poetica*, p. 56.

21. **other.** The form without *-s* is historical (cp. OE masc. pl. *oþre*) ; in Shakespeare there is much variation between *others* and pl. *other*.

23. **deliverers,** ' transmitters '.

24. **challenge,** ' claim '.
    fathers in learning. Cp. Plato, *Lysis*, 214 ; Wills, *De re poetica*, p. 78.

28ff. **Amphion.** ' Jove's son by Antiope : for which reason Lynceus, King of Thebes refused her.' So Vives, *Of the Citie of God*, p. 684,who adds many particulars. ' Pliny saith he invented Music. lib. 7. Some say the Harp also : and some say that Mercury gave him the Harp. He was the author of the Lydian tones. . . . Amphion built Thebes (saith Solinus), not that his Harp fetched the stones thither, for that is not likely, but he brought the mountaineers, and highland-men unto civility, and to help in that work.' Amphion is often coupled with **Orpheus** to exemplify the power of music and poetry ; so B. Daniello, *La Poetica* (Venice, 1536), pp. 11f. ; Minturno, *De poeta*, p. 15 ; Wilson, *Rhetorique*, p. 47 ; Rainolds, *Oratio*, p. 76 (and see Ringler's note) ; Puttenham, *Arte*, p. 6 ; Sidney's Third Song in *Astrophil & Stella*. No doubt the reference best known to 16th c. writers was Horace, *Art of Poetry*, 391–403 :

> Orpheus, a priest, and speaker for the gods
> First frighted men, that wildly lived at odds,
> From slaughters and foul life ; and for the same
> Was tigers said, and lions fierce to tame.
> Amphion, too, that built the Theban towers,
> Was said to move the stones by his lute's powers
> And lead them with soft songs, where that he would.
> This was the wisdom that they had of old,
> Things sacred from profane to separate ;
> The public from the private ; to abate
> Wild raging lusts ; prescribe the marriage good ;
> Build towns, and carve the laws in leaves of wood.
> And thus at first, an honour and a name
> To divine poets, and their verses, came.
> Next these, great Homer and Tyrtaeus set
> On edge the masculine spirits, and did whet
> Their minds to wars . . . .
>
> (Ben Jonson's trans.)

This passage from Horace was also important in suggesting a method of classifying poets and was adapted by Scaliger (*Poetices*, I, ii ; see **97**/1ff. note).

31. **Livius Andronicus and Ennius** are both mentioned by Scaliger in *Poetices*, I, ii, pp. 10–11. Livius Andronicus (*c.* 284–204 B.C.), a Greek, the first Latin poet, who wrote both tragedies and comedies and made other adaptations from the Greek. Ennius (239–169 B.C.), the greatest of the early Latin poets, friend of the Scipios (see **127**/25ff. note), teacher of Roman youth. Only fragments survive of his work, which included an epic *Annales* on the history of Rome.

33f. Sidney intends us to recognise **Dante** (1265–1321), **Boccaccio** (1313–75), and **Petrarch** (1304–74) as didactic poets and the establishers of the Italian language, and also as the authors of works of learning and general philosophic importance (e.g. Dante with *De monarchia*, Boc-caccio as commentator and encyclopaedist, Petrarch in his religious and philosophic tracts). Similarly with the English poets : Chaucer's intel-lectual interests are everywhere evident apart from his prose translations. The philosophically minded Gower introduced *Confessio amantis* (*c.* 1386) as a work which ' to Wisdom all belongeth '.

36. **fore-going,** ' precedent '.

38ff. **philosophers . . . under the masks of poets.** The corollary of the argument noted above on 12, often adduced in Renaissance criticism (e.g. by Minturno, *De poeta*, pp. 13ff., Puttenham, *Arte*, pp. 8–9, and Boccaccio, *De genealogia deorum*) as providing the ultimate justification of poetry (see **28f.**).

p. 97

1ff. Sidney with his examples seems to be following Scaliger's classifica-tion of poets (see notes on **96/28ff.** and **101/37ff.**), where Scaliger dis-tinguished (i) ' scientific ' poets, such as Empedocles, Nicander, Aratus, Lucretius ; (ii) poets of moral philosophy, concerned either with politics, as Solon and Tyrtaeus, or with economics, as Hesiod ; (iii) poets concerned directly with ethics, such as Phocylides, Theognis, Pythagoras (*Poetices*, p. 11) ; cp. Minturno, *De poeta*, p. 15. Sidney confined his selection to ' the philosophers of Greece ' (**96/38**), who are thought of now as little more than reputations associated with fragmen-tary passages of early Greek verse ; but in the 16th c. a substantial body of philosophical verse was ascribed to them (collected by Henri Estienne, *Poesis philosophus* (1573)). **Thales** of Miletus (*fl.* 585 B.C.), of whom some anecdotes but no writings survive, was said to have composed a work on *Nautical Astronomy* and on *First Causes*. **Empedocles** of Acragas (*fl.* 450 B.C.) of whose poems *On Nature*, and *Purifications*, fragments survive. **Parmenides** of Elea (*fl.* 475 B.C.), founder of the Eleatic school of philosophy, who handed down his teaching in epic form. **Pythagoras** of Samos (*fl.* 530 B.C.). Sidney no doubt had in mind a set of moral verses, the so-called Golden Sayings ascribed later to Pythagoras. But the philosopher seems to have left nothing in writing, to have insisted on secrecy, although his disciples are associated with the composition of the Orphic poetry (see **96/17ff.**, note). **Phocylides** of Miletus (*fl.* 560 B.C.), a gnomic poet. **Tyrtaeus** of Aphidnae (*fl.* 670 B.C.), an Athenian (and, according to later tradition, a lame schoolmaster) who inspired the Spartans to victory through his verses. **Solon**, Athenian legislator (*fl.* 600 B.C.). The miscellaneous scraps of verse associated with his name give no ground for accepting Plato's story in *Timaeus* that Solon learned about the lost continent of Atlantis (8) from the priests of Egypt.

10ff. That Plato who condemned poetry was himself essentially a poet was often maintained by Renaissance writers. See Daniello, *La poetica*, p. 22 : 'Plato . . . is esteemed as a poet by all who understand him. There is not one of his Dialogues . . . in which he does not express his conceptions under a fabulous veil' ; and cp. Minturno, *De poeta*, p. 16 ; Scaliger, *Poemata* (Geneva, 1591), i, 13. This opinion concerning Plato went back to antiquity : see Quintilian, *Institutes*, V, xi, 39 ; X, i, 81 : cp. W. Ringler's note to Rainolds, *Oratio*, p. 74. Scaliger, *Poetices*, I, iii, pp. 12–13, supplies a brief, learned account of the character and origin of dialogue as a poetic form. Plato in his dialogues usually gave some sort of social setting to the philosophical discussion, and this example was followed by the humanists in their use of dialogue form (e.g. Erasmus in *Colloquies* ; Dryden's *Essay on Dramatic Poesy*). Plato's discussion on love (*Symposium*) has the banquet for setting (18) ; *Phaedrus* begins with a country walk (18).

13. **standeth upon,** ' is constructed upon, depends upon '. A common idiom.

18. **delicacy,** ' delight ', ' pleasantness '.
  interlacing, ' intermingling ' ; syntactically dependent on *describing* (16).

19. The story of **Gyges' ring** in Plato, *Republic*, II, 359, tells of a descent into the Underworld whence Gyges, a shepherd, steals a ring which enables him to become invisible and so win a kingdom ; and 16th c. readers would be familiar with the tale through Cicero, *De officiis*, III, 9.

22. **verity be written in their foreheads,** as an advertisement of frankness and honesty. Sidney uses a common idiom (see Tilley, F 590) ironically.

23. **fashion,** ' form '.

24. The *History* of Herodotus of Halicarnassus (484–*c*. 406 B.C.), ' the father of history ', was divided by later scholars of Alexandria into nine Books, each named after a Muse.

26. **passionate describing of passions.** Sidney frequently uses this figure of paregmenon in *Arcadia*, less frequently in the *Apology* ; but cp. **100**/32 ; **101**/35–6 ; **102**/19 ; **105**/4 ; **109**/17 ; 19–20 ; **113**/8–9 ; 31–2 ; **115**/33–4 ; **120**/2 ; **123**/15–16 ; **125**/14 ; 32–3 ; **132**/8–9 ; **138**/23. In writing and criticising histories, humanists before Bodin's time took great pains with evocative description and with ' long orations ' (28) ; cp. **36** and note.

33. **passport,** ' password '.

33ff. Cicero in *Pro Archia poeta*, ix, 18–19, observed that 'even barbarians do not dishonour the name of poet' and many 16th c. writers elaborate this theme : so Scaliger, *Poetices*, I, ii, p. 8 ; Minturno, *De poeta*, pp. 9ff. ; Spenser, Argument to October, *Shepherd's Calendar*. Puttenham, *Arte*, p. 10, notes the cultivation of poetry even among ' the American, the Perusine & the very Cannibal'.

36. In the 16th c. Europeans had a lively sense of the power and danger of the infidel Turks who were counted proficient in the arts of war and deficient in all other arts ; cp. Montaigne, *Essays*, I, xxiv (quoted in **126**/27 note). For a general account of English interest in Turkish affairs at this time, see Orhan Burian, *Oriens*, **5** (1952), 209–29 ; and for Renaissance sources of knowledge, see V. J. Parry, in *Historians of the Middle East*, ed. B. Lewis and P. M. Holt (Oxford, 1962), pp. 277–89. Languet and Sidney often discussed Turkish affairs, on which Sidney no doubt more fully informed himself during his travels.
  law-giving divines. An accurate definition of Muslim muftis.

37. Sidney's father, Sir Henry Sidney, was Vice-Treasurer in Ireland, 1556–9, and Lord Deputy, 1566–71, 1575–8. From his childhood onwards Sidney was familiar with conditions in Ireland, which indeed he may have visited in 1576. Spenser, who was there from 1580, speaks of Irish poetry in *A View of the State of Ireland*. ' Noe monument remayneth of her beginning and first inhabiting there ; specially having bene in those tymes allwayes without letters, but onely bare traditions of times and remembraunces of BARDES . . .' (Globe ed., p. 625). But

yet ' it is certayne, that Ireland hath had the use of letters very aun-
ciently, and long before England ' (p. 626). The bards still flourish,
' whose profession is to sett forth the prayses and disprayses of men in
theyr poems and rimes ; the which are had in soe high request and
estimation amongst them, that none dare to displease them. . . . For
theyr verses are usually taken up with a generall applause, and usually
songe at all feasts and meetings. . . .' (p. 640).

p. 98

1. Sidney concerned himself directly with the voyages of English adven-
turers to the Americas, invested in them, and sought to participate
(cp. 7) ; but his information here derives from Peter Martyr's account
of American manners in *Decades*, which was inserted in Richard Eden,
Hystorie of the West Indies (1555), p. 125 ; see R. R. Cawley, *MLN* 39
(1924), 121–3. 'Perhaps your holynesse wyll marvell by what meanes
these symple men shoulde of soo long contynaunce beare in minde such
principles, where as they have no knowledge of letters. . . . They gyve
them selves chieflye to two thynges : As generally to lerne thoriginall &
successe of thynges : And particularlye to reherse the noble factes of
their graundefathers, great graundefathers and auncestours as well in
peace as in warre. These two thynges they have of owlde tyme com-
posed in certeyne myters and ballettes in their language. These rhymes
or ballettes they caule *Areitos*. And as owre mynstrelles are accustomed
too synge to the harpe or lute, so doo they in lyke maner synge these
songes.' A fuller account of the *areyto* (a ceremonial ring-dance accom-
panied by song) was given by the Spaniard, G. F. de Oviedo (1535) in
Natural History of the West Indies, trans. and ed. Sterling A. Stoudemire
(University of N. Carolina, 1959), p. 38. Cook (p. 67) supplied D. G.
Brinton's etymology of *areyto* 'from Arawack *aririn*, "rehearse",
" repeat " '.

9. The Sidney family had many associations with **Wales**. Sir Henry
was Lord President of the Marches, 1560 ; his daughter Mary married
the Earl of Pembroke. So Sidney had opportunities for learning about
the poetry of the Welsh. Moreover, like his father, Sidney was much
interested in British history and survivals, to which many Elizabethan
antiquaries devoted attention. Languet and Sidney discussed in their
letters, and discounted (*Works*, vol. iii, 85), the excessive Cambrian zeal
of Humphrey Lhuyd ' of Denbigh, a Cambro-Britayne ' in his *Britanniae
descriptionis fragmentum* (Cologne, 1572), trans. by Thomas Twyne as
Breviary of Britaine (1573). John Caius (*De antiquitate Cantabrigiensis
Academiae* (1568), ed. Venn (1912), pp. 14–16) praises the early British
kings for their learning and patronage of the arts. Most scholars of
Tudor England were tolerant of the myth, so pleasing to patriotic
feeling, that Britain was originally founded by the descendants of the
Trojans under Brutus ; see T. D. Kendrick, *British Antiquity* (London,
1950), especially Chap. III.

18. **but,** ' merely '.

20ff. The old association of prophecy with poetry was not forgotten
throughout the Middle Ages, and Renaissance writers when they em-
phasise the dignity, antiquity, and scope of poetry, and in particular
when they develop their theory of ' divine fury ' (see **63f.**), commonly
reassert the association; see Elyot, *Governour*, **I,** xiii (ed. Croft, i, 122), as
quoted above, **96**/2 note ; Minturno, *De poeta*, p. 15 ; Wills, *De re*

poetica, p. 54 ; Puttenham, *Arte*, p. 7 ; and Harrington (Smith, ii, 205), following Sidney.

23. **heart-ravishing.** Sidney coins an epithet which alludes to the old (false) etymology of *vates* as from *vi mentis*, ' with violence of mind ' ; so Isidore, *Etymologies*, VIII, vii, 3 (*PL* 82, col. 308).

27. **Sortes Virgilianae.** The practice of opening Virgil at random and applying the passage on which the eye first fell to the particular circumstances of the inquirer developed in imperial Roman times ; see examples in *Sex scriptores historiae Augustae : Life of Emperor Hadrian*, II, 8, *Life of Alexander Severus*, XIV, 5, and *Life of Clodius Albinus* (by Julius Capitolinus), which tells how Albinus, brought up in Africa, became governor in Britain. Acclaimed Emperor by his troops in A.D. 193, he was defeated and killed by Septimius Severus at Lyon in 197. Julius Capitolinus recounts (V, 2) that even as a child Albinus shewed signs of a haughty and warlike spirit, for at school, it is said, he used often to repeat to the other children ' With frenzy seiz'd, I run to meet th' alarms ' (*Aeneid*, II, 314) and he repeated again and again the words ' With frenzy seiz'd '.

p. 99

2. **Delphos,** Delphi, a town in a ravine on Mount Parnassus, regarded as the navel of the earth, site of the most famous temple of Apollo, where the priestess (Pythia) declared the prophetic oracles which were then set down in hexameter verse.

 Sibylla's prophecies. The original Sibyl may have been a prophetess in early Greek tradition, but the so-called Sibylline oracles formed a large collection of prophetic writings which were early acquired by Rome, and often revised and augmented until their destruction in the reign of Augustus. But prophetic materials from various sources, Jewish, Egyptian, and Christian, continued to be accumulated, and many were familiar as Sibylline prophecies during the Middle Ages ; in particular the verses on Judgment Day cited by Augustine in *City of God*, XVIII, 23. Notice is frequently taken of sacred ' oracles . . . in verses ' by writers exalting poetry : Horace, *Art*, 400ff. (see **96**/28 note) ; Minturno, *L' arte poetica* (Naples ed., 1725), p. 31 ; Rainolds, *Oratio*, p. 42 ; Puttenham, *Arte*, p. 7 ; Lodge, Smith, i, 71.

4. **conceit,** ' mental conception ', ' invention ' (in its rhetorical sense) ; see **104**/3 note.

7ff. **great learned men, both ancient and modern** (9) had believed that David composed the Psalter by the direct inspiration of God ; so in the earlier period Jerome, Augustine, Isidore, Bede, and many writers into the 12th c. ; see W. Ringler's note to Rainolds, *Oratio*, p. 74. The humanists later, following Petrarch, reasserted the poetic character of the Psalms, which came to occupy a special position in the development of Renaissance literature in the learned languages and in the vernaculars (cp. below 14ff. note). In France the translations (notably the version made by Clement Marot) gave impetus to the work of the Pléiade ; see F. A. Yates, *French Academies of the Sixteenth Century* (London, 1947), pp. 44ff.

11f. **songs . . . written in metre.** ' What else is a Psalm but a holy and spiritual kind of composition for singing ? ' Preface to Part III of Tremellius and Junius' Latin Bible (1607 ed.), f. 106 (see **102**/3 note). From early Christian times attempts had been made to accommodate and understand Hebrew poetry in the terms of classical prosody. Josephus (*Antiquities of the Jews*, II, xvi, 4 ; IV, viii, 8 ; VII, xii, 3) affirmed that the songs of Moses were in heroic verse and that David composed several kinds of odes and hymns, some of them in trimeter, some in pentameter. Jerome (*Epistles*, LIII, ad Paulinum, in *PL* 22, col. 547) believed he saw iambic, alcaic, and sapphic verses in the Psalms similar to those of Pindar and Horace. Lodge (Smith, i, 71), repeating Jerome, indicates how literary men of the 16th c. used these notions ; cp. Harrington (Smith ii, 207) and Puttenham, *Arte*, p. 9, and see I. Barroway, *ELH*, **2** (1935), 66–91. The metrical character and genius of the Psalms remained much debated until the 18th c., when in his Oxford Lectures on the *Sacred Poetry of the Hebrews* (1753) Bishop Lowth provided a fresh analysis which gave impetus to the late-18th c. cult of the sublime and the development of romantic poetic prose.

12. *hebrician* is the usual term in 16th c. for a Hebrew scholar, probably in parallel with *Grecian* for Greek scholar. In the 18th c. replaced by *Hebraist*.

14. **merely**, ' exclusively ' ; cp. *NED s.v.* adv.[2] 1.

14ff. Sidney's careful elaboration of proof to show that the Psalms are a poem indicates the importance he attaches to the point in the general argument of the *Apology*. He has argued (i) from etymology (10), (ii) from metrical form (11), and now proceeds to argue (iii) from ' elocution ' (manner of expression), by marking the uses made of invocation (as in Ps. 57:9) ; interchange of voices (as in Ps. 2) ; other personages as speakers (prosopopeia) (as in Ps. 50) ; ' animation ' (the ' pathetic fallacy '—much used in *Arcadia*) (as in Ps. 29). A stylistic approach to Scripture had been developed from one facet of Jerome's exegesis by many humanists, especially by Erasmus ; and in their great edition of the Bible Tremellius and Junius (see **102**/3 note) frequently gave literary and rhetorical annotation. Similarly in Sidney's circle, Dudley Fenner, *The Artes of Logike and Rhetorike* (1584), took most of his examples from Scripture. Sidney's account was remembered ; see Henry Peacham, *The Compleat Gentleman* (1634), ed. Gordon (Oxford, 1906), pp. 79–80. But the ideal of the poetry of the Psalms was widely disseminated in the 16th and 17th cs. in England : see Hallett Smith, *HLQ* **9** (1945), pp. 248–71 ; Lily B. Campbell, *Divine Poetry and Drama in 16th Century England* (Cambridge and Berkeley, 1959), Chaps. V and VI. The interest was sustained not only by the piety of such men as Sternhold and Hopkins, Thomas Norton, Archbishop Parker, and John Day, but also by the superior literary talents of Wyatt, Surrey, Sidney himself (with his sister), Donne, and Milton who in *Paradise Regained*, IV, 334–52, sketches the theory which promoted the concern

> With Sion's songs, to all true tasts excelling,
> Where God is prais'd aright, and Godlike men,
> The Holiest of Holies, and his Saints :
> Such are from God inspir'd . . . .

18. **poesy** (as Ben Jonson, *Discoveries*, *Works*, ed. Herford and Simpson, vol. viii, 636, defined it), the poet's 'skill or crafte of making'. Sidney regularly gives this meaning to *poesy* (cp. **101**/33, **102**/9, **107**/34, etc.), which he carefully distinguishes in use from *poetry* (**96**/2, 9, **97**/13, etc.), the more general term for the product of the art.

19. **almost**, ' indeed ' ; here used as intensive. Cp. *NED s.v.* 4.

25ff. The increased use of psalmody in public worship was attacked on both wings of the Church of England. Hooker (*Ecclesiastical Polity*, V, 37) rebutted the objection of the puritan Thomas Cartwright to the prescribed use of the Psalter. On the other side, after the publication of Sternhold and Hopkins' *Metrical Psalter* (1562), which claimed that it was ' allowed to be sung in all churches of all the people together before and after evening prayer, and also before and after sermons ', some opponents of Calvinism objected to what they considered a dangerous vulgarisation of liturgical psalmody ; see Jeremy Collier, *Ecclesiastical History*, Part II, iv, 326.

29ff. Sidney is following Scaliger, *Poetices*, I, i ; see **100**/21ff. note, and cp. Minturno, Preface to *L' arte poetica*.

33. **have met with,** ' are in agreement with '.

a maker. Cp. Puttenham's beginning to his *Arte* : ' A poet is as much to say as a maker. And our English name well conformes with the Greeks word.' *Maker* is common in 15th and 16th c. Northern English, and *making*, ' composing in verse ', is found earlier in ME. But in late Southern ME the terms lacked dignity. Chaucer had restricted *maker*, *making*, to reference to vernacular composition and reserved *poet*, *poesye*, etc., for composition in the classical and Italian languages.

34–6. ' I prefer to demonstrate the excellence of poetry by showing how it compares in its aims and range with other [arts and] sciences, rather than by making a simple assertion which, coming from me, would be taken to be prejudiced.'

37ff. The notion that there is no art which is not chiefly directed toward some product and is not itself a product of nature is Aristotelian ; see *Physica*, II, 2, 194–22 (cp. Plato, *Laws*, X, 889). Renaissance writers seeking a return to nature often invoke the principle ; so Castelvetro, *Poetica d' Aristotele* (Basel, 1576), p. 69 : ' Art is not a thing different from nature, nor can it pass beyond the limits of nature, but intends to work to the same end as nature .' M.-A. Muret (see **131**/19 note) in *Oratio*, xi (introducing the *Aeneid*) approaches poetry as Sidney does, arguing first that ' no art is anything but a kind of imitation of nature, for there is no art that does not owe its seeds and principles to nature ' (*Opera*, ed. Frotscher (Leipzig, 1834), ii, 368). See also B. Hathaway, *The Age of Criticism* (New York, 1962), p. 21. Consideration of the relation of nature and art led to frequent debate on the hierarchy of the human arts. Coluccio Salutati, *De laboribus Herculis* (ed. Ullman), I, iii, discusses the relation of poetry to the arts of the *trivium* and *quadrivium*, urging that poetry is an art independent of other arts : ' The principles of all arts are linked with nature and all art imitates nature in such a way that invention is nothing else than a sort of subtle and keen perception of natural operations . . .' (p. 18). But ' the matter of poetry is not anything determinate as is treated in the *real* sciences, but is universal and wide-open, as subject only to the art of words ' (p. 20). Minturno begins *De poeta* with a comparison of the poet with the musician, geometer, astrologer, grammarian, orator, lawyer, philosopher, and returns to these comparisons later (pp. 87–100). The Florentine Benedetto Varchi (1503–66) in his *Lezioni della poesia*, discussing the knowledge which shall convey and teach perfection and beatitude, runs through the claims of the speculative and moral philosopher, the lawyer, the rhetorician, the historian, and comes to rest with the poet, ' whom all arts serve ' (1859 ed., ii, 576). But Sidney is still following the thread of argument of Scaliger, *Poetices*, I, i, pp. 3–6 (see **100**/21ff. note).

p. 100

1. **actors and players, as it were.** Suggested by Scaliger's phrase in *Poetices*, I, i, p. 6 ; see below 21ff. note.

5. **musician in times.** Folio eds. from 1613 onwards read *tunes* (cp. **140/**28 and M. Croll's note in his edition of Lyly's *Euphues*, p. 257) ; but *times* is probably the correct reading. Music was commonly defined in the Middle Ages as ' the science of modulating well ' (Augustine, *PL* 32, col. 800), and *modulatio* concerns rhythm as well as melody. Late-medieval musical theory was especially engaged in the mensural problems of time ; see G. Reese, *Music in the Middle Ages* (New York, 1940), pp. 292–3. For the contrapuntal music of the 16th c. strict measurement of time was of course a practical necessity.

7. **thereon,** ' on that account '.

8. **natural virtues, vices, and passions.** Cp. **103/**29 note ; **108/**16 ; and Sidney's letter to his brother Robert : ' A moral philosopher . . . sets forth virtues or vices and the natures of passions ' (*Works*, vol. iii, 130).

9. **' follow Nature ',** etc. Sidney is drawing on Cicero, *De officiis*, I, xxviii, 10. This Stoic injunction became a Renaissance commonplace and was attached to a variety of ethical programmes ; see H. Haydn, *The Counter-Renaissance* (New York, 1950), pp. 486ff.

10. **determined.** In a technical sense, ' to determine ' is ' to come to a judicial decision ' ; see *NED s.v.* II.5.

11. **Historian.** This form (earliest example in *NED* is from Elyot, 1531) was slow to supersede other forms such as *historiographer* (cp. **97/**31), *historician, historier.*

11ff. **grammarian . . . rhetorician . . . logician.** The students of the *trivium*. Grammar as a discipline was exalted by some of the early humanists, but by Sidney's time it was often decried as the province of pedants ; see W. Ringler's note to Rainold's *Oratio*, p. 78. In Sidney's dealing with the rhetorician and the logician, his wording may suggest Ramus' method of teaching logic. Ramus intended to ground his method in nature ; so Invention was taught before Judgment or Disposition, thus inverting the order in which traditional Aristotelian logic had been taught. The Ramist order, which Sidney appears to accept for both logic and rhetoric, had, however, been the order in which, traditionally, rhetoric had been taught.

15. **the circle of a question.** Cp. ' the boundes of the question ', *Works*, vol. i, 18 ; and the phrase in the letter to his brother Robert : ' not tyed to the tenour of a question as Philosophers use ' (*Works*, vol. iii, 131). In writing as a rhetorician or logician one elects to be limited and circumscribed by the particular rhetorical purpose or logical issue involved. The arts are derived from nature ; but in so deriving them one limits them in order to use them for particular kinds of verbal activity. Sidney seems to blur the traditional differences between logic and rhetoric deliberately. Wilson (following Cicero, *Topics*, xxi) distinguished between ' definite ' questions which are ' comprehended within some end ' (and these are the special province of Rhetoric), and ' infinite ' questions, the province of the Logician, ' who talketh of things universally without respect of person, time or place ' (*Rhetorique*, pp. 2–3). But for Sidney here, as for the Ramists, all issues proceed from the particular (' are compassed within the circle of a question '), so tend to be rhetorical in character and pose in Wilson's term ' definite '

questions. Now that logic is absorbed into rhetoric, Wilson's ' infinite ' questions remain to be dealt with by the special technique which Sidney calls poetry. Cp. 73f.

17. **metaphysic,** 'metaphysician'; see *NED s.v.* 2. Pierre de La Primaudaye, *The French Academie* (English trans., ed. of 1618), i, 72, gives the same simple juxtaposition : ' Physike . . . is the studie of naturall things : Metaphysike . . . of supernaturall things.' Cp. Bacon's use of the term *metaphysics* throughout his writings ; see *Novum Organum* (ed. Fowler, Oxford, 2nd ed., 1889), pp. 64–8. The sense of **supernatural** (19) is no more than 'extranatural', 'outside the physical world ', and so ' entirely mental ' in dealings with (18) **the second and abstract notions.** ' Second notion ', a term in logic, is well defined by Sir William Hamilton (as quoted in *NED*) : ' A first notion is the concept of a thing as it exists in itself. . . . A second notion is the concept, not of an object as it is in reality, but of the mode under which it is thought by the mind.' See also Hathaway, pp. 324–5, on Fracastorius' treatment of ' second intentions '. Metaphysics, which in the Aristotelian scheme of inquiry comes ' after ' physics, is thus concerned with secondary qualities, which are ' not in the reality ' of nature, and are thus entirely mental, and so *supernatural.* Yet, adds Sidney, though metaphysics deals with concepts abstracted from reality, it is from **the depth of Nature** (20) ultimately that this abstraction had to be made. See *NED s.* depth I. 6, for the uses of the word in scholastic philosophy.

21ff. **the poet . . . doth grow . . . into another nature.** The bare gist of Sidney's argument is taken from Scaliger, *Poetices,* 1, i, pp. 5–6, a chapter which Sidney had read with some care. Parts of this chapter are here summarised : ' Do not all learned men of the academy, law court, or theatre have one object, *viz.* persuasion ? We agree that all discourse teaches. The end of teaching is knowledge (*scientia*). *Scientia* consists either in accepting inescapable conclusions or in recognising general notions. The end of persuasion is some mental or physical action. Fine speaking is only an instrument, a means, not an end. The end is persuasion to action. In deliberations and in judicial cases the speaker reacts to the audience. The opposite happens in demonstration : there the mind of the hearer depends upon the speaker. But in all forms of speaking (or writing), methods and issues overlap : all deal with human life, vices, and virtues. In many ways the poet and the philosopher treat their material similarly. Both speak either in their own or in another's person. The philosopher has his interlocutors, the orator his prosopopeias ; the orator sings somebody's praise and goes on to recount his life ; the historian often adds eulogies to his narrative and intersperses it with his own judgments.

' Only poetry embraces all these activities, and as a result it is more outstanding than other arts because all other verbal arts reproduce things as they are, as a sort of picture for the ear [cp. **101**/36], but the poet produces another nature altogether [cp. **100**/23], and a variety of outcomes as a result, and in this process even makes himself almost into another god. For in respect of the things that the Great Artificer established, all other arts and sciences which deal with them are actors or representatives [cp. **100**/1]. But the science of poetry presents more compellingly an actual appearance of what exists, and also of what does not exist. Indeed this art deals with things not as if it were narrating events from the outside as a reciter might do [cp. **135**/6–7], but rather as if it were establishing them in their actuality as another god might do.

As a result the usual name, poet, seems to have been arrived at not by agreement among men, but rather by natural providence. For the learned Greeks most appropriately spoke of poetry as a sort of making. I wonder that our own ancestors were so perverse [cp. **99**/32f.], for the word "factor", which expresses the meaning, they preferred to reserve for oilmen and chandlers.'

On the emergence under neo-Platonic influence of the idea of the artist as an imitator of the creative processes of nature, see E. Panofsky, *Idea* (Leipzig and Berlin, 1924), pp. 52ff., 68ff., 122ff. ; but, as Panofsky pointed out later (*Renaissance and Renaissances in Western Art* (Stockholm, 1960), p. 188 note 3), there was a reluctance in the 16th c. to claim for artists anything like the divine creativity. Sidney makes no such claim ; indeed, he is more discreet than Scaliger, or Puttenham in *Arte*, p. 4 : 'if [poets] be able to deuise and make all these things of them selues, without any subject of veritie . . . they be (by maner of speech) as creating gods'. On the development of the theory of poet as 'creator', see M. H. Abrams, *The Mirror and the Lamp* (New York, 1953), pp. 272–4 and notes. Sidney's account of the 'other nature' is eclectic. He draws from Scaliger, but seems to owe a special debt to the analysis of the mind given by Fracastorius (see **131**/18 note) in his dialogue *Turrius, sive de intellectione* ; see Hathaway, chap. 23, pp. 316–28 (from whom this summary is drawn). For Fracastorius, following Aristotle, knowledge derives from the senses. The mind forms images—' appearances ' of external things, and these ' appearances ' have a sort of independent existence (cp. **101**/1ff.). From these sense images, the mind makes abstractions (i.e. ' the second and abstract notions ', 18) of things that cannot be sensed directly; so a man ' can treat what is separated as if it were joined together, either in place or in subject or otherwise, whereby he makes chimeras and centaurs for himself, and gardens and palaces, and becomes a poet ' (quoted by Hathaway, p. 322, from Fracastorius, *Opera omnia* (Venice, 1555), p. 175v.). Abstraction is essentially a function of the active intellect.

27. **not enclosed within the narrow warrant of her gifts,** ' not dependent upon her restricted patronage and authorisation '.

28. **within the zodiac of his own wit.** On the zodiac as a symbol of perfection and entirety, see D. J. Gordon in *England and the Mediterranean Tradition* (Oxford, 1945), p. 116. Sidney was no doubt aware that many Renaissance mythographers spoke of God in creation working within the ' celestial zodiac ' ; see J. Seznec, *La Survivance des dieux antiques* (London, 1940), pp. 63ff. A figurative use of the zodiac was elaborated in the Latin poem (much used as a school text), *Zodiacus vitae* (1534), by Marcellus Palingenius, translated by Barnabe Googe in 1565.

29. Nature's tapestry is a commonplace with late-medieval and 16th c. poets. So : ' The soyle was overspread with tapites that Nature / Had made her self' (*Lament of the Black Knight*, 51).

32f. **brazen . . . golden.** In literary tradition the age of brass under the rule of Jove was considered the third age, between the age of silver and the present age of iron ; see Ovid, *Metamorphoses*, I, 89ff. The golden age is the primal age, but also the hoped-for age of perfection and immortality ; cp. Virgil, *Eclogues*, IV. For Sidney the world of brass is the world of hard but ultimately deceiving fact ; in the golden world reality does not fall short of our desire for perfection.

34ff. A scriptural theme (cp. Ps. 8:7–8) which Renaissance writers made their own ; see H. Baker, *The Dignity of Man* (Cambridge, Mass., 1947), especially pp. 235–40.

37. Theagenes, the Thessalian hero, lover of Cariclea, in *Æthiopica*, a Greek prose romance by the 4th c. bishop Heliodorus : cp. **103**/23 note. The romance was much esteemed in the 16th c., translated into French by Jacques Amyot, and into English by Thomas Underdown. It was, as Sir John Hoskins, *Directions for Speech and Style*, ed. H. H. Hudson (Princeton, 1935), p. 41, observed, one of Sidney's models for *Arcadia* ; see S. L. Woolf, *The Greek Romances in Elizabethan Prose Fiction* (New York, 1912), pp. 307–8.

Pylades, in the stories of the Greek dramatists, assisted Orestes in avenging the murder of Orestes' father, Agamemnon, on his slayer, Orestes' mother, Clytemnestra. Pylades married Orestes' sister, Electra. The friendship between Orestes and Pylades became proverbial.

38. Orlando. Roland in the old stories of Charlemagne and his paladins ; but, for the well-read Englishman of the 16th c., Orlando would be identified as the hero of the succession of Italian heroic poems, *Morgante maggiore* of Luigi Pulci (1432–84), *Orlando Innamorato* of Boiardo (1441–94), and *Orlando Furioso* of Ariosto (1474–1533). Of this last work, Sidney's literary disciple, Sir John Harrington, published in 1591 a translation ' in English Heroicall verse '.

Xenophon's Cyrus. *Cyropaedia*, by Xenophon, the Athenian soldier (*c.* 444–*c.* 350 B.C.), is a fictionalised political treatise based on the story of Cyrus, founder of the Persian monarchy : ' . . . this man excelled all men of his time in goodly personage, gentleness, prowesse, liberalitie, wisedome and memorie ' (Cooper's *Dictionary* (1565)), and was frequently cited as an exemplary figure by English humanists. See also **103**/19 note.

39. Virgil's Aeneas. For Scaliger the ' other nature ' (see 21ff. note above) was exemplified in Virgil's *Aeneid* (see *Poetices, passim,* particularly III, iv, p. 195) and the perfection of manhood in Aeneas himself ; see particularly *Poetices,* III, xi, p. 207. Cp. **108**/22 ; **119**/30ff. and note. Most humanist authors exalted Aeneas ; see E. Wolf, ' Die allegorische Virgilklärung des Cristoforo Landino ', *Neue Jahrbücher für das klassische Altertum, Geschichte und deutsche Literatur und Pädagogik*, **43–4** (1919), 453–79.

p. 101

1. **works of the one,** works of nature.

2. **essential,** as we should say ' real ', as opposed to existing only ' in fiction '.

2ff. This passage is important for an understanding of Sidney's theory (see **64**ff.) and of his practice where his ' course was (besides reading Aristotle and Theophrastus) to imagine the thing present in his own brain that his pen might the better present it to you ' (Hoskins, *Directions*, p. 42). Sidney's *Idea* (4, 5) is not pure Platonism. His theory of poetry runs parallel to Mannerist theory of painting (**66**). Whereas for the theorists ' of the Early and High Renaissance nature was the source from which all beauty was ultimately derived . . . for these Mannerists beauty was something which was directly infused into the mind of man from the mind of God, and existed there independent of any sense-impressions [cp. Augustine's theory of illumination (**57**)]. The idea in the artist's mind was the source of all the beauty in the works he created, and his ability to give a picture of the outside world was of no importance,

except in so far as it helped him to give visible expression to his idea.
. . . Lomazzo and Zuccaro both perfunctorily define painting as the
imitation of nature, but . . . both had in mind more particularly the
Scholastic idea that art works according to the same principles as
nature . . . [according to the Scholastic phrase, things exist in potency
before they exist in act]. That is to say, they mean that both painting
and nature are controlled by intellect—in the one case human and in
the other divine intellect—that both obey certain laws of order. . . .
The emphasis is on the idea in the artist's mind, which is the proper
object of imitation' ((Sir) Anthony Blunt, *Artistic Theory in Italy
1450–1600* (Oxford, 1940), pp. 140–1 ; see also E. Panofsky, *Idea*,
pp. 39ff.). In the 1570s Sidney's interests in painting probably brought
him in touch with painters developing Mannerism. R. C. Strong, *JWCI*
22 (1959), 359–60, has shown that Zuccaro's acquaintance during his
visit to England in 1575 was limited to members of Leicester's party.
However, there were more general intellectual forces at work in the
16th c. which could have guided Sidney towards his theory of poetry,
notably Florentine Neo-Platonism. ' Each cause which operates by art
or intelligence must first of all contain the form of that which it wishes
to produce. This form is called by the Platonists the Idea or exemplar
. . . which is often more perfect and authentic than its realisation '
(Pico della Mirandola, *Commento*, ed. E. Garin (Florence, 1942), II, 6,
pp. 467–8). Similarly, Ficino in arguing that beauty is incorporeal
shows that there is a close correspondence between the originating
concept and the final form ; see *Commentary on Symposium*, ed. Marcel
(Paris, 1956), IV, 4, pp. 173ff. Similar ideas were commonly expressed
in the 16th c. (cp. Scaliger, *Poetices*, II, 1, pp. 124–5 ; Fracastorius,
Naugerius (see **102**/25ff. note); and in particular, Paolo Beni, *In Aristo-
telis poeticam commentarii* (Padua, 1613), pp. 57ff.), and in relation to
literary composition can be traced back through the Middle Ages to
classical times ; cp. Geoffrey of Vinsauf, *Poetria nova* (ed. Faral),
43–56 ; Seneca, *Epistles*, 65. In any case Florentine Neo-Platonic
thinking in Sidney was bound to be modified by his own English
academic upbringing which was in part at least Aristotelian, even
scholastic, and by his Protestantism, which laid a heavy emphasis on
the personal mental act in theology and in worship and could thus
assimilate without strain elements of the Platonic theory of knowledge.
Du Plessis' theology is thoroughly Platonised in the work which Sidney
with Golding translated as *On the Treweness of the Christian Religion* ;
here cp. : ' For as the craftsman maketh his worke by the patterne
which he had erst conceyued in his mynde, which patterne is his inward
word : so God made the world and all that is therein ' (*Works*, vol. iii,
328). In many respects Sidney's thinking about poetry could coincide
with rather than derive directly from Mannerist theories of painting.

7. **wholly imaginative**, ' existing only in the imagination ', ' fantastic '
(see *NED s.* imaginative. 4 ; and cp. the distinction made **125**/25f.),
contrasting here with *substantially* (9).

8. **build castles in the air**, ' daydream ' ; see Tilley, C 125, 126.

12. **that maker**, ' the poet ' ; here Xenophon, who wrote the *Cyropaedia*,
as 16th c. readers believed, to teach a king his duties.

16. **heavenly Maker**, etc. God as the author of nature, which is itself a
creative but secondary process—*that second nature* (18). **that maker**
(17) then, will be ' nature ', not ' the poet '. Sidney is again adumbrating
a Mannerist doctrine, according to which man's artistic activity repro-

duces mentally in miniature the creative process of God. God produces nature, which in turn has this secondary creative power in producing ' pleasant rivers, fruitful trees, sweet-smelling flowers ' (**100**/30f.) ; but man with his intellect works in the same way (although on an infinitely reduced scale) as God worked in the first creation. Poetry is the product of this Godlike intellectual activity in man. It shows us perfection, which of course God's first creation would have possessed. That in ' second nature ', in the world around us, imperfection is apparent is, Sidney argues, a clear indication of the Fall of Man by which all nature was impaired.

17ff. who having made man, etc. Cp. Gen. 1:26 ; Hebr. 2:7, and particularly Ps. 8.

19. he, man.

21. her, nature's.

22ff. erected wit . . . infected will. *Erected* by ' the force of a divine breath ' (20). The theology is traditional ; but the emphasis on the corruption of nature and the vestiges of reason manifested in the arts recalls Calvin : ' For because everywhere are seene deformed ruines [Paul] saith that all things in heaven and earth doe endevour to the renewing. For sith Adam by his fall dissolued the perfect order of nature to the creatures . . . they naturally couet the perfect estate from which they are fallen ' (*Institutes of the Christian Religion*, III, 25, 2). Similarly : ' All the parts of the soule are possessed of sinne sith Adam fell away . . . the understanding minde is subject to blindnesse and the heart to perverseness . . . whereupon followeth that the soule . . . needeth not onely to be healed, but in a maner to put on a new nature ' (II, 1, 9). ' The will because it is unseparable from the nature of man, perished not, but was bound to perverse desires, that it can couet no good thing . . . the wit of man cannot for dulnesse keep the right way to search out truth. . . . Yet doe not all the travailes of Wit so alwey become voide, but that it attaineth somewhat, specially when it bendeth itself to these inferiour things. Yea it is not so blockish, but that it tasteth also some little of the higher things. . . . For when it is carried up above the compasse of this present life, then it is principally conuinced of her owne weaknesse ' (II, 2, 12–13) ; this is Sidney's ' no small argument to the incredulous ' (21). And Calvin goes on to show that ' men haue naturally a power and facilitie to learne and finde out artes : wherein . . . the liberalitie of God shineth '. ' The knowledge of artes and sciences is the gift of the spirit of God . . . so he doth particularly for speciall purposes powre speciall notions into [men]' (II, 2, 13–17), for instance, in Sidney's belief, ' in Poetry, when with the force of a divine breath he bringeth things forth far surpassing [nature's] doings ' (19–21).

24–7. This concludes the argument from etymology begun **98**/16.

27. name above all names. Cp. Phil. 2:9.

28. opening, ' exposition ', ' unfolding of the case ' ; a lawyer's word.

31. description. From the terminology of logic ; cp. **120**/23.

33ff. William Temple in his Analysis (see **34** note), p. 13, rightly observes that this paragraph in praise of Poesy as Imitation or Fiction designed to teach and delight contains the whole issue (*tota controversia*), of the *Apology*. In this definition Sidney has brought together many of the learned commonplaces of Renaissance criticism ; cp. Aristotle, *Poetics*, I, 1447a : ' Let us consider poetry itself. . . . Epic poetry, tragedy, and comedy too, dithyrambic poetry, and most music on the flute and the lyre all fall into the general class of imitation ' (see **47**ff.) ; for Horace in *Art*

333ff., *dulce et utile* provides the end of teaching and delighting (see **66**ff.). **a speaking picture** (36) goes back ultimately to Simonides of Ceos (*fl.* 530 B.C.), but the saying is frequently repeated by Plutarch in *Moralia* ; *On the life and poetry of Homer*, 216 ; *On the fame of the Athenians*, 3 ; *How to tell a flatterer from a friend*, 15, etc.—notably : 'Realise not only that poetry is articulate painting and painting inarticulate poetry, but learn that we are not only pleased with seeing a beautiful thing but also with seeing a likeness ' (*How the young man should study poetry*, 15 ; see also *Ad Her.*, IV, xxviii, 39 ; Spingarn, p. 270, note 1 ; Smith, i, 342, and note, p. 386 ; **50**f.). Though influential, the parallel was always somewhat factitious ; see T. J. B. Spencer, *Greece and Rome* **7** (N.S.) (1960), 173–86. But in organising a definition of poetry Sidney follows Scaliger, *Poetices*, I, i, pp. 2–6 : ' What is called Poesy describes not only what exists, but also non-existent things as if they existed, showing how they could or should exist. For the whole matter is comprehended in imitation. But imitation is only the means to the ultimate end, which is to teach with delight. . . . Poetry and the other arts represent things as they are, as a picture to the ear.' Cp. *Poetices*, IV, i, p. 401 : ' All discourse consists of idea, image, *mimesis*, just as all painting does : this is what Aristotle and Plato affirm.'

37ff. **three several kinds.** The classification is based on Scaliger, *Poetices*, I, ii, pp. 10–11 (see Spingarn, p. 270). Sidney has been drawing on this same passage earlier ; see **97**/1ff. note. ' Classifying by antiquity there are three ages. First, the primitive, rude and uncultivated age of poetry of which memory leaves only a trace without a name, unless we count Apollo as its originator. Second, a venerable age, the source of Mystery and Theology : among the poets of which time are Orpheus, Musaeus, Linus. . . . Of the third age Homer is author and father : Hesiod also belongs here, and others. But if records did not exist you would have thought Musaeus later than Homer, for he shows more cultivation and polish [cp. **96**/17ff.]. . . . A third kind of classification can be made according to poets' interests, from their subject matter. . . . By means of analysis these can be reduced to three principal types. First, the theological poets [Scaliger draws on Boccaccio, *De genealogia deorum*, XIV, viii, who draws on Augustine, *City of God*, XVIII, 14] such as Orpheus and Amphion whose works were so divine that they are credited with infusing a soul into lifeless things [see **96**/28 note]. Secondly, the philosophical poets, which are of two sorts—the natural philosophers such as Empedocles, Nicander, Aratus, Lucretius, and the moral philosophers again divisible into kinds —the political philosophers represented by Solon and Tyrtaeus, and poets of social economy by Hesiod, the general moralists by Phocylides, Theognis, Pythagoras [cp. **97**/1ff. note]. Thirdly, there are those of whom we are now going to speak.' Ronsard (*Œuvres complètes*, ed. Laumonier (Paris, 1914), iii, 149–52 ; xiv, 5) makes a similar threefold classification. On the manner in which Sidney modifies Scaliger's classifications, see A. C. Hamilton, ' Sidney's Idea of the " Right Poet " ', *Comparative Literature* **9** (1957), 51–9. R. Wills, *De re poetica*, pp. 60f., follows Scaliger closely. Both Scaliger and Wills make verse writing and didacticism the essentials of poetry, and so do not need to characterise the ' right poet ' according to his subject matter very particularly. Sidney on the other hand has already committed himself to a theory of poetry as ideal imitation, and this he proceeds to show will serve to identify the ' right poet ' ; see **102**/24ff.

39ff. **such were David in his Psalms,** etc. Sidney adds these Scriptural examples to Scaliger's purely classical list. He draws here upon the Preface to Part 3 (the Poetic books) of the most esteemed Protestant Latin translation of the Scriptures, *Testamenti Veteris Biblia Sacra*, etc., by Emanuel Tremellius and Franciscus Junius (Frankfurt-am-Main, 1575–9 ; often reprinted). On f. 117 (1607 ed.) it is explained that other books are grouped with the Psalms because they are metrical and not written in prose like the rest of the Bible (although even there are scattered some elegant pieces such as the Songs of Moses (Ex. 15:1–19), of Deborah (Jg. 5), and in this way, as everybody knows, they can best teach, delight, and move. This sacred poetry is a winning summary of the Law and the Prophets set out succinctly, memorably, and effectively in figurative language and giving the same witness of God—expressing the nature of Christ in part of Proverbs, the workings of Providence in Job, union with the Church in the Song of Songs, the vanity of human life in Ecclesiastes, and common morality in the second part of Proverbs.

p. 102

3. **Emanuel Tremellius** (1510–80), a Jew from Ferrara, converted to Protestantism by Peter Martyr and resident then at Oxford until 1553 ; a great Oriental scholar who at Heidelberg worked with the French theologian **Franciscus Junius** the Elder (1545–1602) on the new Latin translation of the Bible from the original languages.

7. The so-called Homeric Hymns are rhapsodic narratives of Greek legends, probably minstrel legends ; they were translated by George Chapman.

9. James 5:13 ; and Sidney echoes the Scriptural phrasing. According to Tremellius and Junius, *Biblia Sacra*, Part 3, f. 105, the Holy Ghost composed the Psalms for our comfort in our state of sin and prescribed them for our use and benefit. In Sidney's circle of acquaintances Psalm-singing Christians must have been numerous. On the appeal of Psalm-singing see D. Stevens, *Music and Poetry in the Early Tudor Court* (London, 1961), pp. 77ff.

15. **Tyrtaeus, Phocylides.** See **97/1**ff. note.

   Cato. The *Distichs* of the 3rd c. Dionysius Cato was a school text-book throughout the Middle Ages and Renaissance from which boys learnt syntax as well as proverbial morality ; on its use in the 16th c. see T. W. Baldwin, *William Shakspere's Small Latine and less Greeke*, i, 595–606.

16. **Lucretius** (95–52 B.C.), the Roman poet, author of the philosophic poem in six Books, *De rerum natura*. It was little read throughout the Middle Ages. By 16th c. critics Lucretius was frequently grouped with Empedocles and Lucan and sometimes denied the title of poet ; see note on Lucan, 17 below.

   Virgil's Georgics were esteemed as an excellent work on agriculture (cp. Elyot, *Governour*, I, x, ed. Croft, I, 63 ; Harrington, Smith, ii, 206–7) well into the 18th c.

17. **Manilius**, a Roman poet of the time of Augustus, who wrote *Astronomica*, an astrological poem in five Books.

   Pontanus. Giovanni Pontano (1426–1503), soldier, statesman, scholar, viceroy to Ferdinand I, King of Naples, and tutor to his son Alfonso. As a Latin poet he was very highly esteemed ; see Scaliger (*Poetices*, VI, iv, pp. 744–9), who discusses in some detail the poem on the stars in five Books, *Urania*, which in Sidney's mind has linked Pontanus with Manilius.

Lucan (A.D. 39–65), the Roman poet, author of the unfinished epic *Pharsalia* on the wars between Pompey and Caesar. Lucan's writing was much admired whenever the late-Roman rhetorical tradition dominated taste in poetry. In the 16th c. critical voices (including Ronsard's and Castelvetro's) disputed his title of poet on the ground that he was essentially a historian. They were elaborating upon a school judgment which can be traced back through medieval scholars to Quintilian (*Institutes*, I, i, 90 ; see Herrick, pp. 37–8). To this debate Sidney refers (23f. below) in terms suggested by Scaliger (*Poetices*, I, ii, p. 11) : ' Surely grammarians quibble in their usual fashion when they object that Lucan wrote history'. Cp. Smith, i, 336 (where Nash is drawing upon Cornelius Agrippa, *Vanitie of the Arts* (trans. Sandford), f. 13) ; Smith, ii, 196. But in the 16th c. the issue arising from this traditional consideration of Empedocles (see **50**), Lucretius (see 16 above), and Lucan, acquired a general importance, *viz.* whether in verse or fabling lay the essential of poetry ; see Hathaway, Chap. 4, pp. 65–80.

21ff. **this second sort,** etc. Philosophical as well as historical poetry is conditioned by its subject matter. Henri Estienne in the Preface to *Poesis philosophus* (1573) makes the same distinction between poetry and those philosophical writings in verse which are not truly poems. Ben Jonson was giving judgment on the same ground when he told Drummond that du Bartas was ' not a Poet but a Verser, because he wrote not Fictions '. Castelvetro (*Poetica d' Aristotele*, pp. 28–9) is the most rigorously exclusive : ' All works with subject-matter drawn from other arts and sciences are not strictly poetry. In these cases the poet is simply wrapping up other people's work in his own words.'

25ff. **Betwixt whom,** etc. The distinction employed here is several times suggested in Aristotle, *Poetics*, in Chap. 15 (as quoted **49**) ; see also Chaps. 2 and 25. An influential reformulation was provided by Cicero, *Orator ad Brutum*, II, 9 : ' Nothing can be formed by copying which cannot be made more beautiful than it is when merely sensed by eye or ear : it is achieved by the thought of the mind. So the statues of Phidias, which are of unsurpassed perfection. For in depicting Jove or Minerva the artist did not study one person for a likeness but let many beauties haunt his mind and derived a likeness by using them all.' This belief that particular graces could be synthesised into a general ideal beauty (usually illustrated in Renaissance times by the story of the painter Zeuxis representing Juno ; see E. Panofsky, *Idea*, pp. 24ff.) was redeveloped and came to underlie most neo-classic theory of art. In his dialogue on poetry, Fracastorius (see **131**/18 note), in *Naugerius* (trans. by Ruth Kelso, p. 60), presents an argument very similar to Sidney's : other writers ' are like the painter who represents the features and other members of the body as they really are in the object ; but the poet is like the painter who does not wish to represent this or that particular man as he is with his many defects, but who, having contemplated the universal and supremely beautiful idea of his creator, makes things as they ought to be '. These other writers ' imitate particulars, that is make use of the naked thing, but the poet does otherwise—he imitates the simple idea clothed in its beauty, which Aristotle calls the universal '.

30. **the constant though lamenting look of Lucretia.** The story of the Roman wife who to redeem her honour killed herself after she had been violated by Sextus Tarquinius, gave a theme for discussion of tragic destiny and suicide in Augustine, *City of God*, I, xviii ; see B. Croce, ' Lucrezia nella poesia e nella casistica morale ', *Anedotti di varia letteratura* (2nd ed., Bari, 1953), pp. 400–10. It was taken as a common

subject by Renaissance painters ; see the lists in A. Pilger, *Barockthemen* (Budapest and Berlin, 1956), ii, 386–90. Paintings of Lucretia by Paul Veronese and Albrecht Dürer well fit Sidney's brief description. It is possible that he saw these pictures on his travels. He is recognising what the Mannerists asserted, that it was the painter's task to show how ' the minde (according to the diverse affections . . . by reason of the apprehensions both sensible and imaginative) dooth diuersly change and alter the bodie with sensible alterations ' (N. Hilliard, *Arte of Limning*, ed. P. Norman (Walpole Society, i, 1912), p. 23).

33. **For these third,** etc. A more sober re-statement of the assertions at **100**/21ff. (*range* (36) echoes **100**/28), a development of Aristotle's treatment of the relation between imitation and verisimilitude (*Poetics*, Chaps. 8, 9, and 25).

38. **the first and most noble sort.** ' Such were David . . . Solomon . . .' (**101**/39ff.).

39. **so these . . . .** The third sort, ' the poets ' who deserve their etymology of ' makers ' ; cp. **99**/29ff.

p. 103

2. **do merely make to imitate,** ' write exclusively with the intention of producing an imitation ' (in the Aristotelian sense). The arrangement *make to imitate, . . . imitate . . . to delight and teach, delight to move, . . . teach, to make them know,* is an example of strict climax, or what Wilson (*Rhetorique*, p. 204) called *gradation,* ' as though one should go vp a paire of stayres and not leaue till he come to the top '. Cp. **139**/20–2.

6. **scope.** A mark for aiming at ; see *NED s.v.* 1.

9. **These,** *scil.* the works of right poets.

10f. **Heroic, Lyric, Tragic,** etc. Sidney distinguishes eight main genres. Harrington follows him (Smith, ii, 209), and so does Francis Meres (Smith, ii, 319). Puttenham (*Arte,* pp. 25–7) jumbles the same list. The history of genre classification is confused ; see I. Baehrens, *Die Lehre von der Einteilung der Dichtkunst* (Halle, 1940). The eightfold classification was apparently originated by an obscure Roman rhetorician, Caesius Bassus, who was quoted in the popular compendium on poetry (written before 1540) of L. G. Gyraldus, *Historia Poetarum tam Graecorum quam Latinorum* (Basel, 1545), p. 87. The division is based on Horace, *Art,* 73–85, where rather unsystematically Horace dealt with epic, elegy, iambic, comedy, tragedy, lyric in respect of their versification. In lines 86–98 he showed how the different verse forms of comedy and tragedy suit their different material. In *Satires,* I, 10, and *Epistles,* II, 2, he gave further hints for classifying. Quintilian in his review of standard authors (*Institutes,* X, 1) dealt with the genres of Latin poetry : heroic, elegy, satire, iambic, lyric, tragedy, comedy ; he does not seem to admit the Latin poets as writers of pastoral, or the Greeks as writers of satire. Sidney's list is traditionally based. Though he classifies by subject matter his system is not entirely freed from Horace's concern with versification ; hence the appearance of iambic as the name of a kind (see **116**/34 note). Sixteenth c. critics usually provide conflated lists of the genres, put together from Horace's account, from Aristotle's division into epic, tragedy, and comedy (*Poetics,* 1), or from the dominant medieval scheme formulated in the 4th c. by the grammarian Diomedes (who classified according to the person of the speaker in the poetic narrative ; see E. R. Curtius, *European Literature and the Latin Middle Ages* (English trans., London, 1953), pp. 440ff.). The resultant heterogeneity can be marked in Scaliger, who devotes most of Book I of his *Poetices*, in 57 Chapters, to a bewildering number of kinds beginning with pastoral (Chap. 4). Benedetto Varchi in his Florentine lectures distinguished the eight genres (heroic, tragic, comic, lyric, elegiac, satiric, pastoral, epigrammatic) in a descending order of dignity (*Lezioni della poesia*, ii, 701). Similarly Sidney's list here gives his own scale of value. In his detailed examination of the genres (**115**/35ff.) he starts with pastoral, the ' lowest ' (**116**/14), and proceeds to ' the Heroical . . . the best and most accomplished kind ' (**119**/26). The position given to lyric above tragedy is an innovation of importance.

15. numbrous, ' metrical '. The evidence provided by *NED s.* number, *sb.* 17 ; numbrous, 2 ; numerous, 5, indicates that these words belonged to the critical vocabulary of the New Poetry associated with Sidney and Spenser.

16. verse being but an ornament and no cause. Cp. 32ff. below. Sidney's judgment follows from his insistence that the matter of the imitation, *viz.* the example, is the substance of poetry. See 74f. ; and for the critical discussion in Italy in late 16th c., Hathaway, Chap. 6, pp. 87–117.

19. many versifiers. See notes above on **102**/16 and 17 for the hesitation of some learned critics as to the status as poets of fact-tellers like Lucan and Empedocles. More generally throughout the Middle Ages verse was taken as the sure sign of poetry. But judicious critics from classical times onwards distinguished good practitioners of the art from bad, and the bad were often denied the honourable title of poet ; so Horace, *Satires*, II, i, 28 ; Quintilian, *Institutes*, X, i (with reference to Cornelius Severus). Scaliger, although he makes verse an essential of poetry (see **121**/36), discriminates between ' those who can attain but little glory, since they recount simple stories in verse and are called merely versifiers ; and those who gain for themselves the help and patronage of the Muses by whose spirit they find out what escapes the others, and are called poets ' (*Poetices*, I, ii, p. 6). Similarly, Elyot (*Governour*, ed. Croft, i, 120) : ' They that make verses, expressynge therby none other lernynge but the craft of versifyeng, be nat of auncient writers named poetes, but onely called versifyers '. Cp. Puttenham, *Arte*, p. 3.

20. Xenophon. See **100**/38 note.

22. as Cicero saith. In *Epistles to his brother Quintus*, I, 1, viii, 19: ' The Cyrus by Xenophon is not drawn according to historical accuracy but in the likeness of a model ruler, in whom the writer associates supreme dignity with outstanding friendliness. With good cause our great Scipio Africanus never let the book out of his hands. In it nothing is omitted which has to do with the office of a loving and temperate ruler.' The *Cyropaedia* was greatly esteemed in the Renaissance on this account ; cp. Hoby's Preface to his translation of Castiglione, *Courtier* ; Elyot, *Governour*, I, xi (ed. Croft, i, 84) ; II, ix (ed. Croft, ii, 104).

23. an absolute heroical poem. *absolute*, ' complete '. Spenser in his prefatory letter to the *Faery Queen* (quoted 86) assumes that *Cyropaedia* is a poem in prose. Francis Meres extracts this passage from the *Apology* concerning Xenophon and Heliodorus, and adds : ' So Sir P.S. writ his immortal poem, *The Countess of Pembrooke's Arcadia* in

Prose ; and yet our rarest Poet ' (Smith, ii, 315–16). On the learned voices in Italy supporting this view, see Hathaway, Chap. 6, pp. 81–117.

Heliodorus. See **100**/37 note. Scaliger (*Poetices*, III, xcv, p. 332) recommends the *Æthiopica* as a most splendid interlaced episodic epic; ' I consider that this book should be very carefully read by the epic poet and that he should set it before him as his most excellent model.'

sugared, ' sweet and with a special refinement '. An exceedingly common epithet of praise in the 16th c. as applied to speech and poetry.

27. **a long gown maketh an advocate,** etc. The comparison maintains what has been asserted above (16f.), that verse is but the dress. The phrase looks like a Protestant adaptation of the old proverb : ' The cowl does not make the monk ' ; but the change may also indicate the audience Sidney had in mind for the *Apology*.

29. **images of virtues, vices, or what else.** C. M. Dowlin, ' PS's Two Definitions of Poetry ', *MLQ* **3** (1942), 573–81, sees in this stress on the imitation of virtues and vices (cp. **100**/8) the influence of Plato and quotes the *Republic*, 598D–E, 600E, 603B, etc. Aristotle, on the other hand, conceives of poetry as imitation of action. There seems, however, no reason to look for a direct reading from Plato here, when, in the 16th c., among others, Scaliger (*Poetices*, VII, iii, p. 832) treated this problem ' whether a poet teaches morals or actions' (see Hathaway, Chap. 5, pp. 81–6). Scaliger argued that the poet portrays actions so that we may embrace the good and imitate them, and may spurn the bad and refrain from vice. Action is the mode of presenting what is to be taught ; the moral attitude (*affectus*) is that which we are taught to acquire. In a story the action described is an exemplification of the attitude we ought to acquire, or an instrument by means of which this attitude is to be acquired. And this is applicable not only to tragedy but to all kinds of poetry. In life on the other hand it is the action which we propose to ourselves as the end, the attitude is simply the condition in which we act. Sidney at **108**/16 (and cp. **107**/29) speaks again of the virtues and vices and passions of man as the subject of poetry ; but these statements rest on the belief that poetry aims beyond the delineation of moral attitudes by moving men to action.

31. **note,** ' distinctive characteristic '.

33. **all in all,** ' all others in all respects ' ; for the phrase see *NED s.* all A.8.d.

35. **peizing,** ' weighing '. This justification of verse, that it enables one to write with greater control, precision, and dignity, was to become a neo-classical tenet. Sidney's contemporary, Vauquelin de La Fresnaye (*L'Art poétique*, publ. Pellissier, Paris, 1885, I, i, 87ff.), described verse as a means of clarifying thought and of making the design more compact, although verse is not essential ; witness Heliodorus and Montemayor. Cp. Pope, Preface to the *Essay on Man*.

38f. **to weigh . . . Poetry by his works and . . . by his parts.** The Enumeration of the sections of the Confirmation to follow (see Summary of Argument, **14**), announcing an analysis by two of the ' places' of logic, *viz.* (i) by mode of operation ; (ii) by constituent parts.

p. 104

1. **anatomies,** ' dissections '.

2. **sentence.** In an earlier legal sense, ' the decision of the court ', not merely the penalty imposed.

3f. wit . . . memory . . . judgment . . . conceit. These comprehend apparently the inner activities of the mind. The syntax (a nominative absolute construction without finite verb) suggests a resolute refusal to be pedantically scientific ; but *memory, judgment, conceit* appear to be the constituents of *wit*. Usually Sidney uses *wit* as the generic term for the understanding (*intellectus*) (cp. **95**/6 ; **96**/27 ; **98**/5 ; **100**/28, etc. ; see note in Cook, p. 59), and sets it against the *will* (*appetitus*) (cp. **101**/22–3). *Wit* is analysed further into (i) *memory* (the passive storing of knowledge) (see notes on **122**/9 and 20ff.) ; (ii) *judgment* (intellectual evaluation (*ratio*) ; cp. **107**/28, 32, etc.) ; (iii) *conceit* (conception, the activity of the mind in forming notions about things, the ' imagination ') (cp. **99**/4 ; **107**/24 ; **110**/25 ; **113**/15 ; **119**/13). But in other contexts *conceit* can mean concept, the product of conception (cp. **113**/19 ; **120**/21, 22 ; **124**/29 ; **139**/9 ; **140**/16) ; for full range of meaning in 16th c. see *NED s.* conceit, concept, conception ; and see W. Rossky, ' Imagination in the English Renaissance : Psychology and Poetic ', *Renaissance Studies* **5** (1958), pp. 49–73. The triad, Memory, Judgment, Conceit, appears in Spenser's House of Alma (*Faery Queen*, II, ix, stanzas 49ff.; cp. Wilson, *Rhetorique*, p. 31). With Bacon also : ' Intellectus or Understanding seems to be the generic term including Memory, Imagination, and Reason ' (*Novum Organum* (ed. Fowler), p. 18). Bacon like Sidney relates the divisions to learning : ' The parts of human learning have reference to the three parts of Man's Understanding, which is the seat of learning : History to the Memory, Poesy to his Imagination, and Philosophy to his Reason ' (*Advancement of Learning*, ed. Wright, II, i, 1, p. 85) ; and on this division Bacon's whole scheme is based. It is sometimes assumed that he derived the triad from the Italian savant and mathematician Cardanus (1501–76) ; see G. S. Brett, *A History of Psychology* (London, 1921), II, 146. Plainly it was common property in the 16th c., and it can be found in medieval writers ; it derives ultimately from a fusion of the anatomical teaching of Galen with Stoic psychology: see R. Klibansky, E. Panofsky and F. Saxl, *Saturn & Melancholy* (London, 1964), p. 69, note 5.

3. enabling, ' strengthening '.

6ff. the . . . end . . . to lead . . . to . . . perfection. According to Plato, (*Phaedo*, 82–3, *Republic*, VII), the true end of man is to attain to a fuller knowledge by escaping upwards from imprisonment in the flesh. Similarly in the 12th c. for Hugh of St Victor (*Didascalion*) the supreme purpose of all human learning is to restore the integrity of human nature after the Fall ; and for Dante, in his letter to Can Grande on the *Divine Comedy* : ' Briefly the end . . . is to rescue those who live in this life from their condition of misery and to guide them to the state of blessedness.' In this estimate of learning, as Erasmus, *Praise of Folly* (English trans., London, 1900), observed, Christians agreed with the Platonists. It became a cardinal principle with Renaissance writers ; see Foster Watson, *Vives on Education, Introduction*, pp. cliii–clvi ; Bacon, *Advancement* (ed. Wright), To the King, p. 2 : ' The mind of man by nature knoweth all things, and hath but her own native and original notions (which by the strangeness and darkness of this tabernacle of the body are sequestered) again revived and restored ' ; Milton, *Tractate on Education* : ' The end then of learning is to repair the ruins of our first parents by regaining to know God aright, and out of that knowledge to love Him.' Many literary critics argued that the end of poetry is 'beatitude': Scaliger, *Poetices*, VII, ii, p. 830; B. Varchi, *Lezioni della poesia*, ii, 576. See also G. W. O'Brien, *Renaissance Poetics and the Problem of Power* (Chicago, 1956), pp. 41ff.

8f. Sidney is perhaps glancing at an account of the psychological origins of the different branches of learning given by the Spaniard, Juan de Dios Huarte, *Examen de ingenios* (1575; trans. by R. Carew, 1594). Huarte distinguished the same triad (see 3f. note), Memory, Judgment, and Conceit, and went on to show how the dominance of one of these faculties in a man inclined him towards a particular branch of knowledge.

13f. **they knew the causes of things.** Cp. Virgil, *Georgics*, II, 490-2.

> Felix qui potuit rerum cognoscere causas. . . .

> Happy the man, who, studying Nature's laws,
> Through known effects can trace the secret cause—
> His mind possessing in a quiet state,
> Fearless of Fortune, and resign'd to Fate.
> (Dryden's trans.)

According to some old commentators, Virgil is distinguishing the two aspects of philosophy—physics (natural philosophy) and moral philosophy. Sidney's distinction, however, is between the natural philosophers and the metaphysicians; see **100**/17 note.

20f. **the astronomer looking to the stars.** Cp. *Astrophil & Stella*, XIX:

> . . . like him that both
> Lookes to the skies, and in a ditch doth fall.

Plato's story in *Theaetetus*, 174, of the philosopher and astronomer Thales (on whom see **97**/1ff. note) was often repeated (cp. Cicero, *De divinatione*, II, 30) as well as being applied to other philosophers: by Erasmus (*Apophthegmes*, I, 17) to Diogenes; by Cornelius Agrippa (*Vanitie of the Arts*, trans. Sandford, f. 43v.) to Anaximenes as well as to Thales. See W. Ringler's note to Rainolds, *Oratio*, p. 83; and D. W. Robertson, *A Preface to Chaucer* (Princeton and Oxford, 1963), p. 273, for medieval citations. This passage in the *Apology* recalls Erasmus' treatment of self-opinionated scientists in *Praise of Folly*, pp. 126ff.

22f. **the mathematician might draw forth a straight line,** etc. Cp. Seneca (*Epistles*, 88): 'You know what makes a straight line; what does that avail you if it does not teach you how to go straight in your life?', which is versified by Fulke Greville, *Treatise of Human Learning* (*Poetry*, ed. Bullough, i, 162). This Senecan Epistle on the uncertain value of the liberal arts when divorced from the practice of virtue lies very close to Sidney's thought.

25. **serving sciences.** Cp. **106**/14. The term appears a deliberate irony for the 'liberal arts'. Earlier (**99**/37-**100**/20) Sidney has shown how the arts and sciences are limited in intellectual scope by reason of their dependence upon a particular aspect of nature; here he shows their moral limitation by arguing, in Seneca's words, that they can only prepare the mind for virtue, they cannot give it. *Serving sciences* are set against **the mistress-knowledge** (27). Sidney now follows the argument at the beginning of Aristotle's *Ethics* (I, 1-2). First Aristotle observed that all arts and sciences aim at some end which is their respective good. 'Now since there are many actions, arts and sciences, it follows that there are many ends. Of medicine the end is health; of

shipbuilding, a ship ; of generalship, victory ; of economy, wealth. But in those cases where some arts combine (as, for instance, under horsemanship is comprised the art of making bridles and all other horse furniture; and this and the whole art of war is comprised in generalship; and in the same manner, other arts combine together)—in all these, the ends of the chief arts [the architectonic arts] are more to be sought than the ends of the subordinate arts, because for the sake of the former, the latter are pursued. . . . If therefore there is some end . . . which we seek for itself, and if we seek for other things on account of this . . . it is evident that this must be the good and the greatest good. . . . This it would appear must be the end of that which is the chief and master science of all [the architectonic art] ; and this seems to be the political science, for it directs what arts should be cultivated by states, what individual people should learn. . . . This end must be the highest good of man.' This doctrine of a guiding principle of virtue in thought and action, in *well-doing* as well as in *well-knowing*, was characteristic of Sidney, as Fulke Greville testified (see **5**), and of many other humanists ; see E. F. Rice, *The Renaissance Idea of Wisdom* (Cambridge, Mass., 1958), pp. 163ff. On the advocacy by Italian literary critics of the late 16th c. of poetry as an architectonic study serving the highest good of man, see Weinberg, i, 28ff.

31. **next,** ' nearest '.

33. **soldiery,** ' military science '.

p. 105

1. **as principal challengers.** The portraits of the moral philosopher and historian that follow here anticipate the Theophrastan character literature of 17th c. writers and recall Erasmus' ironic delineations in *Praise of Folly* (pp. 115ff.) and in many of the *Colloquies*. Sidney serves his cause well by indulging in personalities at the expense of the philosopher and historian.

3. **rudely clothed,** etc. The excessive squalor or plainness of the Cynics and Stoics was notorious ; cp. Boccaccio, *De genealogia deorum*, XIV, v (Osgood, p. 34). M.-A. Muret, *Oratio*, iv (*Opera*, i, 144), refuses to permit philosophy to be dishonoured because philosophers are said ' to live in filth and squalour, with patched clothes, always unwashed, always unshaven, always uncombed '.

5. This recalls Cicero, *Pro Archia poeta*, 26 : ' These same philosophers set their own names even upon the books in which they condemn the pursuit of glory.' Cp. *Tusculan Disputations*, I, xv, 34.

8. **definitions.** Originally formal pronouncements on points of doctrine (cp. **107**/29 ; **113**/25). **divisions and distinctions.** In logic, the parts and successive refinements of an argument. All three terms belong to medieval scholasticism and survive in Elizabethan academic use. Hoskins (*Directions*, pp. 42–5) deals in succession with Distinction, Definition, Division as used in rhetoric.

9. **interrogative.** As noun.

10ff. In dealing with philosophic method Sidney goes through a simplified but traditional list of the ' places of logic ' : definition, causes, effects, adjuncts. Cp. Wilson, *Rhetorique*, pp. 23, 113 ; Cicero, *Topics*, ii-v. Aristotle in *Ethics* proceeded in this way : from the definition of the good in Book I, through the causes and instruments of virtue to the examination of social virtue in later Books.

14. **cumbersome**, ' obstructive ', ' interfering '.

16. **containeth**. With a plural noun ; see Abbott, *Shakespearian Grammar*, § 334.

20ff. Sidney reduces the historian to little more than a self-opinionated antiquarian. Complaints against the partisanship of local or national historians go back to antiquity ; cp. Josephus, *Against Apion*, I, 3–5, on the contradictions, uncertainties, and prejudices of the Greek historians. Bitter partisan disputes were numerous among the historical scholars of the 16th c. Those who sought to defend the usefulness of history argue that even if histories did not always provide the facts it could still give ' examples ' from which men could learn : cp. Elyot, *Governour*, II, xxv (quoted in **108**/7 note); Amyot, in Preface to Plutarch's *Lives* (see **106**/34f. note); Montaigne, *Essays*, I, xx.

24. **accord**, ' reconcile '.

25f. A characteristic statement of Sidney's empiricism : cp. Descartes, *Discours de la méthode* (ed. Charpentier), p. 49, also discussing history : ' When one is too curious about things that took place in centuries gone by, one usually remains remarkably ignorant of what takes place in this.'

29. **in a . . . chafe**, ' in a temper '.

31. **testis temporum**, etc. Cicero, *De oratore*, II, ix, 36 : ' History indeed is the witness of the ages, the light of truth, the life of memory, the governess of life, the herald of antiquity.' The phrases were in common use. See Elyot, *Governour*, I, xi (ed. Croft, i, 82) ; *Amiot to the Readers*, in North's *Plutarch*, I, 16 ; Frontispiece to Raleigh, *Historie of the World* (1613). Bodin, *Methodus ad facilem historiarum cognitionem* (1572), Preface, discusses the phrase *magistra vitae*.

33. **disputative**, ' controversial '. But in this context well rendered by ' academic ', in its vulgar modern sense of ' slightly unreal '.

36. **Marathon** (490 B.C.), where the Athenians repulsed the Persians. **Pharsalia** (48 B.C.), where Julius Caesar defeated Pompey. **Poitiers** (1356), where the small English army under the Black Prince routed a French host and captured the French king. **Agincourt** (1415), where Henry V defeated the French.

39. **goeth beyond**. Ambiguous. Taken literally it continues the sense of the preceding sentence ; but cp. an Elizabethan meaning of ' outmanœuvre ' : see *NED s.* beyond, B.2.d.

p. 106

3. **guide . . . light.** Cook noted that the antithesis is sharpened if Latin *dux . . . lux* are recalled.

4. **conferring**, ' collating ', ' comparing '. Ponsonby reads *confirming*.

6. **Brutus** (85–42 B.C.), the tyrannicide, the Brutus of Shakespeare's *Julius Caesar*. Plutarch in his life of Brutus records that Brutus applied himself to the study of his ancestors' deeds and made them his guide in action ; that before the battle of Pharsalia he occupied himself in epitomising the history of Polybius.

Alphonsus. Alfonso V of Aragon and I of Naples and Sicily reigned 1416–58. An extravagant ruler, but enlightened, a great patron of the arts ; see J. Burckhardt, *Civilization of the Renaissance in Italy*, III. Amyot cites his example : ' That Prince so greatly renowmed in Chronicles for his wisedome and goodnesse, . . . being sore sicke in the citie of

Capua, when his Phisitions had spent all the cunning that they had to recover him his health, and he saw that nothing prevailed : he determined with him selfe to take no mo medicines, but for his recreacion caused the storie of Quintus Curtius, concerning the deedes of Alexander the great, to be red before him : at the hearing whereof he tooke so wonderfull pleasure, that nature gathered strength by it, and overcame the waywardness of his disease.' North's *Plutarch*, I, 17–18. On Sidney's use of Amyot, see Marguerite Hearsey, *SP* **30** (1933), 535–50

8. **maketh a point,** ' comes to a full stop '.

10. **standeth for the highest form,** ' engages the top class '. *NED s.v.* 6.b gives first entry for *form*, ' school-class ' from 1560.

11. **moderator.** Presiding master in academic disputations.

14. **serving sciences.** Cp. **104**/25.

poet . . . historian . . . philosopher. Representing the three traditional disciplines in liberal studies ; see Quintilian, *Institutes*, X, i. Amyot compares the three (see North's *Plutarch*, I, 10–11, quoted in 34f. note). Bacon, *De augmentis*, II, i, assimilates this classification to his faculty psychology (see **104**/3f. note) : ' Wherefore from these three fountains, Memory, Imagination, and Reason flow these three emanations, History, Poesy and Philosophy ; and there can be no others. For I consider History and experience to be the same thing, as also Philosophy and the sciences.'

17f. **the divine ... is ever ... excepted.** Sidney's position (see **30** : cp. **113**/18) is like Bacon's, who rejected Final Causes in the study of nature and firmly restrained the exercise of reason within a secular frame. To exceed this limit was to encourage *philosophia phantastica* as well as *religio haeretica* ; cp. *Novum Organum*, I, lxv, lxxxix. But men may properly study the ends and objects of the parts of nature and the relations and harmony within the whole and gather in these ways a faint conception of the Creator ; see *De augmentis*, III, ii.

20. **And for the lawyer.** Amyot, having compared the usefulness of history and poetry, to the advantage of history, continues : ' Moreover, it doth thinges with more grace and modestie than the civill lawes and ordinances doe : bicause it is more grace for a man to teach and instruct, than to chastise or punish ' (North's *Plutarch*, I, 11). Cp. Boccaccio, *De genealogia deorum*, XIV, iv (Osgood, pp. 21–32), and see Osgood's notes.

21. **justice the chief of virtues.** An Aristotelian position ; cp. *Ethics*, V, 1 : ' Justice is perfect virtue. . . . In a proverb we say, " In justice all virtue is comprehended." And it is more than any other perfect virtue because it is the exercise of perfect virtue ; and it is perfect because the possessor of it is able to exercise his virtue towards another person and not only in reference to himself.' This Aristotelian maxim was taken up by Cicero (*De officiis*, II, xi, 38) and often repeated in socio-political writing of the 16th c. ; so Castiglione, *Courtier* (trans. Hoby), p. 272 ; *Mirror for Magistrates* (ed. Campbell, Cambridge, 1938), p. 65.

23. **formidine poenae . . . virtutis amore.** Horace, *Epistles*, I, xvi, 52–3 :

> Oderunt peccare boni virtutis amore :
> Tu nihil admittes in te formidine poenae.

[Good men hate to sin through love of virtue ; but you will admit nothing in yourself from fear of punishment.] Lodge uses this couplet similarly (Smith, i, 81). The argument that virtue cannot be enforced by law appears frequently in 16th c. debate on freedom of conscience in relation to the demands made by church and state, e.g. in Thomas Starkey, *Dialogue between Cardinal Pole and Thomas Lupset*, written *c.* 1536–8 (EETS, E.S. 12 (1871), 206); the Printer to the Reader in Thomas Blennerhasset, *A Revelation of the True Minerva*, 1582 (Scholars' Facsimiles and Reprints, New York, 1941), insisting that ' the politike laws of any common weale ' cannot ' beate downe sinne ', for ' the bodie cannot be brought to obey anie lawe except that the working of the conscience bee the chief cause thereof '. This Thomas Blennerhasset was a member of Sidney's circle.

26. **him.** The lawyer.

28. **these.** The philosopher, the historian, and the poet.

29. **naughtiness,** ' wickedness '.

30. **cabinet,** ' private chamber '.

31. **manners,** ' morals '.

34f. **The philosopher . . . the historian . . . the one by precept, the other by example.** For these distinctions in the 16th c. see Spingarn, p. 20, and Smith, i, 389; but Sidney is adapting *Amiot to the Readers* on history. ' For it is a certaine rule and instruction, which by examples past, teacheth us to judge of thinges present, and to foresee things to come : so as we may know what to like of, and what to follow, what to mislike, and what to eschew. It is a picture [cp. **107**/11] which (as it were in a table) setteth before our eies the things worthy of remembrance that have bene done in olde time by mighty nations, noble kings and Princes, wise governors, valiant Captaines, and persons renowmed for some notable qualitie. . . . These things it doth with much greater grace, efficacie, and speede, than the bookes of morall Philosophie doe : forasmuch as examples are of more force to move and instruct, than are the arguments and proofes of reason, or their precise precepts, bicause examples be the very formes of our deedes, and accompanied with all circumstances. Whereas reasons and demonstrations are generall, and tend to the proofe of things, and to the beating of them into understanding : and examples tende to the shewing of them in practise and execution bicause they doe not onely declare what is to be done, but also worke a desire to doe it, as well in respect of a certaine naturall inclination which all men have to follow examples, as also for the beautie of vertue, which is of such power, that wheresoever she is seene, she maketh her selfe to be loved and liked ' [see **113**/8ff. note, and **119**/20f.] (North's *Plutarch*, I, 10–11). Sidney follows Amyot in arguing that the philosopher provides only precept, and the historian, example, but (36) **both halt,** ' both proceed lamely '—as having only one leg each.

37. **thorny.** The humanists regularly called scholastic argument *spinosus* ; and the literary critics of the 16th c. frequently comment on the aridity of philosophic language as compared with poetic utterance. See Castelvetro, *Poetica d'Aristotele*, p. 29 ; Daniello, *Poetica*, p. 19 ; Minturno, *De poeta*, p. 39 ; Smith, i, 6, 67.

39. **wade in,** ' advance in ' (discussion with).

p. 107

6. **the particular truth . . . not to the general reason.** Cp. 41f. and **109**/23ff. note.

10f. Cp. Amyot's comparison of a history to a picture in **106/34f.** note.

12. **so as,** ' so that '.

14f. **an image . . . a wordish description.** Sidney is making in respect of verbal composition a distinction similar to that he made between ' the meaner sort of painters' and the more excellent who have ' no law but wit ' ; here a distinction between logicians who supply ' accidental definitions ' which merely assign the various inessential qualities and circumstances to things, *their shapes, colour, bigness, and particular marks* (20), and writers who present the vivid ' conceit ' of a thing, the concentration of a thought into a visual image (see **57**ff.). Belief in the primacy of the sense of sight in learning processes was admitted by Plato, *Phaedrus*, 250d, Horace, *Art*, 180–2, Cicero, *De oratore*, III, 161, and was often vigorously re-asserted in the 16th c. ; see Jean H. Hagstrum, *The Sister Arts* (Chicago, 1958), pp. 68ff. Cp. Elyot, *Governour*, I, viii (ed. Croft, i, 45) : ' Finally every thinge that portraiture may comprehende will be to him delectable to rede or here. And where the liuely sprite, and that whiche is called the grace of the thyng, is perfectly expressed, that thinge more persuadeth and stereth the beholder, and soner instructeth hym, than the declaration in writynge or speakynge doth the reder or hearer.'

19. **an elephant or a rhinoceros.** Traditional enemies. Bishop Cooper in his *Dictionary* defined a rhinoceros : ' A beaste enemie to the Elephant, and hath an horne in his snout bending upward'. There are several 16th c. accounts of the rhinoceros ; see e.g. *The Voyage of John Huyghen van Linschoten to the East Indies*, II, Hakluyt Society, **71** (1895), 8–9. But it was in 1684 that the diarist John Evelyn reported he had seen the first ' rhinoceros or unicorn ' that was ever brought to England. In 1515, however, the German artist Albrecht Dürer had published a famous woodcut of the rhinoceros, drawn according to travellers' tales out of his imagination, and this woodcut, which it is likely Sidney had in mind, remained the basis of representations of the animal into the 18th c. ; see F. J. Cole, ' The History of Albrecht Dürer's Rhinoceros in Zoological Literature ', in *Science, Medicine, and History* (Essays Written in Honour of Charles Singer), ed. E. Ashworth Underwood (London, 1953), i, 337–56.
  exquisitely, ' discriminatingly '.

21. **architecture,** ' architect '. Sidney's form, found in other 16th and 17th c. writers, derives through Fr. *architecteur* from Med. Lat. *architector* ; see *NED s.* architector.

28. **so no doubt,** etc. Here is the consequence clause required by the opening *For as in outward things*, etc. (18ff.). The scheme is : As a description is surpassed by a picture in effectiveness, so a philosopher affording rules is outgone by the poet offering examples.

29. **virtue, vices,** etc. Cp. **100/8.**

30ff. **the memory . . . the imaginative and judging power.** Cp. **104/3f.** note. Poetry brings the imagination and judgment into active play upon matters which otherwise would lie inert in the memory.

33. **the speaking picture.** Cp. **101/36.**

35. Here begins a section illusrating the effectiveness of poetic handling of lessons in virtue and vice : love of country, the nature of anger, etc.
  Tully. Cicero gives many examples of patriotic fervour from Greek and Roman history ; see particularly *De officiis*, I, xxiv, 83–4 ; xlv,

159–60 ; III, xxiv, 93 ; xxv 95 ; xxvii, 100 ; *De oratore*, I, 196–7 ; *De finibus*, III, 64.

37. Anchises speaking. *Aeneid*, II, 634–50.

38. Ulysses with the nymph Calypso on the island Ogygia. *Odyssey* V, 149ff. and 215.

p. 108

1. Anger . . . a short madness. Horace, *Epistles*, I, ii, 62 ; Seneca, *De ira*, I, 1. A very familiar tag throughout the Middle Ages.

2. Ajax on a stage. But in Sophocles' play, *Ajax*, the killing and whipping are not presented on the stage but are reported. Sidney probably never saw the play performed, nor even read it, for Myrick, *Sir P. S. as Literary Craftsman*, pp. 100–5, argues that he is drawing here directly on Minturno, *De poeta*, p. 41.

6. genus and difference. In scholastic logic, *differentiae* were the attributes by which *species* within a *genus* were marked off from one another.

7ff. wisdom and temperance in Ulysses and Diomedes, valour in Achilles, etc. The list of exemplary figures seems to be Sidney's own, and similar lists were common in 16th c. writers treating similar themes. Cp. Castiglione, *Courtier*, p. 70 : ' What minde is so fainte, so bashful and so bare in courage that in reading the acts and greatness of Caesar, Alexander, Scipio, Hannibal and so many others, is not infected with a most fervent longing to be like them ? ' ; Elyot, *Governour*, III, xxv (ed. Croft, ii, 398f.), also in praise of history : ' Admytte that some histories be interlaced with leasynges, why shulde we therefore neglecte them ? sens the affaires there reported no thynge concerneth us, we beyng thereof no parteners, ne therby onely may receyue any damage. But if by redynge the sage counsayle of Nestor, the subtile persuasions of Ulisses, the compendious grauitie of Menelaus, the imperiall maiestye of Agamemnon, the prowesse of Achilles, and valiaunt courage of Hector, we may apprehende any thinge wherby our wittes may be amended and our personages be more apte to serue our publike weale and our prince ; what forceth it us though Homere write leasinges ? ' (With this passage cp. Sidney's argument **109**/35ff.) Elyot's figures **are** Homeric : in Sidney, Ulysses, Diomede, Achilles, Nisus, and Euryalus all belong to the Trojan story but are probably recalled from post-Homeric accounts of the war, where Ulysses and Diomede are linked in the theft of the Palladium. For Nisus and Euryalus, see *Aeneid*, IX, 176ff., 433ff.

9. an apparent shining, ' a visible splendour '.

10. remorse of . . . Oedipus. As portrayed in the plays *Oedipus* of Sophocles or Seneca.

pride of Agamemnon. As in *Agamemnon* by Aeschylus or Seneca.

11. According to Aeschylus, *Agamemnon*, 1568ff., Agamemnon's father **Atreus** served up Thyestes' own children as a banquet for Thyestes ; for which deed Thyestes laid the ineluctable curse on Atreus and his kin.

12. the two Theban brothers. Eteocles and Polynices, twin sons of Oedipus, whose quarrels in the government of Thebes brought about the expedition under Polynices of the Seven against Thebes, as recounted in Aeschylus' play of that name and in Seneca's *Thebais*.

13. sour-sweetness. An oxymoron ; cp. **118**/13. ' Revenge is sweet ', a 16th c. commonplace ; see Tilley, R 90.

Medea. George Buchanan (see **131**/20 note) translated Euripides' *Medea* (published by Henri Estienne, 1567). Seneca also wrote a *Medea*.

14. **Gnatho.** In Terence, *Eunuch* ; often used as a type-name for a parasite : cp. **117**/22.

Pandar. The common noun ' pander ' is an Elizabethan coinage from Pandarus the go-between in Chaucer, *Troilus and Criseyde*.

16. **all virtues, vices, and passions.** Cp. **100**/8.

19. **the . . . determination of goodness.** Sidney has shown that poetry presents individual human affections ; now he proceeds to show the superiority of poetry in delineating patterns of absolute goodness.

21. Cp. **100**/38 note.

22. **Aeneas.** Cp. **100**/39 and **119**/30.

23ff. **Sir Thomas More's Utopia.** The Latin text of *Utopia* was first printed at Louvain in 1516. Ralph Robinson's English translation appeared in 1551 and More's collected works, English and Latin, in 1557 and 1563. In some prefatory verses to the Latin editions of Utopia from 1518 there is a word-play on *Utopia*, ' no-place ', and *Eutopia* ' good-place '. Both Olney and Ponsonby print *Eutopia* here. Sir Thomas More (1478–1535), executed on a charge of high treason, was unlikely to command Sidney's political sympathy ; but the quality of More's mind was readily recognised in the 16th c. Bodin, like Sidney, disapproved of the political doctrine underlying *Utopia*. Chapter 6 of Bodin's *Methodus* (1572) begins with the complaint that the true nature of a commonwealth has never been investigated except by a few authors (and More is named), and these authors have occupied themselves in creating ideal commonwealths—fictions unfounded upon rational experience ; and Bodin proceeds to rebut More's theory that the supreme authority in a commonwealth could be vested in more than one organ of state. Sidney also preferred strong, responsible, monarchical government. Somewhat ambiguous praise for More and his *Utopia* is afforded by Thomas Wilson in dealing with ' feined narrations and wittie inuented matters ' which can ' help wel to set forward a cause, and haue great grace in them. . . . *Luciane* passeth in this point : and Sir Thomas More for his *Eutopia*, can soner be remembered of me, then worthely praised of any, according as the excellencie of his inuention in that behalfe doth most iustly require ' (*Rhetorique*, p. 199).

26. **absolute,** ' perfect ', ' consummate '.

33. Horace, *Art*, 372–3 :

> But neither men, nor gods, nor pillars meant
> Poets should ever be indifferent.
>
> (Ben Jonson's trans.)

That is, mediocrity in poets is rejected by all, including their booksellers (whose wares were displayed in Rome around the columns of buildings).

37ff. This introduces the supreme evidence that poetry can teach even the highest spiritual truths by means of examples. That the parables were poetic had been recognised by some medieval writers (see J. Pépin, *Mythe et allégorie* (Paris, 1958), pp. 252–9) and was generally accepted during the Renaissance ; see Boccaccio, *De genealogia deorum*, XIV, ix (Osgood, p. 49), and Osgood's note, p. 166, citing Petrarch as well as Augustine ; Minturno, Dedication to *L' arte poetica*. Bacon, *Advance-*

ment of Learning (ed. Wright, II, i, 1, p. 85), speaks of ' parables which is divine poetry '.

p. 109

1ff. **Dives and Lazarus.** Luke 16 : 19–31.
 discourse of the lost child, Luke 15 : 11–32. Harrington (Smith, ii, 205–6) follows Sidney in this passage very closely.

10. **acts.** Records of things done.

14f. **the poet . . . the right popular philosopher.** Cp. in cancelled passage of *Arcadia* quoted in **140/26ff.** note ; and Harrington (Smith, ii, 199).
 Plutarch, *How the young man should study poetry*, particularly towards the end (37), expatiated on this theme which was well enough known through the Middle Ages ; see Curtius, Chap. 11, pp. 203–13. It is a commonplace with 16th c. writers. Smith (i, 389) quotes Minturno, *De poeta*, pp. 38–40, beginning : ' Yet the people are to be taught and instructed in virtue, not by the precepts of the philosophers, but by examples of the poets, not historians. . . . Poets should feign and set out such fables as will please people. . . .' See also D. L. Clark, *Rhetoric and Poetic in the Renaissance* (New York, 1922), pp. 110–15.

15. **Aesop's tales.** Latin versions in verse or prose of the fables ascribed to the Greek slave (who was said to have lived in 6th c. B.C.) remained the first reading books in children's formal education right through the Middle Ages, and indeed up to the 19th c. in England. See T. W. Baldwin, *William Shakspere's Small Latine and lesse Greeke*, i, 607–40. Their moral usefulness, especially for the little learned, was always recognised ; as by Quintilian, *Institutes*, V, xi, 1 ; Elyot, *Governour*, I, x (ed. Croft, i, 56).

17. **formal tales of beasts.** Tales ostensibly about beasts. See *NED s.* formal. 2.c.
 beasts . . . more beastly than beasts. Cp. **97/26** note.

18. **hear the sound . . . from . . . dumb speakers.** A characteristic wordplay, p. **95/27c** note.

21f. **images of true matters . . . not . . . fantastically or falsely . . . done.** Cp. **125/25** note.

23ff. **Aristotle.** *Poetics*, 9, 1451b : ' . . . the poet's function is to describe, not the thing that has happened, but a kind of thing that might happen, i.e. what is possible as being probable or necessary. The distinction between historian and poet is not in the one writing prose and the other verse [cp. **103/16**]—you might put the work of Herodotus into verse, and it would still be a species of history. It consists really in this, that the one describes the thing that has been, and the other a kind of thing that might be. Hence poetry is something more philosophic (*philosophoteron*, 25) and of graver import (*spoudaioteron*, 25) than history, since its statements are of the nature of universals (*katholou*, 28), whereas those of history are singulars or particulars (*kathekaston*, 29). By a universal statement I mean one as to what such or such a kind of man will probably or necessarily say or do—which is the aim of poetry, though it affixes proper names to the characters ; by a singular statement, one as to what, say, Alcibiades did or had done to him.' The meaning and implications of this passage were often elaborated in Renaissance criticism ; see Hathaway, Part 2, and pp. 132–4 for bibliographical information.

33f. **thus far Aristotle,** etc. An acknowledgment of Sidney's general Aristotelianism in artistic matters, though he never goes so far as Scaliger, who at one point in *Poetices* (VII, ii, 1, p. 858) speaks of Aristotle as ' our director, the perpetual dictator of all good arts '.

35ff. Sidney's argument goes : If history were to be equated with truthfulness, then much could be said in favour of its superiority ; but two points must be considered. (i) Men require not simply a *statement* of truth ; they need to accept truth to make it a basis for action and conduct. (ii) In any case, history does not provide a statement of truth in relation to the whole structure of things ; it can provide only isolated and often insignificant detail. Thus Sidney takes up a position against the new school of historians emerging at the end of the 16th c. Bodin, for example, asserted that history was essentially *vera narratio* (*Methodus*, Chap. I) ; this Sidney would deny. And all Bodin's *Methodus* rests on a fundamental assumption that some primary influences in human history are to be looked for in nature (in climate, geography, etc.) : for Sidney this is the determinist view of nature ' which we call fortune ' (**110**/30), which he repudiates (see **52**f.).

38f. **Vespasian's picture right,** etc. Cp. Aristotle, *Poetics*, 15, 1454b, quoted **49**, on the need for a painter to improve on a likeness. On Renaissance attitudes towards this problem see Rensselaer E. Lee, ' Ut pictura poesis : the humanistic theory of painting ', *Art Bulletin* **22** (1940), 197–269, especially pp. 203ff. ; A. Blunt, *Artistic Theory in Italy 1450–1600*, pp. 14ff., 88ff. Suetonius, *Life of Vespasian*, 20, described the appearance of this Roman Emperor (A.D. 9–79).

p. 110

2f. **as it should be, or as it was.** Cp. Robortello, *De arte poetica* (Florence, 1548), p. 87 : ' The poet deals with things as they ought to be. Even if he narrates the fact he still presents it as it might or ought to happen. In inventing he must follow the law of possibility, or necessity, or probability. Thus Xenophon describing Cyrus depicted him not as he was, but as the best and noblest king can and ought to be.' Both the doctrine and the example (see **100**/38 note) became very familiar in the 16th c. (see Hathaway, pp. 145f.) and it cannot be asserted incontrovertibly that Sidney was drawing directly on Robortello here.

3. **doctrinable,** ' able to teach ', ' instructive '.

4. **true Cyrus in Justin.** Justin (of uncertain date in the Christian era) in his *Histories* abbreviated the lost Greek *Philippic Histories* of the Augustan historian Trogus Pompeius. Arthur Golding translated Justin's *Histories* into English (1564). Justin's account of Cyrus occurs in Book I, caps. iv–viii : it is brief, picturesque, as unhistorical as Xenophon's, but without Xenophon's serious purpose.

5. **the right Aeneas in Dares.** To Dares the Phrygian (mentioned in *Iliad*, v, 9) was attributed throughout the Middle Ages an eye-witness account of the Trojan War, made available in a Latin narrative ascribed to the Roman historian Cornelius Nepos. Most 16th c. authors rightly doubted the authenticity of this narrative ; so Vives, *De tradendis disciplinis* (trans. Foster Watson), p. 239. Sidney of course improves his argument considerably by contrasting the noble fictions of Xenophon and Virgil with the bald narratives of the historiographers Justin and Dares.

6. **to fashion her countenance to the best grace,** ' to have the most graceful model for her face '. But cp. *NED s.* fashion, *v.* 1.e.

7. Canidia. Horace in *Epodes*, V, gives an extravagantly horrific account of the attempts made by the witch Canidia to regain her lost beauty ; cp. also *Satires*, I, viii ; *Epodes*, III, xvii.

10f. Tantalus, Atreus. Cp. Wilson, *Rhetorique*, p. 197, where he is commending the usefulness of poets' fables : ' If a man could speake against couetous caitiues, can he better shew what they are, then by setting forth the straunge plague of *Tantalus*, who is reported to be in Hell, hauing Water comming still to his chin, and yet neuer able to drinke : And an Apple hanging before his mouth, and yet neuer able to eate ? ' Horace, *Satires*, I, i, 18, also cites Tantalus as a warning against covetousness. According to some stories Tantalus, an intimate of Jove, had served up his own son Pelops at a banquet of the gods, in hope of gain. On Atreus also of the house of Pelops, see **108**/11 note. Horace, *Art*, 188, claims that when villainy is presented on the stage,

> What is shown thus, I'll not believe, but hate,

and cites the example of ' the ill-natured and wicked Atreus '.

12. where, ' whereas ' ; similarly **114**/19 ; **119**/1 ; **128**/26 ; 33 ; **136**/7.

13f. cannot be liberal . . . of a perfect pattern, ' has not the freedom to idealise completely '.

14. without, ' unless ' ; similarly **122**/4 ; **124**/11.

15. Alexander or Scipio. A sensational life of Alexander the Great was written by the Roman historian Quintus Curtius (1st c. A.D.), purporting to show how power and conquest corrupted him. Scipio Africanus (234–183 B.C.) (cp. **128**/2 note), the Roman general and the conqueror of Hannibal, is the central heroic figure of Livy, *Histories*, XXI–XXXIX. But in his later years he was accused of various political malpractices.

19ff. Sir Walter Raleigh, *Historie of the World* (1652 ed.) I/II, cap. 21, vi, pp. 458–60, names Sidney and refers to his argument here on the nature of history. Raleigh is writing as a practical historian struggling to unravel the Books of Kings in the Bible, and he argues that the conscientious historian has to do the best with the material he has, and his best will be useful—' to teach by example of times past such wise-dome as may guide our desires and actions '. The historian ' does not feign, that rehearseth probabilities as bare conjectures : neither does he rave the Text who attempts to interpret and illustrate them as rationally as possible '. Raleigh in fact accepts Sidney's strictures ; but his profounder scepticism about human affairs makes him view the scope of historical writing differently. The history of the world is worked out under the inscrutable prescience of God through the ignorance, folly, and waywardness of men. No man can tell the truth about the process, but he can be truthful enough to be modestly useful. Sidney would be dissatisfied with this position, for he looked for a more certain truth and some knowledge of perfection.

21. doth warrant a man more in that, ' serves as a better guarantee to a man for what . . .'.

24. a gross conceit, ' an undiscriminating understanding '. With his reference to English weather Sidney has reduced the predictive useful-ness of the historical method to an absurdity. But the intellectual problem is real enough and became prominent in Baconian thought. All argument by example, such as Sidney is considering, was traditionally thought of as having the nature of induction and of falling into one of two types : ' one consisting in the mention of actual past facts [as in history], the other in the invention of facts (e.g. Aesop's fables) ' (Aristotle, *Rhetoric*, II, 20, 1393a ; on Sidney's interest in the *Rhetoric*, see **72f**.). Sidney sees that an induction from any single case has no logical validity ; but an example has some pragmatically predictive value. On poetry as proof, see Hathaway, p. 147, and his note 6 for further references.

25. an example only informs, ' an example gives nothing more than the character of '. *Rhetorica ad Alexandrum* (ascribed to Aristotle), 8, 1429a, defines Examples as ' actions which have taken place in the past and are similar to, or the contrary of, those about which we are speaking. They must be used when your statement is not credible by itself and you wish to establish its truth when it does not gain credence from the argument of probability ; the object being that your hearers learning that another action similar to that of which you are speaking has been carried out in the way in which you declare it to have been done, may be more ready to believe what you say.'

27. him, i.e. the historian ; but the antecedent must be extracted from *history* (**20**).

30. fortune. Cp. **111**/28 ; **127**/17 ; **41** ; **52**ff.

33ff. Cp. Aristotle on the two types of example (see **25** note above) ; also Fracastorius, *Naugerius*, trans. R. Kelso, p. 68 : ' But it makes no difference whether we see the emperor give such and such counsels for victory, or are shown them by the poet'.

37ff. Zopyrus. The story is told by Justin (I, x), who derives it from Herodotus (*History*, III, 153–60).

p. 111

5. Livy, *Histories*, I, liii–iv, tells how Sextus, son of Tarquin the Proud, last of the Roman kings, pretended to be a deserter from Rome to Gabii, in order to deliver the town to his father.

6. Abradatas. In *Cyropaedia*, V–VII, king of Susa, husband of Panthea, ally of Cyrus in whose cause he is slain. But Xenophon records no such stratagem involving Abradatas. Sidney has confused him with (i) Gadatas who (V, iii, 8–19), out of hatred for the Assyrian king, agrees with Cyrus' ruse to surrender an Assyrian fort, and with (ii) Araspas who (VI, i, 39ff.) agrees to pretend to flee from Cyrus in order to spy for him.

13. whatsoever action, or faction, etc. Cp. Sidney on history, in his letter to Robert : ' In that kinde yow have principally to note the examples of vertue or vice, with their good or evell successes, the establishments or ruines of greate Estates, with the cawses, the tyme and circumstances of the lawes they write of, the entrings, and endings of warrs, and therin the stratagems against the enimy, and the discipline upon the soldiour ' (*Works*, vol. iii, 130–1). **faction,** 'proceeding', 'course of conduct' ; see *NED s.v.* 1.

18. That Sidney had read Dante's *Divine Comedy* would appear also from his reference to Landino (**142**/5). His claim that the subject matter of poetry is uncircumscribed would not have been admitted by all Renaissance critics ; but cp. Giraldi Cinthio, *Discourse on Romances* (Gilbert, p. 265) : ' For there is nothing above the heavens or below, nor in the very gulf of the abyss, which is not ready to the hand and choice of the judicious poet. . . .'

20. . . . again, I speak of the art, and not of the artificer. Cp. 108/35 above ; and for the phrase, cp. Castiglione, *Courtier*, p. 79 : '. . . but I speake of the arte and not of the Artificers '. In *Ad Her*. II, xxvii, 44, it is counted a fault in pleading to disparage an art or science because of those engaged in it, as in the case of those who blame rhetoric because of the blameworthy life of some orator.

22. to, ' as to '.
the praise of histories, such as is provided by Elyot in *Governour*, III, xxv, and *Amiot to the Readers* in North's *Plutarch*, I, 10ff., asserting that historical examples show the beauty of virtue and that history ' also hath his maner of punishing the wicked '. Bacon (*Advancement*, ed. Wright, II, iv, 1–2, pp. 100–1) elaborates on Sidney's distinction : Poesy ' is nothing else but feigned history . . . as well in prose as in verse . . .' which gives ' some shadow of satisfaction to the mind of man in those points wherein the nature of things doth deny it. . . . Therefore because the acts or events of true history have not that magnitude which satisfieth the mind of man, poesy feigns acts and events greater and more heroical. Because true history propoundeth the successes and issues of actions not so agreeable to the merits of virtue and vice, therefore poesy feigns them more just in retribution, and more according to revealed providence.'

27. her, *viz*. virtue's.

29. Ulysses in a storm. In *Odyssey*, V.

33ff. as the tragedy writer answered, etc. As reported in Plutarch, *How the young man should study poetry*, 4 : ' Euripides . . . said to those who railed at his Ixion as an impious and detestable character : " But I did not remove him from the stage until I had fastened him to the wheel." ' Renaissance critics usually asserted the morality of dramatic punishments and rewards ; see Madeleine Doran, *Endeavors of Art* (Madison, Wisconsin, 1954), Chap. V, pp. 85–100.

37. a terror from, ' a dissuader from ', i.e. by terrifying.

39. valiant Miltiades, the victor of Marathon, was subsequently imprisoned by his own people ; cp. Cicero, *Republic*, I, iii, 5 ; Justin, II, 15 ; *Mirror for Magistrates*, ed. Campbell, 334.

p. 112

1. Phocion, Athenian general, an ' excellent guardian of the virtues of justice and sobriety ', opposed Demosthenes and was condemned and drank poison 316 B.C. The proceedings against Phocion, Plutarch observes in the *Life*, ' put the Greeks in mind of those against Socrates. The treatment of both was equally unjust.'

2. the cruel Severus. Lucius Septimius Severus, Emperor A.D. 193–211, an African who successfully disposed of his rivals, Julianus in 193, Pescennius Niger in 194, Clodius Albinus in 197 (see 98/37 note) ; a brilliant and ruthless general ; died at York. In the 16th c. a popular moralised life was elaborated by the Spaniard Guevara in *La década de los Césares* (1539), trans. E. Hellowes, *Chronicles . . . of tenne Emperours of Rome* (1577), pp. 266–330.

3. the excellent Severus, Alexander Severus, Emperor A.D. 222–35, murdered in his thirtieth year by mutineers. In the 16th c. Guevara

developed his reputation (see E. Hellowes, *Chronicles* . . ., pp. 433–84), and he came to be regarded by Elizabethan writers as the very type of the grave and righteous ruler ; see M. Lascelles, *RES* N.S. **2** (1951), 305–18.

Sylla. Lucius Sylla (138–78 B.C.), dictator of Rome, whose bitter struggles with Caius **Marius** (157–86 B.C.) and the Marian party filled all Italy with strife and terror for twenty years. Marius died of pleurisy during his seventh consulship. Sylla abdicated his dictatorship and died in retirement after a lingering sickness.

4. Pompey the Great (106–48 B.C.), defeated by his rival Julius Caesar at Pharsalia in 48 B.C., fled to Egypt and was killed there.

Cicero (106–43 B.C.) retired from public life after Pharsalia, except for a brief period after the death of Julius Caesar. He was put to death by the triumvirate of 43 B.C.

5. Cato of Utica (95–46 B.C.), the stern and aristocratic Stoic who opposed the triumvirate of Caesar, Pompey, and Crassus, but later supported Pompey against Caesar. After Pharsalia he continued to resist until Caesar had subdued all Africa except Utica, where Cato committed suicide.

7. his name, *viz.* Caesar as title [OE *casere*, ME *kaiser* ' emperor '].

8. Caesar's own words. Suetonius, in *Julius Caesar*, 77, reports this saying, *Sullam nescisse literas, qui dictaturam deposuerit*, with the play on the word ' dictation ' : ' Obviously, Sylla did not know even the alphabet of politics since he let others do all the dictating'. Erasmus (*Apophthegmes*, II, 19) had extracted and explained this witticism.

9. who, with antecedent *Caesar*.

his, Sylla's. After the death of Sylla Caesar as a young man supported the opponents of Sylla's aristocratic policy (see Suetonius, *Julius Caesar*, 5)—according to Sidney, his only honourable political act. On principle Sidney would condemn Caesar both as usurper and as tyrant ; see note on 13 below.

11. by, ' in respect of ' cp. 13, 14. A usage going back to OE.

12. new punishments . . . for tyrants. As by Homer in *Odyssey*, XI ; Virgil in *Aeneid*, VI, 621 ; Dante in *Inferno*, xii, 104.

13. Philosophy . . . teacheth occidendos esse. Tyranny was discussed by Cicero, *De officiis*, III, 6 (cp. *Pro Milone*, xxix, 80) ; Seneca, *De clementia*, I, xiff. ; Dio Cassius, *Orationes*, VI and LXII ; Plutarch, often incidentally in *Moralia* (cp. his *Life of Publicola*, who gave his name to the Valerian Law by which it was made lawful to kill a man who should seek supreme power) ; but the first philosophical doctrine on tyrannicide was formulated by John of Salisbury, *Policraticus* (1159), VIII, 17ff., according to whom ' it is just for public tyrants to be slain ' ; cp. Thomas Aquinas, *De regimine principum*, I, 3 ; 6 ; 9ff. The morality of tyrannicide was vigorously debated in the 16th and 17th cs. by, for example, Erasmus, John Knox, George Buchanan, the Huguenots, Milton ; see J. W. Allen, *A History of Political Thought in the Sixteenth Century* (revised ed. 1957), *passim* ; and with particular reference to the drama, W. A. Armstrong, ' Doctrine of the Tyrant in the Renaissance ', *RES* **22** (1946), 161–81. On Sidney's concern with tyranny and a subject's duty under it, see I. Ribner, *JHI* **13** (1952), 257–65.

15. **Cypselus** and his son **Periander** ruled Corinth as tyrants for most of the 7th c. B.C. **Phalaris**, tyrant of Sicily in the 6th c. B.C., who roasted his victims in a brazen bull, became a by-word for cruelty in a ruler. **Dionysius** the Elder, tyrant of Syracuse in the 5th c. B.C. for 38 years. Sidney to prove his point has selected four tyrants who in the eyes of historians would appear successful rulers. Herodotus specifically states that Cypselus ' died happy '. Periander, Phalaris, and Dionysius all acquired reputations as patrons of arts and learning.

16. **kennel,** ' pack ' ; cp. Fr. *canaille.*
   speed, ' prosper '.

19. **setting . . . forward,** ' promoting ' ; see *NED s.* set. *v.* 145.

22. **laurel crown.** See **120/34** note.
   victorious . . . of, ' victorious . . . as concerns '.

24. **questionable,** ' arguable '.

28. **philophilosophos,** ' lover of the philosophers '.

30ff. See **69ff.** Sidney like other Renaissance critics speaks of the triple aim of teaching, delighting, and moving ; see Scaliger, *Poetices,* III, xcvi, p. 334 ; Minturno, *De poeta,* p. 102 ; and B. Varchi, *Lezioni della poesia,* ii, 576, who believes that the poet passes beyond instruction and pleasure-giving (Horace's *utile* and *dulce* : see **101/33ff.** note), and induces also certain passions in the audience, inciting their minds to a degree of admiration (see **118/1** note)—in particular to an admiration which leads to active emulation. Thus poetry is rhetorical ; like oratory it is persuasion (cp. W. Ringler's note to Rainolds, *Oratio,* p. 66). The triple aim of teaching, pleasing, and moving had been ascribed to oratory from classical times ; see Cicero, *De optimo genere oratorum,* I, 3 ; *Orator ad Brutum,* 69 ; *De oratore,* II, 121. Quintilian admitted the aims for oratory, limiting poetry to delighting. Augustine, *De doctrina christiana,* IV, 12, transferred the aims to Christian preaching. Rudolph Agricola (*De inventione dialectica* (Paris, 1529 ed.), II, iv, p. 167) argued that the three aims merge into a general persuasion ; and he was followed by Ramus (e.g. in *Scholae Rhetoricae* (Basel, 1569), lecturing on Cicero's *Orator*), who specifically denied the triple aim to the orator. But Sidney here follows the Ciceronian tradition such as was still represented in Wilson : ' Three thinges are required of an Orator. To teach. To delight. And to perswade ' (*Rhetorique,* p. 2). Wilson explains how delighting is involved in moving. ' Nothing is more needfull, then to quicken these heauie loden wittes of ours, and much to cherish these our lompish and vnweildie Natures, for except men finde delite, they will not long abide : delite them, and winne them : wearie them, and you lose them for euer. And that is the reason, that men commonly tarie the ende of a merie Play and cannot abide the halfe hearing of a sower checking Sermon. Therefore euen these auncient Preachers, must now and then play the fooles in the pulpit . . .' (p. 3). Wilson shows that it is primarily by amplification that a writer effects this needful ' moving of the affections ' (pp. 130ff.). Sidney appropriates the traditional teaching on rhetoric to his poetics.

35. **as Aristotle saith.** In *Ethics,* I, iii : ' The end is not knowing, but doing.'

p. 113

5. **painfulness,** ' painstakingness '.

8ff. Cp. **119**/20f. It was an idea familiar in antiquity (so Plutarch, *Life of Pericles* : ' The beauty of goodness has an attractive power ; it kindles in us at once an active principle ') and often repeated in the 16th c. (so Castiglione, *Courtier*, p. 268 : ' For in case good and ill were well knowne and perceiued, every man would alwaies choose the good, and shunne the ill ' ; *Amiot to the Readers*, North's *Plutarch*, p. 11 ; quoted **106**/34f. note). In 16th c. England the confidence which Sidney expresses in the efficacy of *the inward light* (11) established in man's nature (12) is highly characteristic of Protestant thought. Hooker (*Ecclesiastical Polity*, I, 8) restates the belief (which had been developed by some medieval theologians) in terms with which Sidney would have agreed : ' Law rational therefore, which Men commonly use to call the Law of Nature, meaning thereby the Law which human Nature knoweth itself in reason universally bound unto, which also for that cause may be termed, most fitly, the Law of Reason ; this Law, I say, comprehendeth all those things which Men by the light of their natural understanding evidently know, or at leastwise may know, to be seeming or unseeming, virtuous or vicious, good or evil for them to do.'

14. **words of art,** *scil.* the technical terms of the scholastic philosophers ; see *NED s.* art. 3.c.

15. **out of natural conceit,** i.e. by their innate gifts of reason. Philosophy like the other arts, as Sidney has noted **100**/7ff. above, is grounded in ' nature '.

17. **hoc opus, hic labor est.** Virgil, *Aeneid*, VI, 129 : ' In this the task and mighty struggle lies '.

18. **I speak still of human,** *scil.* not of divine knowledge ; cp. **106**/17f.

25. **blur the margent.** As in an old book where a portion of text on a page is surrounded with commentary.

26. **doubtfulness,** ' ambiguity ' ; cp. Thomas Wilson, *Logique* (1580), f. 65b : ' Of no one thyng riseth so moche controversie, as of the doubtfulnesse, and double takyng of a worde'.

29ff. These illustrations of the winning power of poetry were borrowed by Harrington (Smith, ii, 208) ; and cp. Shakespeare, *Love's Labour's Lost*, II, i, in Rosalind's description of Biron, whose fair tongue

> Delivers in such apt and gracious words
> That aged ears play truant at his tales,
> And younger hearers are quite ravished.

31–2. **pretending no more, doth intend . . .,** ' claiming to be nothing more than a story, yet inclines towards . . .'.

34. **hiding them in . . . a pleasant taste.** The sugar-coating of a medicine afforded critics a common explanation of the way in which poetry works; see Gilbert, Index s. *Poetry, a pleasant medicine* for many references, and Smith, i, 390. The illustration goes back at least to Lucretius, *De rerum natura*, I, 936–50 ; IV, 11–25 ; and was familiar to the Middle Ages. Cook, p. 90, quotes from the Preface to Part III, the Poetical Books, of Tremellius and Junius's Latin translation of the Bible (see **101**/39 note), where the editors explain (*ed. cit.*, f. 105) how the Holy Ghost in these poetical books has sweetened doctrine as experienced doctors do medicine by smearing the lip of the cup with honey.

36. **rhubarb.** Formerly one of the commonest purgatives, made from the bitter, so-called Chinese rhubarb. Sidney (*Astrophil & Stella*, XIV) speaks of the corrective medicine of ' rubarbe wordes '. Cp. also Harrington (Smith, ii, 208).

p. 114

5ff. **That imitation . . . hath the most conveniency to Nature.** That is, poetry in its mode of imitation takes into consideration the demands of nature ; thus in delineating a horror it does not produce horror, for men by their natures would shrink away from horror. **conveniency,** ' congruity ', ' suitability ', ' decorum '. William Webbe (Smith, i, 292) explains the Aristotelian term *to harmoston* which is interpreted ' *convenientiam*, fitness ' ; cp. also, Horace, *Art*, 119.

6ff. **as Aristotle saith.** In *Poetics*, 4,1448b, quoted in part on **47** : ' Imitation is natural to man from childhood. . . . It is also natural for all to delight in works of imitation. . . . This is proved by experience. The pictures of those very things which in themselves are disagreeable to look at when they are painted with utmost accuracy, we delight to gaze on, such for example, as those of the vilest animals or of dead bodies.' Plutarch (*How the young man should study poetry*, 3) repeats this argument more naively. In *Arcadia* Sidney often exemplifies his remark in *Astrophil & Stella*, XXXIV :

> Oh, cruell fights well pictured forth doe please.

9. **Amadis de Gaule.** A late chivalric prose romance, of Spanish origin, which in the French translation (1540) of Nicolas de Herberay des Essarts had a great European success. Sidney borrowed many incidents for *Arcadia* ; see R. W. Zandvoort, *Sidney's Arcadia* (Amsterdam, 1929), pp. 193–5.

12f. **Aeneas carrying . . . Anchises.** *Aeneid*, II, 705–84.

15ff. **the tale of Turnus.** Told in the last six Books of the *Aeneid* ; how Turnus, king of the Rutuli, betrothed to Lavinia, Aeneas' destined bride, was eventually slain. Sidney quotes from the speech of Turnus (*Aeneid*, XII, 645–6), who is anticipating the disasters to come :

> Shall this land see him flying hence,
> In such a plight is death so hard to bear ?

21. **whether virtue be the chief or the only good.** This was an old proposition often debated by the Stoics (cp. Augustine, *City of God*, XIX, i). Cicero, as he says in *De officiis*, II, 35, had often argued the question, on which the 2nd c. Neo-Platonist Maximus Tyrius wrote a disputation. The discussion continued through the Middle Ages ; see O. Lottin, *Psychologie et morale aux XIIᵉ et XIIIᵉ siècles*, IV (Louvain and Gembloux, 1954), pp. 549–663. In More's *Utopia*, ' they reson of vertue and pleasure. But the chief and principall question is what thinge, be it one or moe, the felicitye of man consistethe ' (p. 72) ; see E. Surtz, *The Praise of Pleasure . . . in More's Utopia* (Cambridge, Mass.,1957), Chap. 3.
whether the contemplative or the active life do excel. This Aristotelian (see *Ethics*, I, 3) and medieval question continued to be debated by generations of humanists ; see E. F. Rice, *The Renaissance Idea of Wisdom*, Chap. 2, pp. 30–57 ; Francis A. Yates, *French Academies of the Sixteenth Century*, pp. 6f. ; and 21ff.

22. **Plato and Boethius well knew** that if, as philosophers, they had scorned to delight, they would have remained very unconvincing philosophers. Plato used poetic fables, as Sidney has already noticed

7 *a*

(97/10ff.) ; Boethius in *Consolation of Philosophy* alternated the prose arguments of Mistress Philosophy on the *summum bonum*, on virtue and fate, with passages in verse. Here, cp. in particular, *Consolation*, I, prose i.

25. **virtue a school name.** Cp. Horace, *Epistles*, I, vi, 32 ; and *Arcadia* (*Works*, vol. i, 80), where Pyrocles is defending himself against the charges of Musidorus : ' For if we love vertue, in whom shall we love it, but in a vertuous creature ? without your meaning be, I should love this word vertue, where I see it is written in a book.' Cp. also original *Arcadia* (*Works* vol. iv, 301) ; and 1593 *Arcadia* (*Works*, vol. iii, 133), in the description of Timantus a nobleman ' of extreme ambition ', ' a man that could be as evill as he listed, and listed as much, as any advancement might there be gotten. As for vertue, he counted it but a schoole name.' On the advocacy of libertinism current in Sidney's time, see H. Haydn, *The Counter-Reformation*, Chap. 7, pp. 380ff. ; and cp. Hooker's denunciation of ' their brutishness which imagine that Religion and Virtue are only as the will account of them ' (*Ecclesiastical Polity*, I, 8).

26. **indulgere genio.** From Persius, *Satires*, V, 151, where *Luxuria* exhorts men ' to follow their own devices ', to get what they can out of life, for it is all they have.

29. **good-fellow.** Sidney combines the two current meanings : (i) boon companion, (ii) thief (hence *steal*, 30).

30f. Cp. 113/8ff.

35ff. **The one of Menenius Agrippa.** This was certainly a story ' often remembered ' : told by Livy, *Histories*, II, xxxii ; Plutarch, *Life of Coriolanus* ; John of Salisbury, *Policraticus*, VI, xxiv ; Boccaccio, *De genealogia deorum*, XIV, ix (Osgood, p. 50) ; Erasmus, *Praise of Folly*, pp. 46–7. Quintilian, *Institutes*, V, xi, 1, uses Aesop's fables and this story of Menenius to illustrate the moving power of poetry, and the story was included in J. Camerarius, *Fabellae Aesopicae*, a popular school-book. Richard Rainolds includes it in *Foundation of Rhetorique* (1563), f. vib ; so does Wilson in *Rhetorique*, p. 159, who compares the persuasiveness of such a ' merry ' and ' foolish ' tale with the ineffectiveness of ' the quiddities of Duns Scotus '. A. Thaler, *Shakespeare and Sir Philip Sidney* (Cambridge, Mass., 1947), pp. 5–7, suggests that Shakespeare in *Coriolanus*, I, i, caught up phrases from Sidney's telling of the story.

p. 115

4. Plato, who regarded God as a geometer, based his idea of a liberal education on a study of proportion (see *Republic*, VII). It was commonly said that over the door of his Academy was written : ' Let no one enter here who knows no geometry ', but the saying was of medieval origin ; see Neal W. Gilbert, *Renaissance Concepts of Method* (New York, 1960), p. 88.

5. **forsooth,** ' indeed ', ' so far from that being the case '. Cp. **121/24** note.

10ff. **In the end ... it was a tale.** The sort of brisk, rather empty word-play which Sidney usually avoids in the *Apology* except in moments of banter and deprecation.

16ff. **The other ... of Nathan.** As told in 2 Sam. 12.

22. **ungratefully**, ' unkindly '.

24. **the second and instrumental cause** is the parable itself. The first cause moving David to repentance would be the Holy Ghost.

25. **psalm of mercy.** Psalm 51, in which ' David prayeth for remission of sins, whereof he maketh a deep confession '. Sidney's sister, completing the translation of the Psalter which she and Sidney had begun together, translates v. 3 of this Psalm :

> For I alas, acknowledging do know
> My filthy fault ; my faulty filthiness
> To my soul's eye uncessantly doth show.

30. **a conclusion,** *viz.* to the argument weighing poetry by its works, beginning **104/2** above.

32. **most familiar to teach,** ' most congenial in teaching '.

38ff. **as in a man . . . one defectious piece.** A reminiscence of Aristotle's treatment of the hero with a tragic flaw in *Poetics*, 13, 1453a.

p. 116

4. **tragi-comical.** See **135/39** note.

5. **mingled prose and verse.** On the *prosimetrum* as a literary form see F. Dornseiff, *Zeitschrift für die alttestamentliche Wissenschaft* **11** (1934), 74. It was used in post-classical times by Petronius, by Martianus Capella in *De nuptiis Mercurii et Philologiae*, by Boethius (see **114/22** note) in *Consolation of Philosophy*, in the 12th c. by Bernard Silvestris and Alan of Lille, and later by Dante, Giordano Bruno, and of course by Sidney in *Arcadia*.

6. **Sannazzaro.** Jacopo Sannazzaro (1455–1530) of Naples was highly esteemed as a poet in the 16th c. His Latin verse includes the *Piscatory Eclogues* (in which fishermen replace the traditional shepherds), which were much admired and imitated. Scaliger accounted him ' in pastoral poetry the only poet worth reading after Virgil ' (*Poetices*, VI, iv, p. 753); see **133/28** below. Besides some Italian verse Sannazzaro wrote a Latin religious epic, *De partu virginis*, and a pastoral romance in *prosimetrum*, *Arcadia*, finished in 1485. To this work Sidney refers here, and to it he owed something more than the title of his own *Arcadia* ; see R. W. Zandvoort, *Sidney's Arcadia*, pp. 189–91.
mingled matters heroical and pastoral. As Sannazzaro in *Arcadia*, Montemayor (following Sannazzaro) in *Diana* (1559 ?) ; and Tasso in *Gerusalemme liberata* (completed 1575), to which Spenser was greatly indebted in the *Faery Queen*.

14. **where the hedge is lowest,** etc. Cp. Harrington (Smith, ii, 195) ; for other instances of this proverb, see Tilley, H 364. Throughout the Middle Ages and beyond, pastoral poetry (the *Eclogues* of Virgil of course, but also those of Theodulus (10th c.) and in Elizabethan times of Mantuan (1448–1516)) was among the first poetry read by a schoolboy. It was poetry ' *of the poor pipe* ' (15), i.e. in ' low style ' ; see V. Rubel, *Poetic Diction in the English Renaissance* (New York and London, 1941), Chap. X ; **84f.** But in theory as well as in practice Sidney and many other Elizabethan poets of the 1580s found in the conventions of pastoral the means of bridging the gap between the ideal which poetry effects and the actual with which poetry works.

15. In Virgil, *Eclogues*, I, Meliboeus, representing the people of Mantua, laments being dispossessed of land and cattle, and Tityrus as Virgil himself rejoices in the freedom and security granted him by Octavianus Caesar.

19. **pretty tales of wolves and sheep.** As for example in Mantuan, *Eclogues*, IX, a satire on the papal court, imitated by Spenser, in *Shepherd's Calendar*, September Eclogue :

> Sike as the shepheards, sike bene her shepe,
> For they nill listen to the shepheards voyce. . . .
> They wander at wil and stay at pleasure . . .
> And ben of ravenous Wolves yrent,
> All for they nould be buxome and bent.   (141ff.)

Cp. *ibid.*, May, 123ff. A contrast between wrong-doing and patience is brought out better in the tales of the Sheep and the Dog, the Wolf and the Wether, and the Wolf and the Lamb in Robert Henryson's *Fables*, of which an English version appeared in London in 1577. The pastoral as Sidney and Spenser conceived of it drew not only upon the Theocritus-Virgil tradition which was vigorously developed by neo-Latin poets in the 15th and 16th cs. (see W. L. Grant, *Renaissance Studies* 4 (1957), 71–100) but also upon a native, quasi-rustic literature of complaint, on which see J. Peter, *Complaint and Satire in Early English Literature* (Oxford, 1956), Chap. 3, pp. 40–59.

21. **contention for trifles.** In Virgil, in *Eclogues*, III, Menalcas and Damoetas propose to stake in a singing-match a calf against beechen bowls ; in *Eclogues*, V, Menalcas and Mopsus exchange gifts ; in *Eclogues*, VII, Corydon and Thyrsis compete. Cp. Spenser, *Shepherd's Calendar*, August Eclogue : and see W. Ringler's note (*Poems*, p. 362).

23ff. This juxtaposition of the great wars of Alexander (who defeated Darius, king of the Persians, 330 B.C.) and the contention of Thyrsis and Corydon is somewhat puzzling. Sidney is arguing that from the pastoral we can learn that a contention for trifles can lead only to a trifling victory ; presumably, he suggests here that we can go on to learn that even in the greatest political struggle of the past all that comes down to the present has the appearance of a trivial dispute, the intensity of contending is forgotten and only the outcome is recalled.

24. **cock of this world's dunghill.** For this common expression, see Tilley, C 486.

25. **afterlivers.** Compounded by Sidney.

26–7. Virgil, *Eclogues*, VII :

> These rhymes I did to memory commend,
> When vanquish'd Thyrsis did in vain contend ;
> Since when, 'tis Corydon among the swains ;
> Young Corydon without a rival reigns.
>
> (Dryden's trans.)

28. **the lamenting Elegiac.** Sidney's rather narrow description of elegy (which Cooper, *Dictionary*, defined simply as ' lamentable verses ') suits his purpose. Puttenham (*Arte*, pp. 25, 48f., 56f.) gives a more comprehensive account, indicating that the subject matter was the passion of love or death. Scaliger treats of the whole variety of elegiac poetry in *Poetices*, I, 1, pp. 117–18. Sidney is concerned to minimise the love-elegy which had gained prominence in Latin through Ovid, Tibullus, and

Propertius. To some educationalists and moralists of the 16th c. this type of poetry was highly suspect ; see 125/2ff. note. Though Sidney glances at this love poetry which paints the weak ' passions of woefulness ', he presents elegiac verse as primarily reflective, moralising verse such as was particularly associated with the distinctive elegiac verse form in Latin literature.

30. **Heraclitus** (c. 500 B.C.) of Ephesus, who according to Cooper's *Dictionary* was remembered as ' A Philosopher, which alwayes wept when he beheld the people, considering how busie they were to gather treasure, and howe negligent in the well bringing up of their children '. Sidney's reference probably derives from Juvenal, *Satires*, X, 28, or from Seneca, *De ira*, II, x, 5. Both contrast Heraclitus's gently contemptuous commiseration for mankind with the scornful, satiric laughter of Democritus.

34. **the . . . Iambic.** From Gk *iambos*, a lampoon poem with a characteristic measure based on speech rhythm. Between *iambic* and *satiric* (37) Sidney is making the distinction made by Scaliger (*Poetices*, I, xii, p. 44) between the direct, pointed attack of Juvenal and Persius ' more aptly called iambus ', which utters abuse and direct affronts, and the mixed, indirect treatment of satire proper, as employed by Horace, whose method is well indicated in the couplet from Persius in *Satires*, I, which Sidney adapts :

> Omne vafer vitium ridenti Flaccus amico
> tangit, et admissus circum praecordia ludit. (116–17)

[Flaccus (Horace) the rascal, probes every fault of his friend while making him laugh ; and once inside he plays with the secrets of his heart.] Cp. Gosson, *School*, p. 31.
  rubs the galled mind. Cp. Skelton, *Garland of Laurel*, 96–7 (on Juvenal) :

> yit wrate he non Ille,
> Saving he rubbid sum on the gall.

gall, an uncalloused sore; as used in this phrase, see Tilley, G 12.

p. 117

4. Persius' words quoted in note on 116/34, above.

5. **headaches.** A rare anticipation of the modern figurative use.

7. Horace, *Epistles*, I, xi, 30 (with *nos* for *te*), implying that even in the squalid and unpleasantly situated town of Ulubrae happiness may be found if we possess calm and equable minds.

8. **the Comic, whom naughty play-makers . . . have justly made odious.** Many Renaissance writers observe that in the first period of Greek comedy the dramatists sought laughs anywhere and were licentious rather than critical ; so Scaliger (*Poetices*, I, vii, pp. 26–7) and Boccaccio had condemned their example because they had presented filthy creatures on the stage and prompted lascivious men to crime (*De genealogia deorum*, XIV, xiv, xv, xix ; Osgood, pp. 70, 72, 93). Sidney applies these condemnations to his own place and time. On the mounting opposition to the new playhouses outside London during the 1570s among most serious-minded men with social or political responsibility, see W. Ringler, *Stephen Gosson* (Princeton, 1942), Chap. IV, pp. 53–82.

9. To the argument of abuse, etc. See 125/2ff.

11. Comedy is an imitation . . . of . . . life. A more precise variation on the usual Renaissance definition that comedy is ' an imitation of life, the mirror of custom and the image of truth ' (see Smith, i, 369), usually ascribed to Cicero. Cp. also Aristotle, *Poetics*, 5, 1449a ; ' Comedy is an imitation of those who are worse than we are but not in every sort of evil, but only in that baseness of which the ridiculous is one form'. Sixteenth c. theorists usually extend the Aristotelian account, as Sidney does, by giving comedy a heavily didactic justification : comedy teaches men virtue by deriding and censuring their foolishness. See Madeleine Doran, *Endeavors of Art*, pp. 105ff. and notes.

15. the oblique must be known as well as the right. Hooker (*Ecclesiastical Polity*, I, 8), commending a maxim of Aristotle, *De anima*, 1, agrees that ' he that knoweth what is straight, doth even therby discern what is crooked. . . . Goodness in actions is like unto straightness.' This idea that good must be learnt through the discernment of evil runs through Protestant thought in the 16th and 17th cs. and became the ground of the Miltonic conception of Christian liberty. See further Cook's note, pp. 94–5.

17f. the filthiness of evil . . . the beauty of virtue. Sidney is probably recalling Elyot's recommendation of History (*Governour*, III, xxv, ed. Croft, ii, 401) which teaches ' the beaultie of vertue and the deformitie and lothelynes of vice '. Earlier in *Governour* (I, xiii) Elyot's line of argument in defence of comedies anticipates Sidney's here : ' Comedies, whiche they suppose to be a doctrinall of rybaudrie, they be undoutedly a picture or as it were a mirrour of man's life, wherin iuell is nat taught but discouered ; to the intent that men beholdynge the promptnes of youth unto vice, the snares of harlotts and baudes laide for yonge myndes, the disceipte of seruantes, the chaunces of fortune contrary to mennes expectation, they being therof warned may prepare them selfe to resist or preuente occasion. Semblably remembring the wise-domes, advertisements, counsailes, dissuasion from vice, and other profitable sentences, most eloquently and familiarely shewed in those comedies, undoubtedly there shall be no litle frute out of them gathered ' (Croft, i, 124–5).

21. Demea. The miserly father in Terence's play, *Adelphi*.

22. Davus. The tricky servant in Terence's *Andria*. **Gnatho,** the hanger-on in Terence's *Eunuchus* ; in the same play appears **Thraso** as the military braggart. The names of some of these personages had been established as common nouns by the 16th c. ; see *NED s.vv.* Gnatho, Thraso. Critics often drew attention to the representative quality of characters in the old comedy ; so Minturno, *L'arte poetica*, p. 39 : ' Terence illustrates . . . in Demea, harshness and avarice . . . in Davus, clever service. . . .' Scaliger (*Poetices*, I, xiii, pp. 44 ff.) deals with the various types of dramatic *personae* and shows how they work. A proper actualising requires that the *persona* should be an animated fiction on the stage. As the distinguishing marks of any man are to be found in his physical make-up and behaviour and in his social position, attention must be directed to these marks in presenting the *persona*. Guided by the traditional rhetorical teaching on *circumstances*, Scaliger deals with the social position, the profession, function, age, and sex of the *persona* ; then with the naming, physical appearance, manners, sayings, deeds, and feelings. He describes the distinctions in dress to be observed. All these marks are ' the badges (*insignia*) of the *personae* ' (p. 48) ; cp. 24.

the signifying badge. The characters should be made recognisable for what they are when they appear on the stage (e.g. a miser, a young lover) by their dress, deportment, etc. On these aspects of dramatic presentation in England see T. W. Craik, *The Tudor Interlude* (Leicester University Press, 1958), particularly Chaps. III, IV. By Sidney's time the demand for decorum in characterisation was well established. Richard Edwards, Prologue to *Damon and Pithias* (1571), had urged the dramatist to ' frame each person so / That by his common talke you may his nature rightly know '. Thomas Whetstone, Prologue to *Promos and Cassandra* (1578), required a strict decorum in presenting ' graue olde men ', ' yonge men ', ' strumpets ', etc.

25. **comedian,** ' comic-poet ' ; see *NED s.v.*

26. **as I said before.** See **117**/12f.

29. **pistrinum.** A mill operated by stamping and pounding, in which, in Roman society, slaves were set to work as punishment. Sidney associates a mill with sacks (through such proverbial expressions as ' more sacks to the mill ') and alludes to the Aesopic fable of the man with two sacks, one filled with his neighbours' faults and constantly surveyed, the other filled with his own faults, carried on his own back and consequently unseen; on the popularity of this fable, see T. W. Baldwin, *William Shakspere's Small Latine and lesse Greeke,* ii, 404-6.

34. **Tragedy.** Elaborating on Aristotle, *Poetics,* 13, 1453a, Renaissance critics insist on the aristocratic nature of the tragic action ; see Vernon Hall, *Renaissance Literary Criticism* (Columbia Univ., N.Y., 1945, repr. 1959), pp. 37ff., 174ff. Tragedy differs from epic according to Scaliger (*Poetices*, III, xcvi, p. 332) in only rarely admitting men of low rank into the action. ' Tragic matters are grand, atrocious, the commands of kings, slaughters, despairs, executions, exiles, bereavements, parricides, incests, conflagrations, battles, blindings, weepings, lamentations, conquests, funerals, epitaphs and memorials ' (p. 333). Tragedy deals with the public figure cut by a man of noble birth. Given the usual didactic turn, this idea of tragedy comes to incorporate a dreadful warning directed towards such personages as its action concerns ; see Gilbert, p. 218, note 10. Thus a major function of tragedy is to make *kings fear to be tyrants* (36) ; cp. Elyot, *Governour*, I, x (ed. Croft, i, 71) : a man shall ' in redyng tragoedies execrate and abhorre the intollerable life of tyrantes '. T. Heywood (*An Apology for Actors*, 1612), still speaks of tragedy

> That held in awe the tyrants of the world
> And played their lives in public theatres,
> Making them fear to sin.

35f. **openeth the . . . wounds, and showeth . . . ulcers . . . covered with tissue.** Cp. Horace, *Epistles*, I, xvi, 39–45 : ' Whom doth false honour please and lying infamy terrify, whom but the villain, who is diseased with vice ? . . . All the family and his neighbours see this man to be polluted within, though seemingly fair of skin.' Cp. *Hamlet*, III, iv, 145–50. D. W. Robertson, *MLN* 56 (1941), 56–61, showed that in Sidney's use of this medical metaphor of the ulcer there is no reference to the Aristotelian catharsis.

p. 118

1. **the affects of admiration and commiseration.** Cp. **135**/35. This is Sidney's rendering (and inversion) of the Aristotelian pity and terror :

' Tragedy is an imitation of an action . . . exciting pity and terror ' and bringing about the catharsis of such emotions (*Poetics*, 6). **affects,** Lat. *affectus*, the emotions, in the terminology of medieval psychology. Like other Renaissance critics, Sidney presents only part of Aristotle's doctrine on tragedy, which was endlessly discussed. For a full account of this discussion among the Italian critics at the end of the 16th c., see Hathaway, Part 3, pp. 205–300. Scaliger (*Poetices*, I, vi, p. 26) quotes and then prunes Aristotle's definition into : ' Tragedy is an imitation through actions of an illustrious fortune, with an unhappy outcome, composed in dignified verse'. Castelvetro (*Poetica d'Aristotele*, XII, p. 268) speaks of tragedy's efficacy in producing fear and pity (note the inversion of order) in the mind of the spectator. The purgation is a general moral after-effect : the delight rises from a recognition of justice done, the usefulness in inuring the mind to the assaults of passion. Minturno (*L' arte poetica*, pp. 76–7), believes that a cleansing from moral faults is effected directly by the contemplation of horrible things. We are constrained to virtue by fear that these things might happen to us ; our pleasure rises from being done good to. Sidney is as moralistic as Minturno but more literary in his approach. He inverts the order of Aristotle's pity and terror and replaces terror by *admiration*. On *admiration* as a critical term, see Gilbert, Appendix, p. 459. For Sidney, *admiration* is a kind of emotional shock, the amazement felt in face of an exceptionally heroic order of behaviour. In thus replacing Aristotle's terror by *admiration* Sidney avoids the difficulty of having to explain how the contemplation of horror can be an instructive or delightful process. The tragic effect as Sidney understands it is primarily in this emotional shock followed by a feeling of pity that men should have to do and suffer horrible things. The tragic effect produces a moral effect. The shock, followed by reflection, brings a man to a consideration of the true nature of life (2f.). Sidney plays down the sensationalism of some of the Italian critics and accentuates the rational usefulness of tragedy.

5–6. Seneca, *Oedipus*, III, 705–6 (with order of *saevus duro* reversed). Sidney uses this couplet as the basis for a love epigram :

> Faire seek not to be feard, most lovely beloved by thy servants
> For true it is, that they feare many whom many feare.

(Poems, ed. Ringler, p. 143)

and quotes it also in his letter to the Queen against the French marriage (*Works*, vol. iii, 59). For the sentiment see also Seneca, *De ira*, II, xi.

7. **Plutarch** tells the story of the tyrant Alexander of Pherae in *On the fortune or virtue of Alexander*, II, 1 ; and more fully in the *Life of Pelopidas* who was slain by this Alexander in 364 B.C. The tyrant, Plutarch recounts, paid so ' little regard to reason or justice that he buried some persons alive, and dressed others in the skins of bears and wild boars and then by way of diversion baited them with dogs and despatched them with darts ; that having summoned the people of Meliboea and Scotusa . . . he surrounded them . . . and . . . put them to the sword . . .; that he consecrated the spear with which he slew his uncle . . . and offered sacrifice to it as to a god. . . . Yet upon seeing a tragedian act the *Troades* of Euripides, he went hastily out of the theatre . . . for . . . he was ashamed that his citizens should see him, who never pitied those he put to death, weep at the sufferings of Hecuba and Andromache.' Muret in his oration on the *Aeneid* (*Opera*, ii, 370) also uses this story to show how poetry can affect conduct.

13. **sweet violence.** Aristotle uses Gk *hadus*, ' sweet ', several times in discussing tragedy. Sidney himself is fond of the oxymoron ; cp. ' a delightful terribleness ' of battle (*Arcadia*, *Works*, vol. i, 42), and also **95/27** note.

19ff. **the Lyric.** Sidney presents the traditional, learned conception of the lyric which can be illustrated from Scaliger, *Poetices*, I, xliv, pp. 105ff. : ' Next after the majesty of the heroic comes the noble lyric poetry'. Such poems were never recited without song and the lyre ; hence the name lyric. 'There are many types . . .': those which sing the ' cares of love ' ; those ' in praise of heroes or of places or of mighty deeds ' ; ' hymns of praise in which thanks are given to the immortal gods for victory ' ; ' hymns recited at the altars to the gods, pieces compounded of the praise of brave men . . . and pieces made up of common maxims and proverbs and of all sorts of exhortation to virtuous living.'

22. **natural problems.** A problem in logic required a solution through analysis ; thus here *problems* are set against *precepts*. In *Astrophil & Stella*, III, Sidney indicates how lyric poets deal with *problems* ; cp. W. Ringler's note, *Poems*, p. 460. Most short Elizabethan poems are made up of statements of moral precepts and expositions of problems of natural philosophy.

24. **barbarousness,** ' lack of literary culture '.

25. **the old song of Percy and Douglas.** Presumably some version of the ballad of Chevy Chase which still in 1711 Addison could call ' the favourite Ballad of the people of England '.

27. **sung . . . by some blind crowder.** Crowd, croud, a Welsh fiddle. Blind minstrels were often associated with the recitation of heroic *gestes* in late-medieval times : we may recall Blind Harry, the reputed author of *Wallace*. Puttenham refers to ' blind harpers ', ' their matters being for the most part stories of old time, as the tale of Sir *Topas*, the reportes of *Beuis* of *Southampton*, *Guy* of *Warwicke*, *Adam Bell*, and *Clymme* of the Clough, & such other old Romances or historicall rimes, made purposely for recreation of the common people at Christmasse dinners & brideales ' (*Arte*, p. 83). In the accounts kept by Thomas Marshall of Philip Sidney's expenses while still a boy, for September 1566, an entry reads : ' Itm gevenne by Mr Philipps commandmente to a blinde harper who is Sr Willm. Holles man of Nottinghmshier . . . xiid.' (Wallace, *Life*, p. 421).

30. **Pindar.** The greatest of the Greek lyric poets, born at Thebes *c.* 522 B.C. Horace (*Carmina*, IV, ii) indicates the kinds of lyric which Pindar composed : hymns to the gods, praises of heroes, *epinicia* celebrating the Olympic victors, funeral songs. Only the *epinicia* survive. Pindar was little known at first hand in England until the late 16th c. ; see R. Shafer, *The English Ode to 1660* (Princeton, 1918), p. 74. In 1584 a John Sootherne, plagiarising Ronsard without acknowledgment, announced in his *Pandora : the Musique of the Beautie of His Mistress Diana*, ' that never man before, /Now in England, knew Pindar's string'.

In Hungary. Sidney spent some weeks there in mid-1573. Towards the end of the 16th c. Hungary experienced a remarkable resurgence of national culture and spirit in reaction to her defeat at Mohacs (1526) by the Ottoman Turks against whom for centuries the old kingdom of Hungary had stood as Christendom's eastern bulwark.

34. The incomparable Lacedemonians. Sidney like other Protestant humanists admired the discipline and efficiency of the Spartans. ' Their songs had a spirit which could rouse the soul, and impel it in an enthusiastic manner to action. . . . There were three choirs in their festivals corresponding with the three ages of man. The old men began

> Once we were valiant youth ;

the young men answered,

> If you will, behold us now ;

and the boys concluded,

> Soon we will be more valiant still. . . .

And the king always offered sacrifice to the muses before a battle. . . . It was at once a solemn and dreadful sight to see them measuring their steps to the sound of music and without the least disorder in their ranks or tumult of spirits, moving forward cheerfully and composedly with harmony to battle ' (Plutarch, *Life of Lycurgus*, 21 ; cp. also *The ancient customs of the Spartans*, 14 ; *On praising oneself inoffensively*, 15).

p. 119

2. victories of small moment. The victories of champions in the Olympic games.

4. Cp. **111**/20.

6. toys, ' trifles '.

7. Olympus for Olympia. But many 16th c. writers thought that the Olympic games were held on Mount Olympus ; so Bishop Cooper, *Dictionary* ; Spenser, *Faery Queen*, III, vii, 41. See D. T. Starnes and E. W. Talbert, *Classical Myth and Legend in Renaissance Dictionaries* (Chapel Hill, 1955), p. 107.

8. his three fearful felicities. Plutarch (*Life of Alexander*, 3) records that Alexander's father, ' Philip had just taken the city of Potidaea and three messengers arrived the same day with extraordinary tidings. The first informed him that Parmenio had gained a great battle against the Illyrians ; the second, that his racehorse had won the prize at the Olympic games ; and the third, that Olympias was brought to bed of Alexander.' The story was extracted by Erasmus (*Apophthegmes*, II, 2, trans. Udall, p. 182). The *felicities* are *fearful* presumably in the sense that such a coincidence of good luck was thought to be ominous.

   did. Substitute for ' awoke ', anticipatory of *to awake* (9).

12. the Heroical. See also below **125**/7f. note. That heroic or epic poetry is the greatest of all forms of writing almost all Renaissance critics agree (Castelvetro is an exception in preferring drama) ; see Vernon Hall, *Renaissance Literary Criticism* (repr. 1959), pp. 46ff., 190ff. For Scaliger, the epic is pre-eminent because of its comprehensiveness (*Poetices*, I, iii, p. 13). Minturno (*De poeta*, p. 105) likewise concludes after some discussion that the epic is the greatest of all types. For Sidney the epic presents the most fully worked out ' example ', a perfected portrayal of the human ideal in action.

15f. Achilles in Homer, *Iliad*, and in Statius, *Achilleis* ; **Cyrus** in Xenophon, *Cyropaedia* ; **Aeneas, Turnus** in Virgil, *Aeneid* ; **Tydeus** in Statius, *Thebais* ; **Rinaldo** in Ariosto, *Orlando furioso*, and Tasso, *Rinaldo*, and *Gerusalemme liberata*.

18f. shine throughout misty . . . and foggy desires. Cp. **106**/38 ; **124**/2 ; **133**/19. For Sidney, obscurity is a moral and intellectual vice.

20. the saying of Plato and Tully. Cicero, *De finibus bonorum et malorum*, II, xvi, 52, and *De officiis*, I, v, 14, in both cases referring to Plato, *Phaedrus*, 250D. Obviously Sidney found memorable this saying of Plato ; cp.

> That virtue if it once met with our eyes,
> Strange flames of love it in our souls would raise.
>
> (*Astrophil & Stella*, XXV)

Cp. also **113**/8ff.

22. this man recapitulates *who* (19), the distant subject of *sets*.

23. deign not to disdain. A word-play for emphasis.

31. tablet, ' notebook ', ' sketchbook ' ; see *NED s.v.* l.c. On the idealising of Aeneas, see **100**/39 note. Passages which expatiate on Aeneas' virtues, as Sidney does here, are common. Boccaccio, *De genealogia deorum*, XIV, xv (Osgood, pp. 74–5) : ' Re-read those lines in the *Aeneid* where Aeneas exhorts his friends to endure patiently their labours to the last. How fine was the ardour of his wish to die a fair death from his wounds to save his country. How noble his devotion to his father when he bore him to safety on his shoulders through the midst of the enemy. . . . What gentleness he showed to his enemy. . . . What strength of character in spurning and breaking the chains of an obstreperous passion. What justice and generosity . . . among friends and strangers at the games.' Pontanus, *De sermone*, ed. S. Lupi and A. Risicato (Lucca, 1954), II, v, pp. 61–2 : ' Indeed what is there in the way of piety, religion, endurance, courage, and again what in respect of the uncertainty of human affairs and the changes of fortune, which Virgil neglects in his treatment of Aeneas ? So that even for those who have departed this life, one may learn in full what rewards there are and to whom they were properly meted out, and the same with punishments. And Horace said about Homer . . .' (quoting the couplet from which Sidney quotes **120**/5). Cp. also Montaigne, *Essays*, II, xxxvi, attaching the same quotation from Horace to a commendation of Homer and Virgil. Scaliger in *Poetices*, III, xi, pp. 207ff., has a lengthy eulogy of Aeneas, proclaiming his excellence in thought and deed, ' in war and peace ', ' as a ruler ', in his piety (p. 209), in his fortitude (p. 213), etc., but affords no close verbal parallel with Sidney here.

33. ceremonies. The material objects associated with worship. For the same use cp. Shakespeare, *Julius Caesar*, I, i, 70.

p. 120

4. as Horace saith. At the opening of *Epistles*, I, ii, addressed to Lollius :

> Trojani belli scriptorem, maxime Lolli, . . .
> Dum tu declamas Romae, Praeneste relegi.
> Qui, quid sit pulchrum, quid turpe ; quid utile, quid non,
> Planius, ac melius Chrysippo et Crantore dicit.

[While you are speaking in public at Rome, Lollius the firstborn, I have been reading at Praeneste the author of the Trojan War over again. He shows what is becoming, what is dishonourable ; what is profitable, and what not, much more openly and satisfactorily than Chrysippus and Crantor.] Chrysippus of Soli (280–207 B.C.), after Zeno the most notable of the early Stoic philosophers. Crantor (*fl.* 300 B.C.), the first of the commentators on Plato.

9. **his,** ' its ' ; but **him** (10) presumably requires us to understand ' a poet ' as antecedent.

11. **fast handle to,** ' firm instrument for '.

12ff. A careful summary of the *Apology* up to this point, in which each clause can be referred back to particular stages of the argument ; cp. Summary, **13f.**

21f. **not learn a conceit out of a matter,** etc. Cp. **100**/21ff. above, arguing again that a poet does not simply verbalise experience but gives an intellectual structure to experience.

33. **dissections.** The products rather than the processes of dissection. *Dissect* is a new word in English in 16th c., and of medical origin.

34. **the laurel crown.** In 1341 Petrarch was awarded a triumph in Rome on the Capitoline Hill such as victorious generals had received in ancient Rome, and similar coronations of poets with laurel became common in 15th and 16th c. Italy ; see J. Burckhardt, *Civilisation of the Renaissance in Italy*, III, 4, and a wide-ranging account by E. H. Wilkins, ' The Coronation of Petrarch ', *Speculum* **18** (1943), 155–97.

37. **But because we have ears,** etc. Beginning the rebuttal of charges against poetry.

p. 121

3. **yielding,** ' admitting '.

4. **mysomousoi,** ' haters of the Muses '. Sidney's coining.

5. **seek a praise,** ' look for eulogy '.

8. **the spleen,** regarded as the seat of ill-tempered laughter ; see *NED s.v.* l.c.

   a through-beholding, ' a thorough consideration of '. Sidney's verbal nouns often retain a verbal strength. Cp. **97**/16, 18 ; **98**/28 ; **99**/15 ; **103**/29 ; **104**/19 ; **116**/32 ; **119**/25 ; 32 ; **140**/15.

10. **Those kind of.** A sense that *kind of* qualified the following noun adjectivally led to such uses as this with plural pronouns ; see *NED s.* kind, 14.

    full of very idle easiness, ' based on a very empty glibness '. Boccaccio, *De genealogia deorum*, XIV, ii (Osgood, pp. 18–19), first attacks as detractors of poetry those ' so garrulous and detestably arrogant ' who condemn ' everything that even the best man can do ' ; who ' seem to cheapen and vilify . . . by obscene raillery '.

14ff. Pontanus, *De sermone*, and Castiglione, *Courtier*, gave elaborate treatment to the art of conversation and carefully distinguished *asteimus*, urbanity, merry jesting, *playing wit*, from *sarcasmus*. Conversation or writing which cultivated raillery to the point of unwearied frivolousness (as, for example, in pieces by the Italian Aretino and many of his compatriots ; on whom see J. Burckhardt, *Civilisation of the Renaissance in Italy*, II, 3), as well as the more weighty humanist literature of sustained paradox (to which More, Erasmus, and Rabelais contributed), could cause moral embarrassment, as Sidney hints, and as Richard Mulcaster (*Elementarie*, 1582, ed. Campagnac, p. 50) explains : ' If anie kinde of writer for vaunt, not for want of wit, or vpon som particular cause else, do practis his pen or whet his tung against the good in learning, as Lucian doth in most places of hole works, as Agrippa doth in his vane book of vanities in science, theie cannot wound learning, tho theie strike at the warts which be in som professors.' And Mulcaster goes on to show that ' euen if the good qualitie transubstantiate the euill' . . . yet ' such fellowes bewrie their own folie, euen in jeast to turn their heles against their own helps, & by their fond doing to stir som fond heads, to mislike that in earnest, which theie ment but in jeast' (p. 51).

15. **praise . . . an ass,** as did Cornelius Agrippa (see 19 below) in the last chapter of *Vanitie of the Arts*. Erasmus, Prefatory Epistle to *Praise of Folly*, p. xviii, recalls that both Lucian and Apuleius celebrated the ass, and that Favorinus (2nd c. A.D.) wrote in praise of a quartan fever. Wilson in *Rhetorique*, pp. 8 and 14, refers to Favorinus' ' trivial cause '. Cook notes (p. 99) that Francesco Berni (*c.* 1496–1535) wrote facetiously on both debt and plague, in the 16th c. revival of the frivolous rhetorical exercises of the post-Augustan schools.

17f. Ovid, *Ars amatoria*, II, 661–2 :

> Dic habilem, quaecumque brevis, quae turgida, plenam :
> Et lateat vitium proximitate boni.

[Call the meagre pretty, and the excessive well-rounded, so that any fault may be concealed by being associated with a virtue.] Sidney adapts the verse to his purpose by replacing *vitium* by *virtus*, and *boni* by *mali*.

19. Cornelius **Agrippa** of Nettesheim (1486–1535), of noble birth, served as secretary to the Emperor Maximilian, studied at various universities, held in European courts a variety of appointments which brought him little personal profit but fame and many quarrels ; among other works he published *De occulta philosophia* (1531–3) and the work to which Sidney refers, *De incertitudine et vanitate scientiarum et artium* (Antwerp, 1530 ; trans. as *Vanitie of the Arts* by J. Sandford, 1569), a sharp satire on contemporary aspirations to learning. On Sidney's use of this work in the *Apology*, see A. C. Hamilton, *RES* N.S. 7 (1956), 151–7.

20. **Erasmus.** *Moriae Encomium* (1511, trans. as *Praise of Folly*, 1549). On the reception and influence of this book in the 16th c., see Walter Kaiser, *Praisers of Folly* (London, 1964).

23. **another foundation.** Sidney saw the point of these books ; many readers in the 16th c. did not and could not.

24. **Marry.** Cp. **132/26.** Sidney uses this type of exclamation (' why, to be sure ') when he wishes to add a tone of amused surprise or contempt ; cp. *forsooth*, **115/5.**

   these other . . . faultfinders. Apparently a third sort—amateur critics who are interested, but ignorant—a type Sidney must have frequently encountered at the Inns of Court.

26. **confirm,** ' firmly establish '.

27. Cp. Prov. 14:6.

29. **good fools:** ' wags '. On this use of *good*, see *NED s.v. adj.* 7.c.

32. **already said.** See **103/16** note.

36. **Scaliger** in *Poetices*, I, ii, p. 6, asserts that historically the poet is named not from making fables, but from his making of verses, which in *Poetices*, II, pp. 124ff., he treats as the essential matter of poetry.

37. **oratio next to ratio.** An educational axiom in the 16th c., for which plenty of support could be found in classical and Christian tradition.

Among the Greeks, see in particular Isocrates, *Nicocles*, 6–10 ; *Antidosis*, 253. In a notable passage in Cicero, *De officiis*, I, xvi, 50, which examines the basis of society, this ' bond of reason and speech ' is shown to be ultimate : in no other way are we further removed from the beasts ; cp. Cicero, *De inventione*, I, iv ; *De oratore*, I, 8 ; Quintilian, *Institutes*, II, xvi ; Augustine, *De doctrina christiana*, I, xxii. Pontanus, *De sermone* (*ed. cit.*), begins : ' Nature gave man reason which perfected him in his animal condition, and also speech ; with this intention : that under guidance of his intellect he should be as like as possible to the angels.' See also T. W. Baldwin, *William Shakspere's Small Latine and lesse Greeke*, ii, 272.

p. 122

3. **his forcible quality,** ' its accent or pitch '.
   his best measured quantity, ' its quantity ' or ' length '. Scaliger (*Poetices*, I, ii, p. 6) argues that verse has a natural music. Each fraction of human utterance is marked by both quality and quantity. Quality depends upon the sharpness or weight of sound. Quantity concerns the passage of time : it relates to the time, the measure, and the movement. See also 140/21ff. notes.

7f. **Music . . . the most divine striker of the senses.** The humanists reasserted Greek ideas of the effectiveness of music. Plato (*Laws*, II, 667–70) and Aristotle (*Politics* 8, 5) taught that music could present to the mind through the sense a direct imitation of anger, courage, temperance, etc., and so reproduce these qualities in the listener. The belief became an Elizabethan commonplace, comprehensively set out by Hooker, who in *Ecclesiastical Polity*, V, 38, remarks the ' admirable facility which Musick hath to express and represent to the Mind, more inwardly than any other sensible mean, the very standing, rising and falling, the very steps and inflections every way, the turns and varieties of all Passions, whereunto the Mind is subject . . . so, although we lay altogether aside the consideration of ditty or matter, the very Harmony of sounds being framed in due sort, and carried from the ear to the spiritual faculties of our Souls, is by a native puissance and efficacy greatly available. . . .' Cp. also E. K.'s gloss on Spenser, *Shepherd's Calendar*, October Eclogue, 27.

9f. **memory . . . the . . . treasurer of knowledge.** A common phrase ; cp. Tilley, M 870. Wilson (*Rhetorique*, p. 209) gives a systematic anatomy of the mind : in front of the brain is the common sense. ' But the memorie, called the Threasure of the minde, lieth in the hinder part. . . .'

16. **accuseth itself,** ' charges itself with the lapse '.

20ff. **the art of memory.** Memory had been the fourth branch of study in the traditional art of rhetoric, but during the later Middle Ages it came to be developed as a separate art, notably by the Catalan Franciscan philosopher Raymond Lull (*c.* 1232–1315), who produced a ' logical algebra ' of mnemonics, long to be known as ' Lully's art '. Lullism was taken up again in 16th c. France ; see Frances A. Yates, *French Academies of the Sixteenth Century*, p. 103, n. 3. Giordano Bruno published a new art, *De umbris idearum* (Paris, 1582). In England, W. Fulwood's *Castel of Memorie* (1562) quickly had three editions. For other English treatments, see C. Camden, ' Memory, the Warder of the Brain ', *PQ* **18** (1939), 63–72. Most Renaissance scholars paid serious attention to the art (see Frances A. Yates, *The Art of Memory*

(London, 1966).) The basis of it remained, as in rhetoric, a doctrine of ' places ' (see *NED s.* place, 7*c*., = Lat. *locus*, in logic or rhetoric), as Sidney explains 21f. In order to memorise his arguments and their proper order, an orator was taught to visualise, say, a room in which certain features of the room were associated with stages of the argument, and certain furnishings were mentally related to these features as a means of recalling specific points. Wilson (*Rhetorique*, p. 213) explains how to dispose images appropriately in ' places ' : ' A place is called any roome, apt to receive images '. The notion of the trained memory as a store-room of images is said to have had its origin in the teaching of Simonides of Ceos (born 556 B.C.) ; it was developed in the treatments of rhetoric (see Cicero, *De oratore*, II, lxxxvi; *Ad Her.* III, xvi–xxiv ; Quintilian, *Institutes*, XI, ii, 18–22). Sidney argues that with verse the positioning and relationship of words, one with another, effect a similar process of recall as is effected by a system of ' places '. Harrington (Smith, ii, 206) follows and simplifies this passage of the *Apology*.

27. **Cato.** Dionysius Cato. See **102**/15 note.

30. Horace, *Epistles*, I, xviii, 69, which, as Cook notes, is quoted and translated by Bacon in *Advancement* (ed. Wright, I, iv, 8, p. 34) : ' An inquisitive man is a prattler '.

31. Ovid, *Remedium Amoris*, 686 : ' While each pleases himself, we are a gullible set'.

33. **all delivery of arts.** Cp. Harrington (Smith, ii, 207). Acting on the principle that verse aids memory, medieval and Renaissance pedagogues versified many branches of knowledge. The most used Latin grammar of the late Middle Ages was the verse *Doctrinale* of Alexander of Ville-dieu (born *c.* 1170). The Latin verses beginning *Barbara celarent*, listing the types of syllogism in logic, are well known. As late as 1570 William Buckley of Cambridge produced *Arithmetica memorativa* in Latin verse. Many medical treatises in English verse as well as in Latin on disease and physiology survive from the 15th c. and earlier, and some 12th c. Latin verses on the art of preserving health, ascribed to the medical school of Salerno, were familiar to Elizabethan men of letters ; see Puttenham, *Arte*, p. 12 ; Smith, ii, 361.

p. 123

1ff. **the most important imputations laid to . . . poets.** The charges against poetry had come down from antiquity. Most of them had been gathered together and answered by Boccaccio, *De genealogia deorum*, XIV, ii–xx (Osgood, pp. 17–96). Erasmus wrote a youthful oration on the subject (see A. Hyma, *The Youth of Erasmus* (Univ. of Michigan, 1930), pp. 239–331), distinguishing (pp. 270ff.) three enemy factions : (i) those who wish the whole republic of letters destroyed— the ignorant who despise all writing as ' poetry ' ; (ii) those who wish literary studies narrowly constricted because poetry is a waste of time which could be better employed ; (iii) those who require all writing to be of one approved modern kind and despise the classics. See also Elyot (*Governour*, I, x–xiii), who finds it necessary to rebut charges that poetry is unprofitable, unworthy of great captains and kings, and de-moralising, containing ' nothynge but baudry . . . and unprofitable leasinges '. Vives, *De tradendis disciplinis* (trans. Foster Watson), p. 121, noted that ' Poetry is openly hated by certain people ; there has been a long and varied dispute on the matter '. The arguments of Erasmus, Elyot, and Vives are pedagogical : they are opposing theories of educa-tion which dismiss poetry as non-vocational and time-wasting. This

198 AN APOLOGY FOR POETRY

constitutes the first charge against poetry dealt with in the *Apology*
The second is that, intellectually, poetry is false (see note on 28f. below).
This charge is the ground upon which the satiric attack on poetry is
made by Cornelius Agrippa, *Vanitie of the Arts*, cap. 4, ff. 11–13v.
The third objection is social : that poetry, especially in popular stage
comedies, affronts public morality. This objection had been officially
maintained by the Church throughout the Middle Ages (see E. K.
Chambers, *The Medieval Stage* (Oxford, 1903), I, 9f. 31ff ; II, 290ff.),
and was reasserted in the 16th c. by many of the stricter moralists both
in the unreformed as well as the reformed Churches (see also **117/8**
note). The most notorious statement of this opposition on social
grounds in England was Stephen Gosson, *The School of Abuse* (1579),
to which a reply was made by Thomas Lodge, *A Defence of Poetry*
(1579).

A full, succinct account of most of the charges brought against poetry
in Elizabethan times, together with a rebuttal of them all, is given by
Richard Wills, *De re poetica*, ed. Fowler, pp. 92–126, drawing (as
Fowler indicates, pp. 25ff.) chiefly on Vives, *De causis corruptarum
artium*, II. Poetry is said to be worthless in itself because in catering
merely for men's pleasure it implies that men are no better than beasts.
It deals with lies and purveys blasphemy and whitewashes bullies and
villains, promotes lust and villainy. Eratosthenes, Plato, and Aristotle
called it lying. Where Lucan and Virgil tell the truth they are accounted
no poets (cp. **102**/17 note above). On the stage poetry has always been
a source of licentiousness and shame. The scandalous nature of love
poetry need not be specified. Long ago Plato expelled poets from the
ideal state. If poetry were a good thing, poets would be good men ;
many of them are notorious drunkards. Finally Democritus and others
have shown that to be a poet one has to be mad. Cp. J. W. H. Atkins,
English Literary Criticism : the Renascence (1947), pp. 104–5.

Sidney's list of charges and his defence are traditional and not to be
derived from a single source. On specific points, however, it is possible
that he recalled passages in Elyot (see **124**/14 ; **125**/2ff. below) and
Agrippa (see A. C. Hamilton, *RES* N.S. 7 (1956), 151–7). It is worth
noting that Harrington (Smith ii, 199), who in his account of poetry
follows Sidney closely, names Agrippa as the accuser and confronts his
arguments directly.

7. siren's sweetness . . . the serpent's tale. We should assume the pun
tail/tale. Agrippa, *Vanitie of the Arts*, f. 29v., speaks of ' a certayne
venemous sweetnesse ' of ' the Mermaides ' who ' with voyces, gestures,
and lascivious soundes, doe destroye and corrupt mens myndes ' ; cp.
Boethius, *Consolation*, I, prose 1. The sirens that troubled Ulysses
(*Odyssey*, XII) were in post-classical times confused with mermaids,
and apparently also with serpents ; see Florence McCulloch, *Medieval
Latin and French Bestiaries* (Univ. of N. Carolina, 1960), pp. 166–70,
and on the allegorisation of these sirens, D. W. Robertson, *A Preface to
Chaucer*, pp. 142–4.

9. to ear, ' to plough '. Cp. Chaucer, *Knight's Tale*, 28 :

> I have, God woot, a large feeld to ere

with reference to the length of story to be told. Sidney's allusion is
simply to the phrase, not to Chaucer's matter.

13ff. they cry . . . as if they outshot Robin Hood. Detractors cry out
vociferously against poetry when they find Plato has expelled poets, as

if they had become wiser than Plato himself. *Tales of Robin Hood* became a byname for claims of extravagant achievement, as in the 16th c. couplet : ' Many men speke of Robyn Hode & of his Bow/Which never shot therewith, I trow ' ; see Tilley, R 148.

14. **Plato banished them.** See **128**/15 note. For the phrase, cp. Gosson, *School*, p. 20 : ' No marvel though Plato shut them out of his school, and banished them quite from his Commonwealth'.

15f. **Truly . . . much truth.** A paregmenon used for irony.

17. **to the first.** That poetry is time-wasting ; cp. **123**/1ff. note. Boccaccio, *De genealogia deorum*, XIV, iv (Osgood, pp. 21–32), associated this charge against poetry with lawyers who cry : ' Oh yes, a very pretty work, but of no use whatever'.

18. **petere principium,** ' to beg the question '.

27. **out of earth.** Again implying that poetry is non-divine learning ; cp. **106**/17 ; **113**/18.

28. **the second . . . they should be . . . liars.** *Should* denoting a reported statement (see Abbott's *Shakespearian Grammar*, § 328). Cornelius Agrippa, *Vanitie of the Arts*, cap. 4, f. 11, had made his primary charge against poetry that it ' doeth deserue to bee called the principall Author of lyes '. But the charge was ancient and had probably always had something of a metaphysical character. The aphorism that poets are liars was ascribed to Solon by Aristotle in *Metaphysics*, I, 2, 983a. Xenophanes of Colophon (*c.* 530 B.C.), himself a poet, assailed Homer and Hesiod for falsehood. Pindar felt obliged to defend himself as a truthteller in his First Olympian Ode. By the time of Plato the debate was a stock theme. The old charge was sharply urged again by Eratosthenes of Cyrene (276–196 B.C.) and controverted as strongly by Strabo (*c.* 54 B.C.–A.D. 24) ; see note on **96**/12. The argument was continued throughout the Middle Ages. John of Salisbury (*Entheticus*, 183ff.) and other 12th c. writers argue that the lies of the poet serve truth by using words figuratively (see Curtius, p. 206) ; Thomas Aquinas on the other hand returns to the old charge ' that Poets lie in many things, as the proverb says ' (see Curtius, p. 218) : and a qualified opposition to poetry remained characteristic of scholasticism and was perpetuated, as many other scholastic notions were, in 16th and 17th c. Puritanism (see note on **125**/2ff. below). From the earliest days of Christianity there had been a steady current of opposition to the falsehoods of the pagan poets. Many (but not all) humanists of the 15th and 16th cs. had denied the charge. Boccaccio, *De genealogia deorum*, XIV, xiii (Osgood, pp. 62–9), gave a general defence. He makes use of Augustine, *De mendacio*, on the varieties of the lie, and shows that as poetry does not aim at conveying literal truth it cannot fairly be charged with not providing it. Coluccio Salutati, *De laboribus Herculis* (ed. Ullman), I, cap. xii, pp. 65ff., also deals with the question and justifies poetry. Pontanus (*De sermone, ed. cit.*, II, cap. v, pp. 61–3) indicates the different sorts of lie and carefully exculpates poetic fictions.

Sidney thus deals with a familiar enough theme. He counters the old charge with a re-statement (as he says, paradoxically phrased) of the Aristotelian handling of Plato's position. Plato had attacked poetry as an imitation twice removed from the truth (*Republic*, X), not so much a lie as an enfeeblement of truth. Aristotle distinguished between the ' real ' which belongs to the realm of intellect and the ' actual ' which deals with matters of sense and experience, and so was able to suggest a definition of imitation which relates it veridically with the ' real ' : ' if it be objected that the description is not true to fact, the poet may perhaps reply, " But the objects are as they ought to be " ' (*Poetics*, 25, 1460b), and what ' they ought to be ' is what they ' really ' are. Sidney's answer also to the charge that poets are liars is contained in his understanding of poetry as ' imitation ', which is basically Aristotelian ; see 71ff.

31ff. **The astronomer, etc.** Cp. Cornelius Agrippa, *Vanitie of the Arts*, cap. xxx, f. 44v : Astronomers ' doe no lesse differ touching the greatnesse and distaunce of the Sunne, the Mone and other Starres, neither is there among them any constancie of opinion nor veritie of celestial things '.

34ff. **the physicians.** According to Cornelius Agrippa : ' when the common people will shewe any that lyeth shamefully, they say to hym : Thou lyest like a Phisition ' (f. 144). ' Well neere alwaies there is more daunger in the Phisition, and his medicine, than in the sicknesse itself ' (f. 142).

35. **Charon,** the ferryman of the dead over the river Styx ; cp. *Arcadia* (*Works*, vol. ii, 390) : ' many of those first ouerthrowne, had the comfort to see the murtherers overrun them to Charons ferrie'.

38. **the poet . . . nothing affirms.** In Minturno, *De poeta*, p. 68, Syncerus, the spokesman for Platonism, asks similarly: ' How can he deceive, who himself invents everything ? ' ; but this type of justification for the poet was implicit in the old distinction between *fabula ficta* ' which contains [from a legal point of view] nothing true, nor anything resembling the truth ' (*Ad Her.*, I, viii, 13), and *historia* as the record of things actually done. Cp. Isidore of Seville, *Etymologies*, II, xli (*PL* 82, col. 122). Augustine (*Confessions*, III, 6) saw the problem clearly, and was troubled that the fables of the poets, admittedly nothing more than fiction, should yet have power to engage him so deeply. ' Verses and poems I can turn to true food, and " Medea flying " though I did sing, I affirmed it not ; though I heard it sung, I believed it not.' Harrington (Smith, ii, 201), follows Sidney's argument here closely.

p. 124

1. **artists.** Masters of any of the liberal arts ; men of learning.
   especially the historian. Still Sidney's chief opponent. Cp. Cornelius Agrippa, *Vanitie of the Arts*, cap. v, f. 14 : ' Historiographers doo so muche disagree among themselves, and doo write so variable and divers things of one matter, that it is impossible, but that a number of them should be very Lyars'. He goes on to show their methods of lying.

4f. **never maketh any circles,** etc. To draw a circle on the ground in necromancy defined the area within which the magic was operative ; cp. Shakespeare, *Henry V*, V, ii, 320 ; *As You Like It*, II, v, 62.

7. **entry,** ' opening words ' ; see *NED s.v.* 6.b.

12. **before-alleged : 115**/16ff.

14. **Aesop.** See **109**/15 note ; cp. Elyot, *Governour*, III, xxv (ed. Croft, ii, 400) : ' I suppose no man thinketh that Esope wrote gospelles, yet who doughteth but that in his fables the foxe, the hare, and the wolfe, though they never spake, do teache many good wysedomes'.

18. **seeing Thebes written . . . upon an old door.** Labelled doors on the stage to indicate the locality of the action were used in court and university plays in Sidney's time, probably following Continental practice ;

see Allardyce Nicoll, *The Development of the Theatre* (3rd rev. ed., London, 1948), pp. 119–20.

21. what . . . what. As relatives after nouns implying narration ; cp. *Hamlet* I, i, 35, and quotation from Ascham in *NED s.* what, *rel. pron.* C. I, 7.c.

25f. use the narration, etc. Recalls the conclusion of Plutarch, *On listening to lectures* : ' Let the listener make his memory a guide to invention : looking on the discourse of others only as a kind of first principle or seed'.

imaginative ground-plot is what the rhetoricians called the ' seat of argument ' (Quintilian, *Institutes*, V, x, 1), where material is hidden and whence it is sought in the process of ' invention '.

31f. John a Stile, ' John (who lives) at the stile ' ; **John a Noakes,** ' John (who lives) at the oaks '. Names which were used in fictitious legal actions. *NED* supplies several 16th c. uses of these names.

38. bishop, which belonged to the Northern European tradition of nomenclature in chess, seems to have ousted ME *alfin* as the name for the piece as a result of new developments in the game of chess in the 16th c. ; see H. J. R. Murray, *History of Chess* (rev. ed., Oxford, 1963), p. 424.

p. 125

2ff. The third argument is that poetry is a school of abuse ; see under **123/1ff.** note. Here Sidney limits his treatment to a rebuttal of the charges of (i) licentiousness (**125/2–126/**16), (ii) enervating effeminacy (**126/**17**–128/**7). Both were charges often made by sober humanists in 16th c. England. Vives, *De tradendis disciplinis* (trans. Foster Watson), pp. 126ff., admits the corrupting power of licentious poetry and the need for careful selection. Similarly Elyot (*Governour*, I, xiii, ed. Croft, i, 123), though denying that poetry is ' nothing but bawdry and unprofitable leasings ', urges the wise man in entering the garden of the Muses to trample the nettles under his feet. His anxiety over the evil effects of licentious poetry went further in his *Defence of Good Women* (1540) ; see G. B. Pace, ' Elyot against Poetry', *MLN* **56** (1937), 597–9.

In the last quarter of the 16th c., during the Counter-Reformation, the scruples of both Roman Catholics and Protestants multiplied. Weinberg (i, 8, pp. 297–348) gives a full account of the swing towards a purified Christian poetic among the Italian theorists. An English Catholic rejection of erotic poetry is afforded by Robert Southwell, Dedications to *Saint Peter's Complaint* (1595) and to *Mary Magdalen's Tears* (1591). On the Protestant reaction (of which the ' Puritan ' attack on the stage is only one aspect) see Lawrence A. Sasek, *The Literary Temper of the English Puritans* (Baton Rouge, 1961), particularly Chaps. 4 and 7. In general most English Protestants (including most of the Puritans) thought poetry of value when it furthered civic virtue, militant patriotism, or respect for religion ; and this is Sidney's position. The *bonae litterae* of the humanists are approved ; reprobation is reserved for the lascivious and the effeminate. In 1582 the Privy Council attempted to replace ' such lascivious poets as are commonly read . . . in . . . grammar-schooles ' by poetical texts ' heroicall and of good instruction ' (see Warton's *History of English Poetry*, sect. liii).

5ff. Comedies . . . the Lyric . . . the Elegiac. In dealing with these earlier (**116/**28ff., **118/**19ff.) Sidney had kept discreetly silent about their concern with love.

7f. even to the Heroical. Harrington (Smith, ii, 209) quotes this passage from the *Apology*. The Italian epic poets of the 16th c. had consciously mingled the martial themes of classical epic with the love interests in medieval romance (cp. Tasso, *Gerusalemme liberata*, I, ii–iii). Often the heroic itself is in the late 16th c. defined in terms of the infinite sufferings of love. Giordano Bruno in *Gli heroici furori* (1585), Dedicatory Epistle (addressed to Sidney), speaks of ' Love having taken to itself wings and become heroical '.

8ff. Alas, Love, etc. Boccaccio, *De genealogia deorum*, XIV, xvi (Osgood, p. 77), answering the same charge that love poetry corrupts, likewise breaks off to exclaim : ' Worthy indeed is their homage to Love, whose power overcame first Phoebus, then Hercules—each victorious against monsters'. Cp. also Spenser, *Shepherd's Calendar*, October Eclogue, 85–114. Rhetorically, an apostrophe (*exclamatio*) is useful, as Quintilian (*Institutes*, IX, ii) observes, in raising the emotional tone. Sidney cannot of course free poetry as he himself conceived of it and practised it from concerning itself with love ; instead he seeks to exalt love, and he accommodates his style to his intention by using highly-figured speech (reminiscent of many passages in *Arcadia*), with the word-play of *defend* and *offend* ; the succession of *grant . . . grant . . . grant* (a recognised figure of ' admittance ' ; see Puttenham, *Arte*, pp. 227–8) ; the antithesis of *beastly fault . . . only man, and no beast* ; by paregmena, *beastly . . . beast, lovely . . . Love, grant . . . granted*. In such ways he gives impetus to a vulnerable argument, and yet by the humour and irony saves this elaborate construction (11–23) from pomposity.

12. love of beauty. Cp. *Arcadia* (*Works*, vol. i, 113) : ' O Zelmane, who will resist [Loue], must either haue no witte, or put out his eyes. Can any man resist his creation ? certainely by love we are made, and to love we are made. Beasts onely cannot discerne beauty, and let them be in the role of Beasts that doo not honor it ' ; cp. *ibid.*, p. 403. But the general idea that only man discerns beauty which is both the cause and the product of love is a Renaissance commonplace.

25f. eikastike, ' imitative '. **phantastike,** ' fanciful ', ' imaginary ' (here with derogatory sense). The terms are presumably Greek feminine adjectives agreeing with *Poesy*. The distinction was made by Plato in *Sophist* (235) between the art of making likenesses and the art of making appearances or the phantastic, and he concludes (266ff.) that this art of the phantastic is unworthy and indeed harmful. See Hathaway, pp. 14–16, for the development among 16th c. Italian critics of this distinction, which was also appropriated by the Pléiade. So Ronsard, *Abrégé de l'art poétique françois*, defines Invention as the natural faculty of an imagination conceiving ideas and the forms of everything that can be imagined, earthly and heavenly, living and inanimate, in order to represent, describe, and imitate them; but by the invention is not implied fantastic and melancholic imaginings. The fullest use of the distinction is made by Jacopo Mazzoni in the debate during the 1580s in Italy on the poetic stature of Dante ; see Weinberg, ii, 636–46, 877–83. Naturally enough contemporary theorists of painting also employed the terms, in contrasting the imitation of existing things with the representation of the non-existent ; see E. Panofsky, *Idea*, note 144, pp. 96–8 (quoting Gregorio Comanini, *Il Figino* (Mantua, 1591)). The use of the distinction in the *Apology* not only indicates Sidney's awareness of contemporary European art theory but also exemplifies his own literary theory, which asserted the claims of the ' real ' over the ' wholly

ımaginative ' ; see **101**/7 ; and **55**ff. With his position should be com-
pared that of Puttenham (*Arte*, p. 18), who seeks to establish a worthy
sense of ' the phantasticall ' in poetry ; and so in some measure antici-
pates the position taken up by the ' fantasticks ' of the 17th c. (by some
of the metaphysical poets), whose poetry Sidney like Milton would have
certainly condemned for intellectual irresponsibility and capriciousness.

27. fancy. As in scholastic psychology, the mental apprehension of an
object of perception ; the faculty of forming mental representations of
things not present to the senses.

28ff. the painter . . . should give to the eye, etc. Early theorists of the
Renaissance regarded painting as an activity combining practical obser-
vation and artistic representation : ' Painting is a science because of its
foundation on mathematical perspective and on the study of nature ',
according to A. Blunt, *Artistic Theory in Italy, 1450–1600*, p. 26. Hence
the concern with mathematics, perspective, proportions, as well as with
domestic, civic, and military design. The final fruits of Albrecht Dürer's
astonishing career as an artist were practical treatises, *Instruction in
Mensuration with Compass and Triangle* (1525), *The Theory of Fortifica-
tion* (1527), and *Four Books on Human Proportion* (1528).

30. Abraham sacrificing. The Sacrifice of Isaac (Gen. 21–2) was a com-
mon theme in medieval and Renaissance art. Théodore de Bèze (see
131/17 note) wrote an influential play in French, *Abraham sacrifiant*
(1550), translated by Arthur Golding (published 1577).

31. Judith killing Holofernes was often represented ; see the list of
paintings in A. Pilger, *Barockthemen*, i, 191–6. Salluste du Bartas
treated the subject in his poem *La Judit* (1574).
    David . . . with Goliath (1 Sam. 17). For paintings see A. Pilger,
Barockthemen, i, 138–9. Drayton wrote an epic narrative *David and
Goliath* (not published till 1630). Sidney's insistence on careful choice
of subject and his condemnation of indecorous themes are in line with
the artistic developments of the Counter-Reformation ; see A. Blunt,
Artistic Theory in Italy, 1450–1600, chap. viii, pp. 103–36. But Boc-
caccio, *De genealogia deorum*, XIV, vi (Osgood, p. 38), in condemning
artists who abuse art by their licentiousness, makes a similar reference
to painting.

32. ill-pleased, ' pleased by evil sights '.

34. shall the abuse . . . make the right use odious ? This question is also
answered negatively by Isocrates (*Nicocles*, 4) and by Aristotle (*Rhetoric*,
I, i). Quintilian (*Institutes*, II, xvi) denies that because rhetoric can be
put to wrong uses it is necessarily bad. ' For if this line of argument
were followed, neither generals, nor magistrates, nor medicines, nor
wisdom itself were praiseworthy. . . . The sword is not made simply
for the soldier—a thief can use the same weapon.' **126**/4ff. amplifies
Quintilian.

37. army of words. Cp. Shakespeare, *Merchant of Venice*, III, v, 72.

38. concluding, ' finally proving '.

p. 126

2. title, ' recognised right to possession '.

4. rampire, ' defence '.

10ff. **a needle cannot do much hurt,** etc. The illustration continues the argument of **125/34**. Although a thing insignificant in itself (as expressed in the phrase ' not worth a needle ') cannot do much significant harm or good, a sword (a very large needle) can do much harm and also very much good. Similarly with poetry. If its detractors assert that it can do great harm, they are implying its great potential for good. The argument involves the principle that the worst is a corruption of the best.

14. **the fathers of lies.** Gosson's phrase, *School*, p. 66, with which cp. Sidney's own phrase **123/5**, ' the mother of lies '.

17ff. The charge that poetry (and other forms of learning) produces and is the product of effeminacy was often raised in antiquity. See **127/31**, **129/13** notes ; cp. Cicero, *Tusculan Disputations*, II, ii, 27. Gosson laboured the point in *School*, p. 34. See also **127/6** note.

21. **Sphinx.** As the propounder of an ancient riddle.

24. **Albion.** According to medieval historians this island was called Albion before it acquired the name Britain from settlement by Brutus and his Trojans. Bishop Cooper in his *Dictionary* suggests that earlier Greek adventurers ' wondering and rejoycing at their good arrival nameth this Ile in Greek Olbion . . . *happie*, Felix '.

25. **a chainshot.** Cannon balls linked by chain which on discharge were intended to wrap round the target.

26. **bookishness.** Already in the 16th c. *bookish* was an adjective of disparagement.

27ff. **certain Goths . . . in the spoil of a famous city.** The story is told by the continuator (Petrus Patricius) of Dio Cassius, *Roman Histories*, LIV, 17, of the sack of Athens by the Goths in A.D. 267. But it appears also in Montaigne, *Essays*, I, xxiv, *Of Pedantisme*. Montaigne has gently boasted that Frenchmen of old did never take any great account of letters. ' Examples teach us both in this martiall policie, and in all such like, that the studie of sciences doth more weaken and effeminate mens minds, than corroborate and adapt them to warre. The mightiest, yea the best setled estate that is now in the world, is that of the Turkes, a nation equally instructed to the esteem of armes and disesteeme of letters ' [cp. **97/36**]. ' When the Gothes over-ran and ravaged Greese : that which saved all the Libraries from the fire was that one among them scattered this opinion, that such trash of bookes and paper must be left untouch and whole for their enemies, as the only meane and proper instrument to divert them from all militarie exercises, and amuse them to idle, secure and sedentary occupations.' P. Villey, *Revue d'histoire littéraire de la France* **23** (1916), p. 215, noted Montaigne's source in C. Ventura, *Thesoro politico* (Venice, 1602 ed.), II, cap. 2, pp. 4–7v. Sidney may have read the story in an earlier edition of this work.

29. **hangman,** ' degraded villain ' ; used as a term of general abuse. See *Poems*, ed. Ringler, p. 22, and note.

34. **the ordinary doctrine of ignorance.** That all reading is a waste of time. ' These persones that so moche contemne lernyng ' are considered by Elyot in *Governour*, I, xii (ed. Croft, i, 98ff.) ; and see J. H. Hexter, ' The Education of the Aristocracy in the Renaissance ', *Journal of Modern History* **22** (1950), 1–4. The boor Damoetas expresses the ' ordinary doctrine ' in *Arcadia* (*Works*, vol. i, 152).

37. **but Poetry,** ' excluding poetry '.

p. 127

4. Cp. Horace, *Satires*, I, i, 53 :

. . . iubeas miserum esse libenter,

which Sidney adapts to mean ' I bid him cheerfully remain a fool '.

6. **Poetry is the companion of . . . camps.** A refusal to see a discrepancy between the profession of arms and the art of letters marked a strain of English chivalry throughout the Middle Ages which 16th c. educationalists like Elyot and Ascham developed. The ideal of the highly literate military gentleman is exemplified in George Gascoigne with his motto *tam Marte quam Mercurio*, in the soldier-scholar, George Whetstone, by many men in the Sidney circle, and of course by Sidney himself. See further Smith, i, 395. The concord between Mars and the Muses was everywhere a favourite Renaissance topic ; so Scaliger, Oratio ii (against Erasmus) (Toulouse, 1621), p. 16 : ' The most honourable business of war, which raises men to the rank of gods, ought not to remove anyone from literary glory, since letters are often received and cherished in the bosom of armies'. George Buchanan in the Preface to *Jephthes* (1566) speaks of the closest agreement between military matters and literary studies and of a sort of secret sympathy between them (cp. also Buchanan's account of James I of Scotland, quoted in note on **131**/16). M.-A. Muret in Oratio xxiii (*Opera*, i, 275), compares the arts of letters and arms at length.

7. **Orlando Furioso.** The title of Ariosto's romantic epic, published 1516 and in final form in 1532.

honest has a tone of condescension. By Sidney's time the old Arthurian stories were dismissed by the brighter spirits as hopelessly unfashionable (see Wilson, *Rhetorique*, p. 145), and by the stricter moralists (such as Vives and Ascham) as corrupting nonsense (see Vernon Hall, *Renaissance Literary Criticism*, pp. 203–7).

8. **the quiddity of ens and prima materia.** Scholastic terms : *quiddity*, the essential nature, that which makes a thing what it is ; *ens*, being, pure existence ; *prima materia*, first matter (*hyle* in Aristotle), the mere possibility of being. Defenders of poetry usually made scornful reference to the jargon of the schools ; cp. Lodge (Smith, i, 67) castigating ' your dunce Doctors in their reasons *de ente, et non ente*'.

10. **even Turks and Tartars.** See 97/36.

15ff. **Alexander . . . by Plutarch,** etc. Plutarch wrote two tracts *On the fortune or the virtue of Alexander* in which he showed that personal qualities accounted for Alexander's achievements, not luck.

18. **though Plutarch did not,** ' even if Plutarch had not done so '.

19. **the phoenix,** with reference to the uniqueness, not the resurgence, of the bird.

This Alexander, etc. Plutarch, *Life of Alexander*, 7–8, treats of Alexander's education. He gained from Aristotle ' not only moral and political knowledge, but was also instructed in those more secret and profound branches of science. When Alexander was in Asia he wrote home to Aristotle chiding the philosopher for having published openly this sublimer knowledge and adding : " I had rather excel the bulk of mankind in the superior parts of learning than in the extent of power and dominion". Alexander loved polite learning too, and his natural curiosity made him a man of extensive reading. The *Iliad* he thought as well as called, a portable treasure of military knowledge ; and he had a copy corrected by Aristotle which is called " the casket copy ". One-si-critus informs us, that he used to lay it under his pillow with his sword.' Alexander's admiration for Homer (noted also in Cicero, *Pro Archia poeta*, x) is very frequently adduced in Renaissance defences of literature : Elyot, *Governour*, I, x (ed. Croft, i, 59) ; Lodge (Smith, i, 64) ; see Smith's note, i, 364 ; W. Ringler's note on Rainolds, *Oratio*, p. 85 ; E. K.'s Gloss to Spenser's *Shepherd's Calendar*, October Eclogue ; Wills, *De re poetica*, p. 78, and Fowler's Introduction, p. 28.

21. Callisthenes. An austere Macedonian who opposed the absolutism of Alexander the Great. Plutarch, *Life of Alexander*, recounts the story of his downfall ; see also Justin, *History*, XII, vi ; Cicero, *Pro Rabiro Postumo*, ix, 23 ; Elyot, *Governour*, II, vi (ed. Croft, ii, 57).

23f. to wish . . . Homer . . . alive. The anecdote is given by Plu-tarch, *Life of Alexander*, and *How a man may become aware of his progress in virtue*, 16, and by Cicero, *Pro Archia poeta*, x, 24, and was often reproduced in the 16th c., e.g. by Erasmus, *Apophthegmes*, III, 36 (trans. Udall, p. 223), Montaigne, *Essays*, II, xxxvi, E. K. in Gloss to Spenser's *Shepherd's Calendar*, October Eclogue.

26ff. Cato misliked Fulvius. M. Fulvius Nobilior, consul 189 B.C. ; conqueror of the Aetolians in Greece. In this campaign he was accom-panied by the poet Ennius (239–169 B.C.), a Calabrian by birth who be-came a Roman citizen and the first of the Roman poets. Cicero in *Pro Archia poeta*, xi, 27, recalls the encouragement Fulvius gave to Ennius ; and the story of Cato's dislike was often repeated. See Cicero, *Tusculan Disputations*, I, i, 3 ; Cornelius Agrippa, *Vanitie of the Arts*, cap. 4, f. 12v. ; Gosson, *School*, p. 21 ; Smith, i, 233 ; E. K.'s Gloss to Spenser's *Shepherd's Calendar*, October Eclogue.

29f. the excellent Cato Uticensis. See 112/5 note. Sidney is distin-guishing this later member of the famous Roman family from the Cato contemporary with Fulvius (see next note). Cato of Utica has been much celebrated in European literature as a model of superhuman republican virtue, for example by Cicero in *Cato*, by Lucan in *Pharsalia*, by Sallust in *Catiline*, 54, by Dante in *Purgatory*, i, by Addison in *Cato*.

31. the former. Cato the Censor (234–149 B.C.), the great-grandfather of Cato of Utica, notable for his strict morality and his fierce opposition to what he considered the enervating influences of Greek sophistication ; ' yet [according to Plutarch, *Life of Cato the Censor*] it is said that he learned Greek very late in life '. During his censorship in 184 (at that time the highest civic office in Rome) he made a point of showing his contempt for philosophy, polite studies, and all luxury, of never sacri-ficing to the Graces (33). To ridicule the slow methods of Isocrates' teaching, he remarked that Isocrates' scholars grew old in learning their art, as if they intended to exercise it in the shades below (cp. 35. *Pluto*, as god of the shades).

38. unmustered, ' unenrolled ', ' unenlisted '.

p. 128

1. Scipio Nasica . . . the best Roman. Livy (*Histories*, XXIX, 14) tells how when, acting on the words of the oracle, the Senate in 204 B.C. required a special envoy, they chose P. Scipio. ' They judged him to be the best of all the good men in the whole state.'

2. the other Scipio brothers. The brothers P. Cornelius Scipio Africanus (234–183 B.C.) and L. Cornelius Scipio Asiaticus, cousins of Scipio

Nasica. P. Scipio acquired his surname Africanus by the defeat of
Hannibal at Zama, 202 B.C. L. Scipio was called Asiaticus after his
victory over Antiochus at Mount Sipylus, 190 B.C. Cicero in *Pro
Archia poeta*, ix, 22, recalls that the poet Ennius was buried in the
sepulchre of the Scipios. Boccaccio in *De genealogia deorum*, XIV, v,
xix, repeats the story, and so do many later writers, including Wills,
De re poetica, p. 80 ; and see W. Ringler's note to Rainolds, *Oratio*,
p. 86.

9f. **whom . . . I have ever esteemed.** There is plenty of evidence in the
Apology (e.g. **97**/8ff. ; **129**/28ff.) for Sidney's admiration of Plato ;
see Irene Samuel, ' The Influence of Plato on Sir P. S.'s *Defence of
Poesy* ', *MLQ* **1** (1940) 383–91.

11. **of all philosophers . . . the most poetical.** Cp. **97**/10ff. ; **114**/22ff.

12. **the fountain** of Helicon. Cp. **132**/11 note, and Elyot's praise of
' noble Homer ' (*Governour*, I, x, ed. Croft, i, 58ff.) ' from whom as
from a fountaine proceded all eloquence and lernyng '—drawing on
Ovid, *Amores*, III, ix, 25.

15. **a philosopher . . . a natural enemy of poets.** Cp. **105**/1ff. Plato
(*Republic*, X) testifies to this opposition to poetry : ' With reason we
then dismissed it from our Republic [II, III]. . . . Reason obliged us to
do so. And let us add, lest we be accused of a kind of barbarousness
and rusticity, that there is an old variance between philosophy and poetry.
For such lines as

> That bawling bitch, which at her mistress barks, etc.

and a thousand similar are marks of an ancient opposition.' On the
history of this opposition up to the triumph of philosophy with scholasti-
cism, see Curtius, Chap. 11, pp. 203–13, and R. McKeon in *Critics and
Criticism*, ed. R. S. Crane (Chicago, 1952), pp. 297–318.

25. **for Homer seven cities strave.** This story, originating in a group of
epigrams of the *Greek Anthology*, XVI, 295–9, and told by Cicero in
Pro Archia, viii, 19, became a Renaissance commonplace. See Landino,
Preface to Dante, sig. BB3v ; Boccaccio, *De genealogia deorum*, XIV,
xix (Osgood, p. 90) ; Coluccio Salutati, *De laboribus Herculis* (ed.
Ullman), I, 4 ; Wills, *De re poetica*, p. 78 ; Montaigne, *Essays*, II,
xxxvi ; and W. Ringler's note to Rainolds, *Oratio*, p. 87. The seven
cities are Smyrna, Rhodes, Colophon, Salamis, Chios, Argos, Athens.

26. **many cities banished philosophers.** E.g. Empedocles was excluded
from Acragas ; Damon, Anaxagoras, and Protagoras were banished
from Athens.

28ff. As told by Plutarch in the *Life of Nicias*, who led the Athenians in
their defeat by the Syracusans. Of the Athenians ' some owed their
preservation to Euripides. Of all the Grecians his was the Muse with
whom the Sicilians were most in love. From every stranger that landed
in their island they gleaned every small specimen or portion of his works
and communicated it with pleasure to each other. It is said on this
occasion a number of Athenians upon their return home went to
Euripides, and thanked him in the most respectful manner for their
obligations to his pen.'

30. **philosophers unworthy to live.** Socrates most notably ; but Prodicus
of Ceos was also sometimes said to have been put to death with Socrates.

31. **Simonides** of Ceos (*c.* 555–468 B.C.), the first of the great lyric poets of Greece, resident for a time in Athens, then in Sicily, where he enjoyed the patronage of the tyrant Hieron. In 476 Simonides effected a reconciliation between Hieron and his brother Theron. Hieron's court was a centre of art and literature ; several of the odes of **Pindar** (see **118**/30 note) celebrate his achievements. Landino, Preface to Dante, *Comedy*, sig. BB3v., cites the influence of the two poets on Hieron.

33. **Dionysius,** tyrant of Syracuse, 405–367 B.C. (see **112**/15 note), is said to have given Plato to the ambassador of Sparta, who sold him as a slave. Cicero in *Pro Rabirio Postumo*, ix, 23, alludes to the story.

34. **who should do thus.** *Viz.* a man who ' might maliciously object ' (14 above).

36. **cavillation,** ' faultfinding '.

37ff. Sidney is borrowing from Scaliger, *Poetices*, I, ii, p. 10 : ' Plato should look to himself and see how many foolish, filthy stories he brings in. How frequently does he insinuate opinions which stink with the vice of the Greeks. Certainly it would be praiseworthy never to have read the *Symposium*, the *Phaedrus*, and other enormities.' Parts of the *Symposium* and *Phaedrus* can be read as exalting homosexual love.

p. 129

3. **community of women.** See Plato, *Republic*, V.

6ff. **I honour philosophical instructions,** etc. Sidney conducts the defence against Plato's charge skilfully. So far he has not confronted the charge at all, and has relied upon counter-attacking philosophy. He now goes on to allow that philosophy, although attacked by St Paul, can be a worthy study ; but then, he argues, why should not poetry also be a worthy study, even if it has been attacked by Plato—who is, after all, a less eminent authority than St Paul.

9–10. **(who yet . . . a prophet).** Omitted in Ponsonby.

10. **twice two poets,** etc. Acts 17:28 : ' For in him we live, and move, and have our being ' closely resembles verses in (i) the astronomical poem *Phenomena* of the 3rd c. Greek poet Aratus, and (ii) the *Hymn to Zeus* by a Stoic, Cleanthes, of slightly later date. The third poet referred to by Paul is the shadowy philosophic figure of 5th–6th cs., Epimenides of Crete, in Titus 1:12 : ' One of themselves, a prophet of their own, said, Cretans are always liars, evil beasts, idle gluttons'. The fourth poet is the comic dramatist Menander of the 4th c. B.C., whose play *Thais* provides 1 Cor. 15:33 : ' Evil communications corrupt good manners'. St Paul's uses of the Greek poets had been noted by Jerome in his commentaries (see *PL*, 26, col. 606), by Boccaccio, *De genealogia deorum*, XIV, xviii (Osgood, p. 86). Puritan educationalists rely heavily on these passages to justify Christian use of pagan learning ; see L. A. Sasek, *The Literary Temper of the English Puritans*, pp. 80ff.

11. **setteth a watchword upon,** ' utters a warning against ' ; see *NED s.* watchword, 4, ' cautionary word or speech'. The reference is Col. 2:8 : ' Beware lest any man spoil you through philosophy and vain deceit, after the tradition of men, after the rudiments of world, and not after Christ'.

13. **Plato found fault,** etc. Now Sidney first meets what he considers the main charge made by Plato. It is indeed one of the charges made

by Plato against poetry (*Republic*, II) ; but he made others, *viz*. that it renders the soul effeminate by using lax sounds and rhythms ; that the imitation it provides is twice removed from the truth ; that it feeds and develops unruly passions. On these grounds, Plato argued, poets (except for those who write the praises of the gods and heroes) should be banished. In answering only the first specific charge Sidney follows the common line of medieval discussion which tested the claims (and usually found them wanting by standards of Christian veracity) of the poet-theologians of antiquity ; see Curtius, pp. 215–21. Josephus in *Against Apion*, II, 36–7, had explained that the expulsion of the poets was to prevent the destruction of true notions of God by fables ; cp. also Augustine, *City of God*, XVIII, xii–xviii. Cornelius Agrippa, *Vanitie of the Arts*, ff. 11–12, castigates the poets' lies about divinity and recalls their expulsion by Plato. Renaissance apologists for poetry, however, turn the argument. Salutati in *De laboribus Herculis* (ed. Ullman, I, cap. 12, p. 62) makes a defence that poets did not invent the stories, that *physici* and theologians were as much to blame. See Weinberg, i, 254, for an anticipation of Sidney's argument in Francesco Patrizi, *De institutione reipublicae* (1534) ; and cp. Vives, *De tradendis disciplinis* (trans. Foster Watson), p. 127, where, urging the moderate usefulness of the old poets, he argues, like Sidney, ' that if these tales could formerly injure students, they can do so no longer, for we know that those gods were bad and wicked beings who deserved ruin not heaven '.

21. **according to their nature of imitation,** i.e. in as much as they produced the images of others' fantasies and illusions.

22. **Plutarch,** in the treatises in *Moralia*, *De Iside et Osiride* ; *De defectu oraculorum* ; *De sera numinis vindicta*.

27. **better . . . than the philosophers.** The religious beliefs of the Greeks (and the Romans) as perceived through their mythologies are usually considered to have been eroded by the teachings of rationalising philosophers, particularly by the Stoics and Epicureans.

28. **atheism.** A new word in late-16th c. English, brought in from the French ; see *NED s.* atheism, atheist, atheonism.

31. **Scaliger** (*Poetices*, I, ii, p. 10) in classifying poets speaks of those divinely inspired, as Plato says, ' whose authority certain barbarous and uncouth men seek to use in order to expel poets from the republic'. Scaliger goes on : ' Even if he condemns some of the books, we need not go without the rest, for they are very often adduced by Plato himself in support of his arguments'.

34. **without further law,** ' without more ado '. The sense underlying this use of *law* seems to be that from which an old meaning ' allowance in the start of a race ' in sport was developed ; see *NED s.* law. 20.

38. **Ion.** One of the shorter Platonic dialogues which explores rather inconclusively the nature of rhapsody and poetic inspiration. Whatever Plato intended, the dialogue was never taken ironically by 16th c. readers, who all found in it many passages commending poetry. See Landino, Preface to Dante, *Comedy* (see 142/5 note), Francesco Patrizi and other writers of Platonised poetics (see Weinberg, i, Chap. 7, pp. 250–96), Minturno, *De poeta*, pp. 74–6.

p. 130

4. **under whose lion's skin,** etc. Aesop's fable of the ass in the lion's skin has the moral that each should content himself with his own

praiseworthy achievements and not seek to appropriate the merits or characteristics of another.

7ff. **he attributeth unto Poesy . . . a very inspiring of a divine force.** In ' the forenamed dialogue ', *Ion*, Socrates discoursed on poetry with a degree of irony : ' For the authors of those great poems which we admire, do not attain to excellence through the rules of any art, but they utter their beautiful melodies of verse in a state of inspiration, and, as it were, possessed by a spirit not their own . . . like the Corybantes, who lose all control over their reason in the enthusiasm of the sacred dance. . . . For a poet is indeed a thing ethereally light, winged and sacred, nor can he compose anything worth calling poetry until he becomes inspired and as it were, mad, or whilst any reason remains in him. . . . Every rhapsodist or poet . . . is excellent in proportion to the extent of his participation in the divine influence. . . . And thus it appears to me that the god proves beyond a doubt, that these transcendent poems are not human as the work of men, but divine as coming from the god. Poets then are the interpreters of the divinities—each being possessed by some one deity ; and to make this apparent the god designedly inspires the worst poets with the sublimest verse.' Sidney denies that the poet receives ' a very inspiring of a divine force '. As a critic, he thinks of poetry as a human activity aiming at excellence through ' rules of art ' and the exercise of intelligence ; as a Protestant, he restricts direct inspiration to the composition of the Scriptures (see **63**). Though his attitude was thoroughly consistent it was somewhat unusual : in the 16th c. the notion of the poet's ' divine fury ' was commonly acceptable. On the development of the notion, see Curtius, pp. 473–5 ; Weinberg, i, Chaps. 7, 8 ; Hathaway, Part 5, and particularly, Chap. 34, pp. 437–59, for rationalist rejection of the theory ; and for some account of the notion in England, see F. L. Schoell, *Études sur l'humanisme continental en Angleterre à la fin de la Renaissance* (Paris, 1926), R. Wills, *De re poetica*, pp. 72ff., 124ff., and Fowler's Introduction, pp. 29–34.

11. Omission of a relative (after *honours*), especially when the antecedent is emphatic and immediate, is common Elizabethan practice ; see Abbott, *Shakespearian Grammar*, § 244.

13. **Alexanders, Caesars, Scipios.** See **127**/19 : **128**/2 ; **131**/13 below : cp. Harrington's phrase, ' so many Alexanders, Caesars, Scipios ' (Smith, ii, 195).

14. **Laelius . . . the Roman Socrates.** Cp. Cicero, *De amicitia*, vi, and *De officiis*, I, xxvi, 90 : ' It is a fine thing to keep an unruffled temper, an unchanging mien, and the same cast of countenance in every condition of life : these, history tells us, were characteristic of Socrates and no less of Gaius Laelius'. Laelius (born *c.* 186 B.C.), friend of Scipio Africanus the younger, a prominent member of the philosophic Scipionic circle, and himself a great patron of literature, was introduced as interlocutor in several of Cicero's dialogues, notably in *De amicitia* and *De republica*. Cicero recalls (*Letters to Atticus*, vii, 3, 10) that the plays of Terence were by many ascribed in whole or in part to his friend Laelius. Terence hints at his debts in the Prologues to *Heautontimoroumenos* (*The Self-Tormentor*) and *The Brothers* ; cp. Vives, *De tradendis disciplinis* (trans. Foster Watson), p. 136.

17ff. **Socrates . . . the only wise man.** See Plato, *Apology*, 21 (with Socrates speaking) : ' Chairephon made a pilgrimage to Delphi. . . . He actually asked if there was any man wiser than I. And the priestess [of Apollo] answered, No.' Sidney, *Astrophil & Stella*, XXV, again refers to

> . . . the wight most wise
> By Phebus doome.

In Plato's dialogue, *Phaedo*, 60, Cebes asks Socrates why, since he has come to prison, he has ' put into verse those fables of Aesop and the Hymn to Apollo '. Socrates answers that it rose from the insistence of his *daimon* in a recurrent dream. Harrington follows Sidney with the same allusion (Smith, ii, 204), adding ' as Plutarke testifieth ' (*How the young man should study poetry*, 2). There is no doubt that for Sidney Plutarch is as likely a source as Plato's *Phaedo*.

23. **Plutarch.** In *How the young man should study poetry*. But, as Sidney observes (24f.), Plutarch throughout *Moralia* and the *Lives* quotes poetry frequently.

26. **guards,** ' ornamental borders ', ' trimmings '.

26ff. **But I list not.** . . . The transition to the Summary of the second part of the *Apology*.

28. **fit soil for praise to dwell upon.** Cp. Milton, *Lycidas*, 78.

32. **low-creeping.** Cp. **142**/20, and Horace's phrase ' serpit humi ' (*Art*, 28).

37. **engarland.** Apparently Sidney's invention ; used again *Astrophil & Stella*, LVI.

38. **laureate, as . . . triumphant captains.** Cp. **120**/34ff. ; and see note there.

p. 131

8f. **being . . . makers of themselves, not takers of others.** A brief re-statement of Sidney's theory of imitation ; cp. **100**/21ff. ; **120**/21f.

10. Virgil, *Aeneid*, I, 12 :

> O Muse! the causes and the crimes relate ;
> What goddess was provok'd, and whence her hate.
> (Dryden's trans.)

Virgil of course had in mind the hostility of Juno to Aeneas. By abstracting the line from its context Sidney is seeking the meaning : ' O Muse, bring to my mind the causes by which *your* power has been offended.'

11. **Sweet Poesy,** etc. A justification of poetry by adducing the eminent men who had cultivated it formed part of Cicero's defence of the poet in *Pro Archia*, viiff. Many Renaissance writers use this topic of praise to defend poetry ; see e.g. Boccaccio, *De genealogia deorum*, XV, xiii (Osgood, pp. 138–40). Elyot, *Governour*, I, xii (ed. Croft, i, 99ff.), gives an account of great rulers of antiquity down to Charlemagne who cherished the arts ; Thomas Drant in his Dedication to the Earl of Ormond of his translation of Horace's *Art of Poetry* (1567) instances among other patrons Bembo and King Francis I of France. See also Wills, *De re poetica*, pp. 78ff. ; E. K.'s Gloss on October in the *Shepherd's Calendar* ; Webbe (Smith, i, 233) ; Meres, copying from Sidney (Smith, ii, 322) ; Puttenham, *Arte*, pp. 16–22, concluding (p. 22) : ' Since therefore so many noble Emperours, Kings and Princes haue been studious of Poesie and other ciuill arts & not ashamed to bewray their

skills in the same, let none other meaner person despise learning.' See also W. Ringler's note to Rainolds, *Oratio*, p. 85 ; Bacon, *Advancement of Learning*, I, vii (ed. Wright), pp. 51–67.

13. David. Cp. 99/7 ; **101**/39.

Adrian, the Emperor Hadrian (A.D. 117–38). Elyot, *Governour*, I, xii (ed. Croft, i, 108), praises his learning ; E. Hellowes, *Chronicles . . . of tenne Emperours of Rome* (1577), p. 75, recalls that he ' compounded certaine workes in Heroicall metre ' ; the verses beginning *Animula vagula, blandula* which Hadrian was said to have composed on his deathbed were familiar (and to be translated by Pope).

Sophocles (495–406 B.C.), the Athenian tragic dramatist, was appointed in 440 one of the ten generals in the war against Samos.

Germanicus (15 B.C.–A.D. 19), nephew and adopted son of the Emperor Tiberius. The conqueror of Germany, a favourite with the Roman people, and by reputation, as Elyot, *Governour* (ed. Croft, i. 109–10), observes, ' equall to the moost noble poetes of his time '.

15. Robert, king of Sicily (1309–43). Robert II of Anjou. A lover of fine literature, the great patron of Petrarch (see **120**/34 note) ; eulogised by Boccaccio, *De genealogia deorum*, XLV, ix, xxii.

King Francis I of France. Francis I (1494–1547), a busy, rash, strongly nationalist king, whose military and cultural exploits in Italy brought the Renaissance to France ; a liberal patron of art and literature, encouraging, among others, Rabelais, Erasmus, Budé, the publishing family of the Estiennes, Marot, Leonardo da Vinci.

16. King James of Scotland. Which King James Sidney had in mind is uncertain. The other exemplary figures in this list of the patrons and practitioners of poetry are introduced in pairs. Is this an addition on revision of the text of the *Apology*, intended as an ambiguous compliment to James VI of Scotland ? James VI (b. 1566) was something of a precocious child and was vigorously educated by George Buchanan (see 20 note below) and displayed early his interest in letters. Sidney had some direct contacts with the Scots court during the 1580s ; see A. F. Westcott, *New Poems by James I of England* (New York, 1911), pp. xviii–xxi, and *Poems* (ed. Ringler), p. xlix, note 1. James was to patronise Salluste du Bartas and was highly sympathetic with Sidney's ideals of a Protestant poetry. But behind the likely compliment to a contemporary monarch, Sidney probably had in mind the earlier James I of Scotland (1394–1437). George Buchanan, *Rerum Scoticarum Historia* (Edinburgh, 1582, the year of Buchanan's death), X, xxxviii, speaks of James I busying himself in setting up schools which he encouraged with his liberality and favour and ' not only cherished learned men but was himself present at many of their disputations : and whenever he had freedom from affairs of state he loved to listen to literary talk ; and earnestly laboured to counteract the false opinion of well-born minds that letters draw men away from public affairs to ease and idleness, and soften warlike minds and break up and weaken all their noble impulses '. Cp. Hall's *Chronicle* (1548) (London, 1809), pp. 39, 120. James I was for nearly twenty years a prisoner in England and is usually regarded as the author of *The Kingis Quhair*, a stanzaic poem in the courtly Chaucerian style. James IV of Scotland (1473–1513) is less likely to be Sidney's reference. His real achievements in Scotland as king and as patron of learning were probably invisible to Englishmen in the years after Flodden (cp. Buchanan, *Historia*, XIII, lii).

Bembus. Pietro Bembo (1470–1547) cleric, humanist, and courtier at the courts of Estes, Montefeltros, and Medicis ; secretary to Pope

Leo X ; cardinal 1539. His literary importance lies in his establishment of standards of style and composition both in Latin and in the Italian vernacular. Scaliger (*Poetices*, VI, v, p. 738) calls him ' Cicero's ape '.

17. Bibbiena. Bernardo Dovizi, Cardinal Bibbiena (1470–1520), humanist in the service of the Medicis, secretary to Lorenzo the Magnificent, general and diplomatist, made cardinal in 1513 ; author of a five-act comedy, *La calandra*, in the style of Plautus.

Beza. Théodore de Bèze (1519–1605), a Burgundian of good birth, educated at Orléans and Paris in letters and the law, became professor of Greek at Lausanne, published the tragedy *Abraham sacrifiant* and an edition of the New Testament. An active associate of Calvin, and after Calvin's death (1564) (thus at the time of the composition of the *Apology*) leader of the Calvinists.

18. Melanchthon. Philip Melanchthon (1497–1560), German reformer and humanist. Educated by his uncle, the great Biblical scholar Reuchlin, and at several German universities ; professor of Greek at Wittenberg, becoming Luther's chief associate in reform ; one of the great Renaissance educationalists, both in advancing scholarship and in developing educational method. For several years he lived with Hubert Languet, Sidney's mentor. As a poet he received Scaliger's commendation (*Poetices*, VI, iv, p. 736).

Fracastorius. Girolamo Fracastoro (1483–1553), humanist and natural philosopher. Studied at Padua under Pomponazzo ; professor of logic ; a musician, a physician, a poet ; a precursor of the new science ; author of a medical poem *Syphilis*, eulogised by Scaliger (*Poetices*, VI, v, pp. 753–8). His dialogues (published 1555), *Naugerius* and *Turrius*, on the mind, were probably known to Sidney and certainly suggest his style of thinking. They are products of the influential mid-century neo-Aristotelian school of Padua (see Hathaway, pp. 306ff.), where Sidney studied for some months in 1574.

19. Scaliger. Julius Caesar Scaliger (1484–1558). Claimed for himself an aristocratic Italian birth ; settled at Agen on the Garonne in France in his fortieth year ; a bitter controversialist but a scholar of genius. His *Poetices Libri Septem* (1561), with which Sidney was well acquainted, is the most learned and in many respects the most penetrating and comprehensive of all 16th c. treatises on poetry (see Weinberg, ii, 743–50). Scaliger wrote much poetry and some works on natural philosophy.

Pontanus. Giovanni Pontano (1426–1503), scholar, soldier, diplomatist at the court of Naples and president of the Academy there ; one of the great Latin poets of the Renaissance (see Scaliger, *Poetices*, VI, iv, pp. 744–9) ; his astronomical poem *Urania* was particularly esteemed ; author also of histories and of political and philosophical treatises.

Muretus. Marc-Antoine Muret (1526–85), French humanist, a colleague of Buchanan at Paris 1544. Driven out of France for immorality ; later in Italy as a Jesuit wrote a defence of the Massacre of St Bartholomew. It seems unlikely that Sidney knew much about the later career of this contemporary. Muret edited many of the Latin poets ; much of his other writing is in the form of elegant academic lectures.

20. George Buchanan (1506–82). Scottish poet and pedagogue, probably the greatest of British humanists. Most of his early manhood was spent in France. He became a Protestant in 1563 ; tutor to the young James VI ; later Privy Seal. An outstanding Latin poet, in lyric verse, in satire, and in drama (see **137/17**) ; the author of a famous translation of the Psalms into Latin verse (cp. **99**/7ff. ; 11f. notes), of *De jure regni apud Scotos*, a treatise influential in the development of the idea of British political liberty ; of a much-read history of Scotland. He was in England on several occasions, and was on friendly terms with Roger Ascham, Walter Haddon, Anthony Cooke (tutor to Edward VI). His political, religious, and cultural sympathies must have made him an extremely attractive elder to Sidney ; see further James E. Phillips, ' George Buchanan and the Sidney Circle ', *HLQ*, **12** (1948), 23–55.

21. Hospital of France. Michel de l'Hôpital (1503–73). Chancellor of France 1560–8 ; one of the great practical lawyers of 16th c. France, a reformer of the administration, who made unavailing attempts to promote toleration. He was a considerable patron of literature, and a minor poet.

25. poetise. Apparently Sidney's invention and taken up by other Elizabethan writers.

28. decketh our soil with fewer laurels, ' affords fewer triumphs '. But the phrase may not be entirely metaphorical. Nowadays the true laurel (*laurus nobilis*, the bays of the poet) is not particularly common in England. The word *bays* has a lexicographical history going back to OE, but the name laurel has been usurped by the common or cherry laurel (*laurus cerasus*) which seems to have been introduced into western Europe from Turkey in 1576 by Charles de L'Écluse, a friend and correspondent of Sidney. No testimony has been found to indicate that the true laurel was more plentiful in England before Sidney's time, although there is evidence that it suffered from periodic blight ; see Shakespeare, *Richard II*, II, iv, 8, drawing on second ed. of Holinshed's *Chronicles* (1586–7) ; and John Evelyn, *Sylva*, ed. A. Hunter (York, 1776), i, 396.

30. those times when the trumpet of Mars did sound. What time Sidney looks back to, or whether he intends any clear reference at all, is uncertain. The French wars culminating in Henry V's victories seem the likely reference. Certainly much writing during the hundred years 1350–1450 reflects a strong new nationalist and martial spirit in England.

32. strew the house, ' prepare a welcome '. Paul Hentzner, who visited England in 1598, reported that even the royal presence chamber at Greenwich was strewed with rushes and flowers ' as is the custom in England '.

33. mountebanks at Venice. The loquacious stallholders of Venice seem to have made a particularly sharp impression on English travellers. Shuckburgh (p. 142) quotes from *Coryat's Crudities* (1611) : ' Truly I often wondered at many of these natural orators. For they would tell their tales with such admirable volubility and plausible grace, even extempore, and seasoned with singular variety of elegant jests and witty conceits, that they did often strike great admiration into strangers that never heard them before.' They ' sell oyles, soveraigne waters, amorous songs printed, apothecary drugs, and a common-weale of other trifles '. See also K. M. Lea, *Italian Popular Comedy* (Oxford, 1934), ii, 358–62.

34ff. ' Though from one point of view the inaction in England at present and the silence of the poets can be considered as a commendation of the character of poetry, from another we can see why poets now attain small esteem, for if they functioned properly they would be disturbers of the public lethargy.' Similarly E. K. in the Gloss to October in *Shepherd's Calendar* observes that his poet ' sheweth the cause of the contempt of Poetry to be idelnesse and basenesse of mind '. Sidney's

advocacy for a militant national policy during the 1580s is well attested ;
see Fulke Greville, *Life*, Chaps. viii–x.

35ff. The story how Vulcan, Venus' husband, made a net to catch Venus
and Mars in adultery is drawn from Homer, *Odyssey*, VIII, 266–367.

p. 132

1. **grateful,** ' acceptable '.

5. **Epaminondas** (d. 363 B.C.). Theban general and statesman who raised
Thebes to a temporary supremacy in Greece. Sidney has in mind the
account in Plutarch, *Precepts of statecraft*, 15 ; ' Epaminondas being
appointed *telearch* by the Thebans through envy and contempt, did not
reject it, but said that the office does not make the man, but the man the
office. He brought the office of *telearch* into great and venerable repute,
which was before nothing but a kind of duty of carrying off the refuse
from the narrow streets and lanes of the city and of maintaining the
gutters.'

11. **they,** *scil.* the bastard poets (10).
   Helicon. Like many medieval and Renaissance poets (Dante and
Spenser among them), Sidney speaks as if Helicon itself were the Muses'
well or stream ; but properly it is the range of mountains in Boeotia on
which the Muses' fountain Hippocrene was located. Sidney exploits
further associations. The Muses' fountain sprang from the imprint of
Pegasus' hoof, and in medieval verse (cp. Dante, *Paradise*, xviii, 82)
Pegasus becomes the favourite steed of the Muses and the poet's own
mount in his poetic flights. Sidney's ' bastard poets ' are mounted on
jades.

12. **post-horses.** Horses used in relay and ridden to exhaustion.

14. Adapted from Juvenal, *Satires*, XIV, 33–5. Juvenal is excepting
from the general unhappy effects of bad example one or two ' whose
souls informing better clay Prometheus has shaped '. Montaigne,
Essays, I, xxiv, applies this quotation to the scholar Turnebus, another
of the Buchanan circle.

16. **knights of the same order.** Cp. *Amiot to the Readers*, North's
Plutarch (1579), p. 13 : ' . . . such as speake of matters of government
and state, but specially of matters of warre by the booke, speake but as
booke knights. . . .' Ben Jonson, *The Silent Woman*, II, ii (*Works*,
ed. Simpson and Herford, v, 186), probably had this passage of the
Apology in mind, when to the somewhat incredulous question : ' A
knight live by his verses ? ' comes the answer : ' The noble Sidney lives
by his.' On the status of the amateur author, see E. H. Miller, *The
Professional Writer in Elizabethan England* (Cambridge, Mass., 1959),
pp. 23ff.

18ff. Here, where the vein of mockery running through the *Apology*
reappears, cp. Erasmus, *Praise of Folly*, p. 120, commenting on those
who set up as authors, ' among which they are more specially indebted
to me [Folly] who spoil paper by blotting it with mere trifles and
impertinences ' ; and Florio in his translation of Montaigne, *Essays*,
II, xxxiii, who finds the historian Bodin 'endowed with much more
judgement than the common rabble of scribblers and blurpapers which
now adayes stuffe stationers shops '.

21. **In despite of Pallas,** ' lacking wisdom ' ; rendering the familiar Lat. tag
invita Minerva (e.g. Horace, *Art*, 385).

24f. so have I neglected the means, etc. This strikes a reader as modesty to the point of disingenuousness. Sidney's poems are not improvisations, but the products of elaborate, careful experimentation and calculated artifice.

28. look themselves . . . if they be inclinable. The construction depends upon an obsolete, transitive use of *look* as ' look into ', ' examine in order to discover ' (see *NED s.v. vb.* 6.b), ' if they have a bent for poetry '.

29. drawn by the ears, ' pulled violently or roughly ' (as in handling animals).

32. a divine gift. According to such learned ancients as Cicero, Horace, and Plutarch (see J. F. D'Alton, *Roman Literary Theory and Criticism* (London, 1931), pp. 472–5), and in the Renaissance, a commonplace particularly among Platonising critics. Sidney denies that poetry is given by direct inspiration from God (see **130**/8f.), that it is the product of a ' divine frenzy ' (see **63–4**). He thinks of it as the product of a certain ' inclination ' (24 ; cp. Horace, *Art*, 294–8), of a certain inborn attitude of mind, or of what the scholastics and some of the Renaissance critics, using Aristotelian terminology, would call a ' habit of the practical intellect ' ; see Weinberg, i, 7, 10, 495–6. It is only in this sense that poetry for Sidney is a ' divine ' (because natural) gift. Poetry does not come simply from acquiring the ' art '—from possessing a knowledge of the rules ; a ' poetic nature ' is prerequisite ; only then can the art be learned. An influential group of Italian critics in the late 16th c. took the same position (see Hathaway, pp. 437ff.). In Tomitano's words : ' We men cannot alter Nature . . . as a work that belongs to God . . . but we can often correct and amend it ' (quoted by Hathaway, p. 441). This passage in the *Apology* is illuminated by Harrington when he is reproving Puttenham for labouring ' to proue, or rather to make Poetrie an art '. What Puttenham does succeed in proving by exhibiting his own bad verses, is, Harrington claims, ' that which M. *Sidney* and all the learneder sort that haue written of it do pronounce, namely that it is a gift and not an art ', something that Puttenham lacks despite all his talk about art (Smith, ii, 196–7).

36. ' An orator is made, a poet born.' A common saying but apparently not of classical origin ; see note, Smith, i, 397. W. Ringler, *JHI* **2** (1941), 497–504, shows that the phrase appears as early as a 3rd c. commentary on Horace's *Art* but came into popular use after it was taken up by Polydore Virgil, *De rerum inventoribus* (1499) and by Badius Ascensius in the Preface to his edition of Terence (1502).

37. manured, ' worked at ', ' cultivated '. For the analogy, cp. Plutarch, *The education of children*, 4, in speaking of natural gifts : ' Man's ground is naturally good . . . and experience tells us that if it be well manured it will be quickly capable of bearing excellent fruit ' (cp. **133**/2f. note). Scaliger develops the theme in his poem ' Ingenium paratur agro ' (*Poemata*, 1591, ii, 187).

38. Daedalus. The great artificer and the originator of arts in classical mythology, who gave wise (though unheeded) advice to his high-flying son Icarus. Horace in *Carmina*, IV, ii, begins : ' Whoever seeks to rival Pindar must fly on waxen wings made with Daedalean art . . . ' ; cp. Pindar, *First Olympian Ode*, 105. According to Natalis Comes, *Mythologia* (Geneva ed., 1636, p. 29), who gives under Daedalus a full account of the artificers of antiquity, Minerva herself was educated by a Daedalean nurse ' who taught her in her tender years all the most ingenious arts '.

p. 133

2f. Art, Imitation, and Exercise. The learning process, especially in rhetoric, was usually analysed into three constituents. The analysis goes back to Greek education. Thus Plato in *Phaedrus*, 269D : ' If you are endowed by nature with a genius for speaking you will become a distinguished speaker if you add thereto theory and practice'. See P. Shorey, *Transactions of the American Philological Association*, **40** (1909), 185–201. Cicero in *De inventione*, I, i, 2, discusses whether eloquence depends chiefly on study, art, and exercise or on innate gifts, and finds (like Sidney) that the original gift is prerequisite, but that it must be trained and perfected by application. But all learning processes were considered essentially similar. Plutarch in *The education of children*, 4, observes that as in arts and sciences so also in the training in virtue three things are necessary : nature, reason or learning, use. ' And as in husbandry it is first necessary for the soil to be fertile, next the husbandman skilful, and lastly the seed good ; so here nature resembles the soil, the teacher the husbandman, the precepts the seed ' (cp. **132**/37). The teachers of rhetoric usually took innate ability (*ingenium*) for granted, and split off imitation as part of the theoretical training necessary ; see R. McKeon, ' Literary Criticism and the Concept of Imitation in Antiquity ', *MPh* **34** (1936), 1–35, especially 27f. Thus *Ad Her.*, I, ii, 3 (which can speak for countless manuals of rhetoric in medieval and Renaissance times) : skill in speaking ' we can acquire by three means, by Art, Imitation and Exercise. Art is a set of rules that provide a definite method and order of speaking. Imitation stimulates us to achieve effects in speaking by careful and conscious following of certain models. Exercise is constant practice and experience in speaking.' On the triad in later teaching, see W. G. Crane, *Wit and Rhetoric in the Renaissance* (New York, 1937), pp. 83ff. Later the rhetoricians' triad is applied to other activities : Ascham in *The Schoolmaster* applies the method to the teaching of grammar, in *Toxophilus* to archery.

3f. these, neither artificial rules nor imitative patterns. In MnE the demonstrative would be repeated within the negation ' neither with these . . . nor with these . . .'. *Artificial rules* and *imitative patterns* explain the first two requisites of ' Art ' and ' Imitation '.

5ff. Sidney's requirements fall in line with some new methods of language teaching practised in the 16th c. (for example, the sixfold method advocated by Ascham in *The Schoolmaster*). But they particularly recall Ramus' system in which analysis was to be completed by an act of genesis or composition ; see Walter J. Ong, *Ramus, Method and the Decay of Dialogue* (Cambridge, Mass., 1958), pp. 263–4.

fore-backwardly, ' starting at the wrong end ', inasmuch, as Sidney explains, as we do not exercise our minds in the active discovery of truth, but instead we manipulate familiar products of analysis irresponsibly, with the result that we reproduce *phantastike* (**125**/26) representations of things that have no real existence—' matter which never was begotten by knowledge '. In effect Sidney is here demanding what Ramus and Bacon demanded—' inductive ' thinking about ' real ' things.

8f. two . . . parts—matter . . . and words. The distinction *res* and *verba*, made by Roman grammarians, was introduced rather loosely into the literary theory of Horace (*Art*, 38–72, 310) and amplified variously by Renaissance critics ; see Weinberg, ii, Index, s. Res : Verba ; A. C. Howell, ' *Res et Verba* : Words and Things ', *ELH* **13** (1946), 131–42.

11. **quodlibet.** With the schoolmen, any question or thesis proposed as an exercise in argument. Sidney is reasserting that contemporary poets take up any theme that comes to hand and assume that if they spin it out in verses it will turn into a poem. They do not realise that without an intellectual ' method ' the elaboration can have little significance for a reader.

14. *Tristia*, IV, x, 26 reads

Et quod tentabam [*variant*, conabar] dicere, versus erat.

[' And whatever I tried to say, turned into verse.'] Ponsonby and Olney have *erit*, and at the same time Olney retains the preterite *conabar*. It is likely that Sidney intended a future construction in adapting Ovid's verse.

17f. Sidney's point is that even the best English poets have never acquired a sufficiently unified sense of purpose, with the results : (i) their compositions do not cohere ; (ii) their use of language falters. Sidney recognised apparently that in *Troilus and Criseyde* Chaucer best displayed his power of organisation. The *great wants* (21) probably refer to diction and metre. Up to 1700 *Troilus and Criseyde* was by far the most popular of Chaucer's poems ; see Caroline F. E. Spurgeon, *Five hundred years of Chaucer criticism and allusion* (Cambridge, 1925), i, lxxvi–vii.

22. **Mirror of Magistrates.** In the ' Fall of Princes ' convention, a collection of narratives on the misfortunes of great men in English history, by several poets in a variety of styles. The work originated with Thomas Sackville, first Lord Buckhurst (1536–1608), joint author also of *Gorboduc* (see 39 note). The *Mirror for Magistrates* (ed. Lily B. Campbell, Cambridge, 1938) first appeared in 1559, but several editions were published with additions up to the end of the century.

23. **Earl of Surrey's lyrics.** Some forty poems of Henry Howard, Earl of Surrey (1517?–47), were printed in Tottel's *Songes and Sonettes* (1557).

25. Spenser under the pseudonym Immerito published *The Shepherd's Calendar* in 1579 (reprinted 1581), and dedicated it to ' the noble and vertuous Gentleman, most worthy of all titles both of learning and chevalerie, Maister Philip Sidney '.

27. **an old rustic language.** In the 1580s advanced literary taste in England no longer favoured the archaism in diction which had been popular earlier ; see V. Rubel, *Poetic Diction in the English Renaissance*, pp. 105, 113. Probably Sidney liked Spenser's use of dialect less than his archaism ; but he himself used the ' old rustic language ' in his pastoral *Ister Bank* ; see *Poems*, 66, and W. Ringler's notes, p. 413. Although Vives in *De tradendis disciplinis* (trans. Foster Watson), p. 137, declines to approve of the practice, he expressed the common recognition (which Sidney does not admit here) that Virgil in his Eclogues ' was striving to catch the charm of the country dialect, in which kind of effort Theocritus allowed himself considerable indulgence '.

28ff. **allow,** ' praise '. Sidney cites the authority of the three outstanding pastoral poets : in Greek, Theocritus, the Sicilian poet of the 3rd c. B.C. ; in Latin, Virgil as author of the *Eclogues* ; in neo-Latin, Jacopo Sannazzaro (1458–1530) (see **116**/6 note), whose *Piscatory Eclogues* were much esteemed for several centuries. Independently of Sidney, Webbe measures Spenser's achievement in the *Shepherd's Calendar* similarly against Theocritus in Greek, Virgil in Latin, but against Calpurnius and Mantuan in neo-Latin (Smith, i, 262).

32f. verses . . . in prose. Cook compared Plato, *Republic*, X, 601 ; cp. also George Gascoigne (Smith, i, 51–2) : ' I would exhorte you also to beware of rime without reason ; my meaning is hereby that your rime leade you not from your firste Inuention, for many wryters, when they haue layed the platforme of their inuention, are yet drawen sometimes (by ryme) to forget it or at least to alter it, as when they cannot readily finde out a worde whiche maye rime to the first (and yet continue their determinate Inuention) they do then eyther botche it vp with a worde that will ryme (howe small reason soeuer it carie with it), or els they alter their first worde and so percase decline or trouble their former Inuention : . . . rather searche the bottome of your braynes for apte wordes than chaunge good reason for rumbling rime.' Gabriel Harvey noted at the end of this paragraph in his copy of Gascoigne's *Certaine Notes* : ' A pithie rule in Sir Philips *Apologie for Poetrie*. The Inuention must guide & rule the Elocution : *non contra* ' (Smith, i, 360).

35. tingling, ' tinkling '. Apparently the earliest use (deriving from the Wycliffite and Tyndale translations of I Cor. 13:1) of this derogatory adjective applied (as became common later) to rhyme.

37ff. Our Tragedies and Comedies, etc. A nominative absolute construction appropriate in discourse pretending to oral delivery.

38. honest civility, ' decent behaviour '.

39. Gorboduc. The tragedy by Thomas Sackville (cp. above, 22 note) and Thomas Norton (1532–84), lawyer, translator of Calvin's *Institutes* (1559). *Gorboduc* was first presented (probably as an exemplary lesson in politics) before Queen Elizabeth I in 1561 by the gentlemen of the Inner Temple ; the text was pirated in 1565, and an authorised edition appeared *c.* 1570 under the title *Ferrex and Porrex*.

p. 134

2ff. climbing to the height of Seneca's style. A well-worn pun on ' style '. L. Annaeus Seneca (*c.* 5 B.C.–A.D. 65), the Stoic philosopher and the tutor of Nero, was as the author of ten tragedies preferred to the Greek tragedians during the Renaissance ; so Giraldi Cinthio (Gilbert, p. 256) : ' He surpasses in prudence, gravity, decorum, majesty, and skill in the use of sentences all the Greeks who ever wrote'. Most Renaissance critics looked, as Sidney does, to tragedy for ' stately speeches ', ' well-sounding phrases ', ' high style ', ' notable morality '. It was not essential, Scaliger observed (*Poetices*, III, xcvi, p. 333), for the outcome of tragedy to be unhappy, as long as the action is grim (*atrox*). A ' notable morality ' is most important ; there are two means of achieving it, and these are the columns on which tragedy is built. First, by using *sententiae*, pregnant moral maxims ; secondly, by vigorous sustained metaphor (p. 334). Trissino (Gilbert, p. 223) also emphasised the importance of *sententiae* in tragedy ; see further W. Clemen, *English Tragedy before Shakespeare* (Eng. trans., London, 1961), especially pp. 69–70.

5. defective competed with *defective* in the late 16th c.; cp. **116/1.**
    circumstances. In rhetoric and logic the term for the adjuncts of any action—time, place, manner, cause, etc.—which provide the means whereby a case can be built up on ' circumstantial ' evidence ; see

Ad Her., II, iv, 6–7. On the doctrine of circumstances taught in Eliza-bethan schools see T. W. Baldwin, *William Shakspere's Small Latine and lesse Greeke*, ii, 311–18. The old rhetorical teaching here contri-buted heavily to neo-classical theory on the dramatic unities. In rhetoric the circumstances were to be exploited selectively to make the case presented as coherent, credible, and persuasive as possible. Renais-sance critics believed that similar care was necessary to establish a dramatic illusion. It was an unwarrantable strain on credibility if a stage, obviously one place, should be used as if it were many places. In the same way it was reasonable to observe **Aristotle's precept** (11) in *Poetics*, 5, 1449b : ' Tragedy attempts to keep within a single revolution of the sun, or to exceed it but little, but the epic is indefinite in time and thus unlike tragedy'. See **82f.**

12. **both many days, and many places.** *Gorboduc* deals with the abdica-tion of a king, the later rivalry of two sons, and a long course of civil war ; and the action takes place in several courts.

inartificially, ' inartistically '. An early use of a term adapted from rhetorical theory ; cp. **138/33.** According to Scaliger in *Poetices*, III, xcvi, p. 334f., the story of a play must be set out to conform as far as possible with reality. For tragedy is not designed simply to excite admiration or amazement, but to teach, and to move, and to delight. We are delighted by jokes in a comedy ; on serious matters we are delighted by accuracy and appropriateness, for most men hate lies. And so those battles at Thebes got through in two hours do not please, and no sensible poet arranges that someone shall make a journey from Delphi to Athens, or from Athens to Thebes, in a moment of time ; as in Aeschylus, when Agamemnon is killed and promptly buried and that so quickly that an actor has scarcely time to draw breath. Nor is it satisfactory if Hercules has to throw Lichas in the sea, for that cannot be represented without a break in actuality. The plot should be succinct and yet be made as varied and multiplex as possible. For example, in the story of Hecuba in Thrace and Polydorus, since dead men cannot be introduced, employ ghosts to tell the action. So likewise in the story of Ceyx and Halcyon. If you were to make a tragedy out of this, don't start with the departure of Ceyx, for since the performance can take only six or eight hours at the most, it is not realistic to have a storm spring up, the ship wrecked in the middle of the sea out of sight of land. Use a chorus and messengers. Again in *Poetices*, VI, iii, p. 708, Scaliger raises similar objections against the Greek dramatists who move Theseus and his army from Athens to Thebes, have them fight a battle, and a messenger report back, all within a few hours. Similar cavils, accom-panying stricter requirements, increase during the second half of the 16th c. ; see Spingarn, pp. 91ff. George Whetstone in the Dedication to *Promos and Cassandra* (1578) castigates the typical English dramatist : he ' is most vaine, indiscreete and out of order : he fyrst groundes his worke on impossibilities ; then in three howers ronnes he throwe the worlde, marryes, gets Children, makes Children men, men to conquer kingdomes, murder Monsters, and bringeth Gods from Heauen, and fetcheth Diuels from Hel ' (Smith, i, 59). And see **135/31** note.

23ff. **two armies . . . with four swords.** Cp. Shakespeare, *Henry V*, IV, *Chorus*

> . . . our scene must to the battle fly ;
> Where—O for pity !—we shall much disgrace
> With four or five most vile and ragged foils,
> Right ill-disposed in brawl ridiculous,
> The name of Agincourt.

Jonson in the Prologue to *Every Man in his Humour*, proclaiming his general assent to Sidney's teaching, scorns

> To make a child now swaddled to shoot up . . .
> Past three score years ; or with three rusty swords . . .
> Fight over York and Lancaster's long jars.

Such contentions make the point not that a confusion of times and places is intrinsically wrong but that by refusing to stick to one place and one span of time a poet is making things much harder for himself and is likely to impair the coherence and thus the effectiveness of his presentation. This argument Shakespeare makes astonishingly clever use of in the Choruses of *Henry V* to justify his flouting of it.

32. **at this day . . . in Italy.** K. M. Lea in *Italian Popular Comedy*, i, 262, suggests that Sidney may well have seen troupes of Italian actors in Venice in 1574. Although many of their plays had extravagant actions, an increasing use was being made at this time of standardised sets for comedy, tragedy, tragi-comedy, and pastoral ; see *ibid.*, i, 325–6. Architectural theory developing from Vitruvius (1st c. A.D.), *De architectura* (printed 1486) encouraged the use of a fixed scene and consequently of an almost unbroken action on the stage ; see Allardyce Nicoll, *The Development of the Theatre* (3rd ed., London, 1948), pp. 81ff.

33ff. **some bring in . . . Eunuchus,** etc. Perhaps a reference to the discussion on the unities by Castelvetro in *Poetica d' Aristotele*, p. 60, where he deals with Terence and Plautus. But as Cook (p. 119) suggested, Sidney is confusing the *Eunuch* with *The Self-Tormentor*. In the *Eunuch*, probably the most popular of Terence's plays, the action appears to be completed in one day, for the lover Phaedria, who intends to go off into the country for three days, quickly returns in a matter of hours. *The Self-Tormentor* plainly occupies more than one day. As Scaliger observed : ' Half the story happens one evening ; the second half takes place in the morning ' (*Poetices*, VI, iii, p. 709). Scaliger probably, and succeeding critics certainly, believed that the play had been produced in two parts on successive days ; see Cook's notes (pp. 119–20) and Smith, i, 400. Yet though the stage action takes no more than two days, the story told concerns the birth, bringing up, and return of the girl Antiphila, and stretches over something less than twenty years. The whole reference is puzzling.

35. Probably *not* should be read before *far short.*

37. **Plautus . . . in one place . . . amiss.** Cp. Scaliger, *Poetices*, VI, iii, p. 708 : ' I can never approve that in the *Captives*, Philocrates goes away and Philopolemus comes back from Aulis to Aetolia in a very short time'.

p. 135

1f. **tragedy . . . tied to the laws of Poesy, and not of History.** Cp. Spenser's Letter to Sir Walter Raleigh on the *Faery Queen* : ' For the method of a poet historical is not such as of an historiographer . . . .' Sidney is reasserting the Aristotelian theory (see *Poetics*, 9, 1451b) of the independence of the poet as against the doctrine put forward by Castelvetro that ' it is fitting that the plot of a tragedy and of an epic should accept such actual events as are common to it and to the truth of history ; . . . the plots should be composed of happenings that can be called historical, although Aristotle had a different opinion' (*Poetica d' Aristotele*, p. 188). Scaliger in his account of tragedy (*Poetices*, III, xcvi, pp. 333–4) seems to hang to Sidney's position, and suggests that although history should not be distorted (and some of the ancients were guilty in this respect) the writer of tragedy should be free to interpret actions poetically to bring out their moral lesson.

6. **difference betwixt reporting and representing.** Sidney neatly summarises Scaliger's argument, referred to above (**134**/12 note). Castelvetro in *Poetica d' Aristotele*, pp. 56f., elaborates on the distinction : ' Dramatic presentation . . . is different from narrative, first in that it uses words and things instead of the original words and things, while narrative uses only words in the place of things, and indirect discourse in place of direct discourse. Secondly, the dramatic method is less ample with respect to places, and times.' In addition, the narrative method relates things that are visible and invisible, audible and not audible, and the dramatic represents only things that are visible and audible. Further, the narrative does not so much move the feelings as does the dramatic method.

8. **Peru** was conquered by the Spaniard Francisco Pizarro (1478–1541).

9. **Calicut.** The first port on the south-east coast of India reached by Vasco da Gama in 1498. It remained, next to Goa, the chief port of intercourse between Europe and India during the 16th c.

10. **Pacolet's horse.** The flying horse of the enchanter Pacolet who appears in the late-medieval romance *Valentine and Orson*, printed at Lyon in 1489. The tale was popular in England from the 16th to 18th c.

11. **nuncius,** ' messenger '. Most Renaissance critics explain the function of the messenger as enabling the dramatist to exclude excessive unpleasantness from the stage ; but Castelvetro (*Poetica d' Aristotele*, pp. 56f.) also recommends it to avoid awkward improbabilities ; see Gilbert, pp. 309f., 355, and cp. Scaliger quoted in **134**/12 note.

14ff. **Horace.** *Art*, 147, where he is condemning the dull cyclic poets and showing that the good epic poet does not start at the very beginning, ' from the egg ', but like Homer hastens to the event and starts *in medias res*. The openings of the classical epic poets had been analysed and European practice codified in the 12th c. Arts of Poetry, but the particular importance in drama of beginning *in medias res* was not much discussed before the 16th c. Scaliger in a chapter of precepts (*Poetices*, III, xcv, p. 331) gives as the first law : ' Never begin from the egg ', and notices that Lucan as well as Virgil observe this law. In the next chapter, on Tragedy and Comedy, he recommends concentrating the action of a play (see **134**/12 note). In III, xcvi, pp. 334–5, he insists : ' The argument of a play should be very succinct, and yet the plot full of variety and interwoven strands. For example : Hecuba in Thrace is forbidden to return by Achilles. Polydorus is already slain. . . . Since the dead cannot be introduced on the stage, their likenesses either as images or ghosts can be used : thus with Polydorus.' Sidney follows Scaliger, but fills out his account from personal knowledge of Euripides' *Hecuba*, by drawing directly upon the opening speech of Polydorus' ghost (*for safety's sake, with great riches* (17), *to make the treasure his own* (20), seem to be taken from this speech). *Hecuba* was popular in the 16th c. ; but in this play Euripides was struggling with somewhat intractable material, and his success in unifying it is less than Sidney suggests. See Myrick, *Sir P.S. as literary craftsman*, pp. 105–7, for discussion of Sidney's knowledge of this play.

31. **kings and clowns.** Cp. George Whetstone, Dedication to *Promos and Cassandra* (continuing the passage quoted in **134**/12) : ' And (that which is worst) their ground is not so vnperfect as their workinge indiscreete : not waying, so the people laugh, though they laugh them (for theyr follyes) to scorne. Manye tymes (to make mirthe) they make a Clowne companion with a Kinge ; in theyr graue Counsels they allow the aduise of fooles ; yea, they vse one order of speach for all persons : a gross Indecorum, for a Crowe wyll yll counterfet the Nightingale's sweete voice ; euen so affected speeche doth misbecome a Clowne' (Smith, i, 59–60). Sidney's phrases were remembered ; cp. *The Pilgrimage to Parnassus* (*c.* 1598–9), ed. J. B. Leishman (London, 1949), p. 129, lines 664–6 : ' Dost thou know a playe cannot be without a clowne ? Clownes have been thrust into playes by head and shoulders, ever since Kempe could make a scurvey face. . . .'

34. **decency,** ' decorum '.

35. **admiration and commiseration** (see **118**/1 note), as the effects of tragedy ; **the right sportfulness** (cp. **117**/10 ff.), as the aim of comedy.

36. **Apuleius** (2nd c. A.D.), Latin rhetorician, author of the *Metamorphoses, or Golden Ass* (translated by W. Adlington, 1566), from which Sidney probably took hints for the denouement of *Arcadia*. Apuleius introduced into his story of Charis' misfortunes the love-story of Psyche and Cupid. Thus the work is a mixture—a kind of picaresque novel— and released from observing the unity of epic. See also Boccaccio, *De genealogia deorum*, XIV, viii (Osgood, pp. 50–1).

39. **Plautus** in the Prologue to *Amphitryon* spoke of his play as a tragicomedy, thinking of it apparently as a mixture of the serious and the humorous, which introduced both the divine personages of tragedy and the slave, the typical character of comedy. So Scaliger (*Poetices*, I, vii, p. 31) explains his intention. Sixteenth-c. discussion of tragi-comedy invariably starts from a consideration of Plautus's play ; see M. Doran, *Endeavors of Art*, pp. 190ff.

p. 136

2. **match hornpipes and funerals.** Cp. *Hamlet*, I, ii, 12–13.

7. **tract,** ' course ', ' treatment '. See *NED s.v. sb.*³ 2 ; but cp. *s.v. sb.*¹ 1 also.

8. **well-raised,** ' exalted ', ' kept at a high level '.

10ff. Exemplifies how courtliness modified literary theory and practice. The basis of Renaissance discussion on the nature of the comic is Cicero, *De oratore*, II, lviii–lxx, 235–80, following Aristotle, *Ethics*, IV, 8. Comedy is built on ridicule ; ridicule is provoked by an exhibition of some shame or deformity (but the shame or deformity must not be to excess) ; the comic effect may be aroused by presenting an action or it may depend upon the way in which words are used. Cicero, urging moderation in all things, objected to scurrility or obscenity as a source of the ridiculous ; but the line of decency was difficult to draw, and some of the *comici* of the classical and medieval world (against whose practice Boccaccio campaigned in *De genealogia deorum*, XIV, xix (Osgood's note, p. 182) ; cp. **117**/8 note), were often scurrilous and obscene. Ridicule continued to be considered the basis of comedy and the source of laughter in the Renaissance. A fresh account of the verbal aspects of the comic is given by G. Pontanus, *De sermone* (1499), Book IV. Castiglione in *The Courtier* (1528), Book II, follows Pontanus;

but the courtly setting of the discussion, his own literary intention, and his personal fastidiousness give a more general and social emphasis to his treatment of the comic. Castelvetro in *Poetica d' Aristotele*, pp. 92ff., presented a full literary analysis. Comedy is based on human turpitude, either of the mind or body. If of the mind, it rises from folly, not vice ; if of the body, it can be evoked only if the shame or deformity is not painful or harmful. The chief springs of comedy are deception and ignorance ; see H. B. Charlton, *Castelvetro's Theory of Poetry* (Manchester, 1913), pp. 134–6. Sidney's formulation of a distinction between laughter and the true delight in comedy is a characteristically courteous modification within the tradition of the theory of laughter set out by G. Trissino in *Poetica*, Part VI (1563). Trissino claims to give a philosophical, not an oratorical, account such as Cicero gives ; but he still draws heavily on *De oratore*. The ridiculous, according to Trissino following Aristotle, is a mild form of the ugly, and the seat of the ridiculous is in ugliness and deformity. It is evident that laughter springs from the pleasure of the senses, or from the memory or anticipation of such pleasure. Such pleasure does not come from every object that causes delight, but merely from those objects that have some share of ugliness ; for if a man see a beautiful woman or a splendid jewel he does not laugh, nor does he laugh on hearing music in his praise, nor in reacting with his senses to things that are pleasant and grateful to the touch, the taste, or the smell. These together with the pleasure evoke ' admiration ' not laughter. But if the object presented to the sense has some mixture of ugliness, then it moves laughter, as an ugly and distorted face does, an inept movement, a silly word, a mispronunciation, a rough hand, a wine of unpleasant taste. Those things especially cause laughter from which better results were expected. The pleasure in the ridiculous comes to us because man is by nature envious and malicious, as is clearly seen in little children, for almost all of them are envious and always delight to hurt. Man never naturally delights in the good of others except through accident, that is, through some good which he hopes to acquire for himself. Hence if anyone sees someone find money, he does not laugh or take pleasure, but rather is envious, but if he sees someone fall into the mud, he laughs, because the harm which does not befall us is always, as Lucretius says, pleasant to observe in others. For if we ourselves suffer, the sight of the same sort of suffering in others does not make us laugh. One hunchback does not laugh at another hunchback. If the evils we see in others are deadly or very painful, as are wounds, fevers, they do not move laughter, but rather pity, because we feel that similar evils will come to us. As man is composed of mind and body, so ugliness in him is double, of the mind as well as of the body, and the special deformities of the mind are ignorance, imprudence, credulity, and the like ; and so in jokes we laugh especially when we see such things in persons who are thought to be substantial and of good intelligence. (Adapted from Gilbert, pp. 227–9.) More briefly, but following Cicero more closely, Thomas Wilson suggests the same sort of doctrine : ' An occasion of laughter . . . is the fondnes, the filthines, the deformitie, and all such euill behauiour, as we see to be in other. For we laugh alwaies at these things which either onely or chiefly touch handsomely and wittily, some especiall fault or fond behauiour in some one body or some one thing ' (*Rhetorique*, pp. 135–6).

Sidney avoids the traditional misanthropy shown by Trissino which makes envy the force behind laughter and seeks an inner, mental sanction for comedy. What Trissino calls ' the share of ugliness ' Sidney thinks of as a *contrariety* (15), something that is ' most disproportioned to ourselves and nature ' (17). The true delight of comedy is in recognition of a splendid conformity with nature. Sidney's speculations are realised in Shakespearian comedy : the delightful tends to eliminate the ridiculous. In addition, in discussing delight Sidney comes near to identifying a special aesthetic sense which is usually thought to have been invented in the 18th c.

27. **go down the hill against the bias.** As in the game of bowls when the slope of the ground (as on a crown green) eliminates the expected swerve of the bowl imparted by its bias.

32. **Alexander.** Plutarch in *Life of Alexander*, 4, gives an account of the portraits of Alexander. That by Apelles was the most famous.

33. **mad antics,** ' dances of madmen '. See R. R. Reed, *Bedlam on the Jacobean Stage* (Cambridge, Mass., 1952), Chap. I, on 16th c. use of lunatic asylums as places of entertainment.

34. **Hercules** after the completion of his Twelve Labours was for a time infatuated with Omphale, Queen of Lydia. Comic treatment of this subject was given by the German painters, Cranach and Hans Baldung. It was used apparently to mock the pagan classicism of the Italians and also as a caution against the seduction of wisdom by wantonness. For a list of paintings with this subject, see A. Pilger, *Barockthemen*, ii, 112–16.

p. 137

4. **Aristotle.** *Poetics*, 5, as quoted in note on 117/11 above. Probably Sidney recalled also the fuller discussion of the necessary decorum in humour given by Aristotle in *Ethics*, IV, 8, 1128a—the discussion from which the Ciceronian and Renaissance accounts of the comic spring (see 136/10ff. note).

7ff. Sidney appears to disapprove of using ' Fortune's slaves ' as comic butts—personages who by birth cannot help being what they are, poor, boorish, or foreign. Comedy should exploit acquired characteristics, what men are as a result of ' circumstance '.

11. Juvenal, *Satires*, III, 152–3 : ' Poverty contains no sharper misery than that it makes men ridiculous.' Sidney adduces contemporary Renaissance types, rather than strict types from Roman comedy. As busy-loving courtiers, both Polonius and Osric qualify.

14. **Thraso** (see 117/22 note) had a large Elizabethan progeny. Sidney in Rhombus in his masque of *The Lady of May* had delineated the type of a **self-wise-seeming schoolmaster**; Shakespeare followed with Holofernes in *Love's Labour's Lost* (cp. also, K. M. Lea, *Italian Popular Comedy*, I, 39). The affected traveller ' returned out of *Italie* worse transformed ' (Ascham, *Schoolmaster* (ed. Mayor, I, 74)) is another Elizabethan commonplace ; see e.g. *As You Like It*, IV, i.

16. **naturally.** In real life.

17. **as in the other,** *viz.* in tragedy. Sidney conjoins tragedy and comedy as a conclusion to his prescriptions for contemporary drama. But the complimentary reference to George Buchanan as a model for the writer of tragedies has something of the appearance of an afterthought (cp. 131/20 note).

20. **they,** *viz.* tragedy and comedy.

23. **honesty,** ' honour ', ' chastity '. Cp. 132/10.

24. that lyrical kind. Apart from the writers of the Pléiaₜₑ in France, most Renaissance critics dealing with the vernaculars worked from a Horatian and Aristotelian base and tended to ignore the lyric. Although Sidney in practice and in theory (see **103**/10f. ; **118**/19ff.) esteemed the genre, he restricts himself to the conventional characterisation of the lyric as song in praise of God or of a mistress ; see Rosamund Tuve, *Elizabethan and Metaphysical Imagery*, pp. 84ff. (cp. **118**/19ff. note). Sidney arranges his arguments with his usual skill, commending and defending the lyric by assuming that it could and should be praise ' of the immortal beauty, the immortal goodness ', and finding fault with the technique of the contemporary English lyric by limiting his examination of it to secular love poetry.

32ff. such writings . . . never persuade. Cp. *Astrophil & Stella*, XV. The lyric in Elizabethan estimation was persuasive, i.e. rhetorical ; cp. Puttenham, *Arte*, Chaps. xx–xxvi.

33. the banner of unresistible love. Cp. Song of Solomon, 2:4.

37. For *me* Penshurst MS reads *my father*.

38. Cp. *Hamlet*, II, ii, 362–3.

p. 138

3. forcibleness or energia. The first appearance in English of a form of the word ' energy ', coming in through Latin rhetoric by a Renaissance modification of the sense given it by Aristotle (*Rhetoric*, III, ii, 1411b). According to Scaliger (*Poetices*, III, xxiv, p. 259), there are four poetic virtues : general wisdom, variety, *efficacia*, and sweetness. *Efficacia* he deals with in Chap. xxvi, pp. 266ff. ; it is his term for what the Greeks call *energia*. It is the power of presenting the subject matter clearly, and refers not to the words used in presenting the subject but to the vivid mental apprehension of things themselves. An excess or a deficiency of *energia* is a fault : an excess is affectation in labouring beyond one's powers (cp. 9 note) ; a deficiency produces languidness, characteristic of modern poets. Virgil in particular strikes the happy mean. So for Sidney ' the forcibleness or *energia* ' is the intellectual clarity with which the poet distinguishes or apprehends the fore-conceit or Idea (**101**/4) ; cp. **101**/2ff. note ; and W. Ringler's note, *Poems*, p. 459.

7. diction: ' choice of words '. The first use of the word in this sense, which during the 18th c. was to become one of the technical words of literary criticism.

9. courtesan-like painted affectation. All these terms became hackneyed in criticism. Cp. Gabriel Harvey, *Marginalia* (ed. G. Moore Smith), p. 189 ; *Hamlet*, III, i, 51–3 ; *Paradise Regained*, IV, 343–5 ; Fulke Greville, *A Treatise of Human Learning*, *Poems* (ed. Bullough), I, 181, where wanton Rhetoric ' staines the Matrone with the Harlot's weed '. *Painted* becomes a stock epithet for a deceiving rhetoric ; see T. W. Baldwin, *William Shakspere's Small Latine and lesse Greeke*, ii, 414–15. Sidney probably uses *affectation* in a technical sense (as in the quotation from Scaliger, on 3, note). Quintilian in *Institutes*, VIII, gave a full treatment of *cacozelia*, or vicious affectation, as a fault in all styles of writing : it includes all that is turgid, trivial, over-ripe, redundant, far-fetched (*arcessita*), extravagant, etc.

far-fetched, a favourite word (in its regular form *farfet*) with Sidney ; cp. **115**/3. Puttenham, *Arte*, p. 183, lists ' the figure Metalepsis which I call the farfet, as when we had rather fetch a word a great way off than to use one nearer hand to expresse the matter as wel and plainer '. On Elizabethan attitudes towards exotic borrowing in vocabulary, see Richard F. Jones, *The Triumph of the English Language* (Stanford, California, 1953), Chap. IV, pp. 94–141. Concern for the vernacular language in which the Scriptures should be fully intelligible to all Englishmen led most influential writers to castigate affectation and excessive borrowing. Arthur Golding, completing Sidney's translation of *The Trewenesse of the Christian Religion*, set out in his dedication to Leicester what were most probably Sidney's own principles. ' If any words or phrases shall seeme straunge (as in some places perchaunce they may) I doubt not but your good Lordship will impute it to the rarenesse and profoundnesse of the matters there handled, not accustomed to be treated in our language. . . . Great care hath been taken, by forming and deryuing of fit names and termes, out of the fountaynes of our own tongue, though not altogether most vsuall, yet alwaies conceyuable and easie to be vnderstood ; rather than by vsurping the Latin termes, or by borrowing the words of any forreine language, least the matters . . . might have bene made more obscure to the vnlearned, by setting them downe in terms vtterly vnknowne vnto them.' Cp. Jones, pp. 122–3, and note 49. As Sidney also disapproved of archaic and dialect words, his respect for ' the fountaynes of our own tongue ' would lead him to advocacy of compounding (see **140**/18 note), if enrichment of the vocabulary was required.

11. **coursing of a letter,** ' assiduously employing alliteration '. The phrase is a variation on the commoner ' hunting the letter '. Cp. Epistle Dedicatory to *Shepherd's Calendar* : ' I scorne . . . the rakehellye route of our ragged rymers (for so themselves vse to hunt the letter)' ; Shakespeare, *Love's Labour's Lost*, IV, ii, 56. In 1560 Wilson in *Rhetorique*, p. 167, found fault that some ' vse ouermuch repetition of some one letter ', and by the 1580s heavy initial alliteration was no longer approved except for comic effects ; cp. Puttenham, *Arte*, p. 174, and Mulcaster, *Elementarie*, p. 286, allowing ' the figure of like letter ' if it is not overdone and ' bewraie affectation ' ; and Campion in 1602 (Smith ii, 330). Sidney in his poetry and Spenser use alliteration constantly, unobtrusively, and cleverly, often to reinforce syntax.

12ff. Cp. *Astrophil & Stella*, XV :

> You that do search for everie purling spring,
>   Which from the ribs of old *Parnassus* flowes,
>   And everie floure, not sweet perhaps, which growes
> Neare therabout, into your Poesie wring ;
> You that do Dictionarie's methode bring
>   Into your rimes, running in ratling rowes : . . .
>
> You take wrong waies, those far-fet helpes be such,
> As do bewray a want of inward tuch.
>   (*Poems*, ed. Ringler, p. 172 ; and see notes, p. 466)

In this sonnet ' the dictionary method ' refers to end-rhymes, not to initial alliteration.

13. **figures and flowers.** Cp. Puttenham, *Arte*, p. 138, on ' figures and figuratiue speaches, which be the flowers, as it were, and colours that a Poet setteth vpon his language of arte '. *Winter-starved* in a collocation with ' flowers ' occurs again in *Astrophil & Stella*, Ninth Song, *Poems* (ed. Ringler), p. 222.

14ff. This defines Sidney's attitude to Ciceronianism, which is the touchstone of Elizabethan verbal sense in verse as well as in prose as here, where Sidney glances in particular at sermon writing. He rejected the extreme Ciceronianism of the mid-century (see the letter to Robert, quoted 5), when in Bacon's words ' did Car of Cambridge and Ascham with their lectures almost deify Cicero and Demosthenes, and allure young men that were studious unto that delicate and polished kind of learning ' (*Advancement of Learning*, I, iv, 2, ed. Wright, p. 29). On this movement see *Gabriel Harvey's Ciceronianus*, ed. H. S. Wilson and C. A. Forbes (Lincoln, Nebraska, 1945), Introduction, pp. 14–30. Unlike the extreme Ciceronians, but like Cicero himself (and Gabriel Harvey) Sidney believed wisdom and eloquence more valuable than eloquence alone, that matter is more important than words. No anti-Ciceronian in his own work and in his influence on his literary associates during the 1580s, yet by his interest in a controlled and somewhat Ramist rhetoric he was revealed as a conscious opponent of the excesses of the extremists. Euphuism (see **139/6ff.** note) he seems to have regarded, and rightly, as an ephemeral form of degenerate Ciceronianism.

20. In a well-known passage, Quintilian (*Institutes*, X, i) reported that Livy in an epistle to his son advised him to take Demosthenes and Cicero as models, and many Renaissance critics repeated Livy's advice.

21. **Nizolian paper-books.** Marius Nizolius, Italian scholar, born in Modena 1498, published *Thesaurus Ciceronianus* (1535), which long retained its usefulness as a Latin phrase-book ; see Q. Breen, *Renaissance Studies*, 1 (1953), 48–58. M.-A. Muret (*Opera*, i, 261) also complains that ' nowadays anyone can make an oration that smells of Cicero by following the rhetorical handbooks and by using the work of Nizolius '. On the practice of filling note-books with choice phrases employed by Elizabethan scholars, see W. G. Crane, *Wit and Rhetoric in the Renaissance*, Chap. 2, pp. 33–48.

22. **attentive translation**, ' studious appropriations '. For this legal sense of *translation*, see *NED s.v.* 5.

23ff. Cp. R. Lever, *The Arte of Reason* (1573), sig. Iv : ' As for Ciceronians and sugar tongued fellows which labour more for finenes of speach than for knowledge of good matter, they ofte speak much to small purpose, and shaking forth a number of choice wordes and picked sentences, they hinder good learning, with their fond chatte'.

25. **like those Indians**, etc. According to the earliest account of Brazil familiar to Englishmen ' the Indians of this countrey have their lips made full of small holes in 4 parts, and through these holes be put small rings and like at their ears ' (*Testimony out of Josephus de Acosta*, *Hakluyt's Voyages* (Glasgow, 1904), vol. xi, 20 ; and cp. *ibid.*, p. 24). Montaigne reflects on this Indian custom in his *Apology for Raymond Sebonde*. In Elizabethan and Stuart England both sexes wore ear-rings.

28ff. Cicero, *In Catilinam*, I. Wilson, *Rhetorique*, pp. 200–1 explains *that figure of repetition, geminatio verborum* : ' Doublettes as when we rehearse one and the same worde twise together. . . . Tullie against Catiline, eneueighing sore against his traterous attempts, saieth after a longe rehearsed matter, and yet notwithstanding al this notorious wickednesse : The man liueth still, liueth ? Naie Marie, he cometh into the counsaile house, which is more.' Sidney quotes from memory this same famous opening to the First Oration against Catiline : ' O tempora, o mores. Senatus haec intelligit, consul videt : hic tamen vivit. Vivit ? immo vero etiam in senatum venit.'

33. artificially, ' through the power of art '. Cp. **134/12.**

34ff. hale . . . collar . . . choleric. Sidney maintains the play on words : *collar,* ' restraint ', ' burden ' (cp. *NED s.v. sb.* 8) against *choler,* ' anger '. *too, too* (Olney, *to too* ; other eds. *too*), is a common mannerism for emphasis in prose and poetry, especially, according to *NED,* between 1540 and 1660.

36–139/5 How well store . . . end of their fineness. Olney omits. Ponsonby's **similiter cadences** is a partial and awkward anglicising of the Latin *similiter cadentia.* The passage continues Sidney's rejection of excessively Ciceronian prose in which rhythmic patterns, especially at the ends of periods, were carefully followed. Gabriel Harvey in *Marginalia* (ed. G. Moore Smith), p. 115, remarked that *similiter cadentia* were ' somewhat ouermuch affected of M. Ascham in our vulgare Tongue '. An account of these *Like ending and like falling* was given by Wilson in *Rhetorique,* p. 202 : ' Then the sentences are said to end like, when those wordes doe ende in like sillables which do lacke cases. Thou liues wickedly, thou speakest naughtely. . . . Sentences also are said to fall alike when diuers wordes in one sentence ende in like cases, and that in rime. By greate trauaile is gotten much auaile. . . .' Wilson is one of the first to object to excessive use of these devices especially in preaching, and he goes on : ' Diuers in this our time delite much in this kinde of writing, which beeing measurably vsed, deliteth much the hearers, otherwise it offendeth, and wearieth mens eares with satietie. S Augustine had a goodly gift in this behalfe, and yet some thinkes he forgot measure, and vsed ouermuch this kind of figure. Notwithstanding, the people were such where he liued, that they tooke much delite in rimed sentences, and in Orations made ballade wise. . . .' Earlier, in dealing with composition, Wilson remarked (pp. 166f.) : ' Some end their sentences all alike, making their talke rather to appear rimed Meeter, then to seem plaine speeche, the which as it much deliteth being measurably vsed, so it much offendeth when no meane is regarded. I heard a preacher deliting much in this kind of composition. . . . Some not best disposed, wished the Preacher a Lute, that with his rimed sermon he might vse some pleasant melody, and so the people might take pleasure diuers waies, and dance if they list ' [cp. **139/24ff.**]. A tradition of highly ornamented prose for sermons persisted throughout the medieval period into the 17th c. ; see M. W. Croll, *Euphues,* Introduction, pp. xliff. Sidney's Puritan and neo-classic sympathies induce him to prefer an eloquent plainness in the pulpit.

38. daintiness, ' fastidiousness ', ' good taste '.

39ff. With Sidney's recounting of this story of a superficial logician, cp. Thomas More, *Confutation of Tyndale* (1532), in *Works* (1559), p. 475/2 : ' For lyke wyse as though a sophyster woulde with a fonde argumente, proue unto a symple soule, that two egges wer thre, because that there is one, and there be twayne, and one and twayne make three ; the simple unlearned man, though he lacke learnyng to foyle his fond argument, hathe yet wit ynough to laugh therat, & to eate two egges himself, and byd the sophyster take and eate the thyrde.' It is not certain that Sidney was drawing here upon More, for stories involving this simple fallacy persisted in schoolrooms for generations.

p. 139

6ff. **similitudes,** ' similes '. The passage is an assault on the so-called Euphuists. Although Lyly in his stories of Euphues was the most outstanding exponent of the style, it is less certain that he originated it ; more probably he polished and gave a personal stamp to a superficial Ciceronianism which at Oxford in the late 1570s was grafted on to the flowery rhetorical prose cultivated in late-medieval times ; see W. Ringler, ' The Immediate Source of Euphuism ', *PMLA* **53** (1938) 678–8b. Sidney's objections are logical. The end of discourse should be effective persuasion, not ' seeming fineness ' (4). Ornamentation for its own sake, in particular the excessive use of simile affected by Lyly (cp. also the criticisms of Hoskins, *Directions*, p. 16) do not reinforce argument. Sidney could have learnt as much from the treatment of simile in Aristotle, *Rhetoric*, III.

Cp. also *A woorke concerning the trewnesse of the Christian religion*, etc. . . . translated by Sir P. Sidney and A. Golding (London, 1587), p. 455 : ' To what end do similtudes serve, but to make things cleere ? ' Bacon in *Advancement of Learning*, II, xvii (ed. Wright), p. 174, discussing intellectual method, quotes the dictum of Aristotle, *Ethics*, VI, 3 : ' If we shall indeed dispute, and not follow after similitudes ', and continues : ' For those whose conceits are seated in popular opinions need only but to prove or dispute ; but those whose conceits are beyond popular opinions, have a double labour ; the one to make themselves conceived and the other to prove and demonstrate. So it is necessary with them to have recourse to similitudes and translations [metaphors] to express themselves.' Although Sidney is considering discourse in general, not poetry specifically, he would apply his argument to poetry. Poetry has the ' double labour ' of which Bacon speaks. Similes are indispensable in expressing the poetic conception, ' to explain to a willing hearer ' (11) ; they are superfluous in proving or demonstrating the adequacy of the conception itself. Rosamund Tuve in *Elizabethan and Metaphysical Imagery*, p. 184, note 6 (and cp. pp. 346ff.), suggests that Sidney's attitude to simile here is influenced by the Ramist insistence that all discourse must be soundly based in dialectic.

7. **herbarists,** ' authors of herbals '. Characteristic of Euphuistic prose is its witty, irresponsible use of material drawn from natural history, in particular from handbooks by Pliny and Erasmus. The learning is negligible ; the brilliance superficial ; the examples often invented. Cp. also *Astrophil & Stella*, III.

9, 13, 15. **conceits . . . memory . . . judgment.** Cp. **104**/3f. note.

16ff. **Antonius and Crassus** were introduced as speakers in Cicero's three dialogues, *De oratore*. Marcus Antonius (143–87 B.C.) (grandfather of Cleopatra's Mark Antony), was renowned as an orator. He held a succession of offices of state and was killed at Rome in the civil wars between Marius and Sylla. L. Licinius Crassus, consul 95 B.C., died 91 B.C. ; accounted by his contemporaries the greatest of Roman orators. In *De oratore* Crassus is usually thought to express Cicero's own opinions. In the second Book Cicero compares the talents of these two orators. ' I used to think that Crassus never acquired more learning than was to be obtained by an elementary education ; and that Antonius had no learning of any sort at all.' But in fact ' the one thought to appear a more responsible man if he despised the Greeks, and the other if he appeared to be completely unlearned '.

20. **credit.** The establishment of an orator's credentials and of a sympathetic *rapport* with the audience (*ethos*) was considered in rhetoric as the essential basis for successful persuasion. See Aristotle, *Rhetoric*, II, 1f. ; Cicero, *De oratore*, II, 189ff. ; cp. F. Solmsen, *CP* **33** (1938), 390–404.

23. **tracks,** ' features ', ' attractions '. So Olney. Other texts read *knacks*, ' fanciful ornaments ', ' tricks '. But *tracks* may well be the true reading ; cp. *NED s.v.* and *s.* tract, *sb.*[3]

24. Cp. Wilson, *Rhetorique*, p. 167, cited above **138**/36 note.

25. **curiously,** ' exquisitely ', ' elaborately '.

28. **smally,** ' little '. An adverb, according to *NED*, in common use 1525–1650. The passage summarises Sidney's position ; and a similar status was maintained with increasing difficulty through the 17th c. by a ' mob of gentlemen who wrote with ease '. See **132**/16 note. But elegant and competent nonchalance in an Elizabethan writer could take different forms. According to Puttenham (*Arte*, p. 302) : ' We doe allow our Courtly Poet to be a dissembler only in the subtilties of his arte : that is, when he is most artificiall ; so to disguise and cloake it as it may not appeare, nor seeme to proceede from him by any studie or trade of rules, but to be his naturall : nor so euidently to be descried, as every ladde that reades him shall say he is a good scholler, but will rather haue him to know his arte well, and little to vse it.' The eloquence of Puttenham's courtier poet is artificial but made to seem natural ; the eloquence of Sidney's has been acquired empirically and thus can be considered more truly natural. This is the distinction Harrington made ; see **132**/32 note.

33. **using art . . . to hide art** recalls *ars est celare artem*, a phrase of post-classical origin. But the idea is old; cp. Ovid, *Metamorphoses*, X, 252 ; *Ars amatoria*, II, 313 (' si latet ars, prodest ') ; Longinus, *On the Sublime*, xvii ; xxxviii.

35. **pounded for straying.** Cattle gone astray were rounded up in the village pound.

37. **in this wordish consideration.** That is, in respect of what Sidney has called *diction* (**138**/7).

p. 140

5ff. Sidney denies the force of what had been common allegations against English : (i) that it was not a pure language ; (ii) that it was not a ' ruled ' language ; see R. F. Jones, *The Triumph of the English Language*, especially Chaps. IV–VI.

7. **a mingled language.** See Sir John Cheke (1514–57) (in Arber's reprint of Ascham, *Schoolmaster*, p. 5) : ' I am of this opinion that our own tung shold be written cleane and pure, unmixt and unmangeled with borowing of other tunges, wherein if we take not heed bi tijm, ever borowing and never payeng, she shall be fain to keep her house as bankrupt ' ; and cp. E. K.'s complaint in Preface to *Shepherd's Calendar* that ' they have made our English tongue a gallimaufray or hodgepodge of al other speches '. But Sidney fairly acknowledges the actual situation in the 1580s. Augmentation of the vocabulary had made English a ' mingled ' language, but a language full of resources.

8. **best of both the other.** As Sidney sets English against Latin and Greek (19 below), he probably intends them here also. It is against these

two languages that Drayton in *Elegy : to Henry Reynolds* claims that
Sidney set up English in successful rivalry.

9, 10. it wanteth grammar . . . it wanteth not grammar, ' it lacks gram-
mar . . . it does not require grammar '—with a play on *wanteth*.
Linguistic interest in English in the first part of the 16th c. was confined
to the enriching of the vocabulary in order to attain full expression and
eloquence. Grammar was studied only in relation to Latin. But after
Sir John Cheke's time a new interest shown in English spelling and
pronunciation, culminating in Richard Mulcaster's *Elementarie which
entreateth chefelie of the right writing of our English tung* (1582), led on
to a consideration of English grammar. In 1580 William Bullokar
promised ' a ruled Grammar for Inglish ' and scantily fulfilled the
promise in 1586. The first systematic grammar is the work of a Ramist,
Paul Greaves, *Grammatica Anglicana* (1594). But in the 1580s poetic
practice and theorising were closely involved with linguistic issues, as
Gabriel Harvey explains in a letter to Spenser : ' There is no one more
regular and justifiable direction, eyther for the assured and infallible
Certaintie of our English Artificiall Prosodye particularly, or generally
to bring our Language into Arte and to frame a Grammer or Rhetorike
thereof, than first of all vniuersally to agree upon ONE AND THE SAME
ORTOGRAPHIE, in all pointes conformable and proportionate to our
COMMON NATURAL PROSODYE ' (Smith, i, 102).

13. Tower of Babylon. Babylon the capital of Chaldaea was believed
to have been built by Nimrod upon the site of the Tower of Babel
(Gen. 10:10).

14f. It was at least a generation after Sidney's time that there was any
demand among educationalists that English composition needed to be
taught in the schools. Richard Carew (1555–1620), who was at Oxford
with Sidney and retained a lively admiration for him, wrote later in the
century an account of the *Excellency of the English Tongue* (see Smith,
ii, 285–94) which was included in Camden's *Remains concerning Britain*
(1614 ed.). He sums up many of Sidney's observations, praising English
for its lack of ' those declensions, flexions, and variations, which are
incydent to many other tongues, but a few articles gouerne all our
verbes, and Nownes, and so wee neede a very shorte grammar ',
and claiming that the language is remarkably easy to learn (Smith, ii,
288).

15. uttering . . . conceits of the mind . . . is the end of speech. An
Elizabethan commonplace. Cp. Wilson, *Rhetorique*, p. 2 ; Gabriel
Harvey, *Marginalia* (ed. G. Moore Smith), p. 115 ; Ralph Lever, *The
Arte of Reason* (1573), Forespeache (in which Lever vigorously pro-
claimed the resources of English for intellectual purposes).

18. compositions, ' compounds '. Joseph Hall, *Vergidemiarum* (1598),
VI, ll. 255–8, noted that Philisides (Sidney's pen-name for himself in
Arcadia) fetched this new elegance from France, and that it had been
grossly over-rated by his successors. On Sidney's use of compounds in
poetry see W. Ringler, *Poems, Introduction*, p. liii, and V. Rubel,
Poetic Diction in the English Renaissance, p. 204. On Sidney's com-
pounds in the *Apology*, see Cook's note, p. 130. In addition to his
inventions in Greek (112/28 ; 121/4), some compounds : death-
bringing, **102**/12 (Lat. *mortifer*), earth-creeping (**142**/20), low-creeping
(**130**/32) (Gk. *hamaitupes*), honey-flowing (**138**/7) (Lat. *mellifluus*), are
directly adapted from the classical languages ; others are native for-
mations : paper-blurrers (**132**/19), poet-whippers (**120**/6), afterlivers,

116/25. W. L. Renwick, *MLR* 17 (1922), 1–16, on the origins of Spenser's diction, sought to show that in compounding as in other features of style the New Poets of the 1580s were imitating the practice of the French Pléiade. Sidney was doubtless aware of foreign example as well as of native possibilities ; but the most potent French influence was that of du Bartas, on whose idiosyncratic practice in compounding see *Works of Guillaume de Salluste Sieur du Bartas*, ed. U. T. Holmes, J. C. Lyons, R. W. Linker (Chapel Hill, 1935), i, 173–8.

21ff. The two sorts of versifying were commonly distinguished as verse (22) and rhythm or rhyme (26 ; **141/5**) ; cp. **122/17**. In med. Latin *rithmi, rithmici versus*, were used to denote the more popular accentual versifying in contrast to the more learned quantitative verse. Common use of similar sounding endings in *rithmi* led to the use of *rime* (later *rhyme*) as the general term for compositions with this particular feature. In the 16th c. *verse* continues to be contrasted with *rhyme* and refers to composition in which more attention is paid to metrical regularity ; cp. the juxtaposition of these terms in Gascoigne, Spenser, Stanyhurst, Harvey (Smith, i, 50, 89, 140, 360).

26ff. Which of the two forms (the accentual or the quantitative) was better for English poetry was much argued in the second half of the 16th c. ; see **87ff.** In a cancelled passage in *Arcadia* (found in Jesus College Oxford MS 150 and Queen's College Oxford MS 301 of the *Old Arcadia*) printed by R. W. Zandvoort, *Sidney's Arcadia*, pp. 11–12, by W. Ringler, *PQ* **29** (1950), 72, and in emended form in *Poems*, pp. 389–90, Sidney presents two such speeches in a debate between the shepherds Dicus and Lalus, ' Dicus likinge the measured And Lalus the riminge '. Dicus argued that as the chief beauty of poetry is its musical quality, poetry should conform with the structure of music : ' so that eyther by [the] time a poet should strayght know how every word should be measured unto it, or by the verse as soone find out the full quantity of the musike. Besides that it hath in it self a kind . . . of secret musike, since by the measure one may perceave some verses running with a high note fitt for great matters, some with a light foote fitt for no greater then amorous conceytes. . . .' Lalus retorts that Dicus ' did much abuse the dignitie of poetry to apply it to musicke, since rather musicke is a servaunt to poetry, for by [the one] the eare only, by the other the mind was pleased '. If the proportions of number are not well represented in music, ' it is the musitions fault and not the poettes, since the poet is to looke but to beawtifie his wordes to the most delight, which no doubt is more had by the rime, especially to common eares to which the poet doth most direct his studies, and therfore is caled the popular philosopher ' (cp. **109/**15). Rhymed verse, Lalus adds, has an enriched character of its own. This passage, as well as the *Apology* here, indicates Sidney's serious interest in naturalising classical measures. On the general background to Sidney's experimentation and for an assessment of his success see W. Ringler, *Poems*, pp. 390–3. Discussion on the relative merits of the two prosodies turns on the function of music in poetry. Since, as Lalus claims, poetry speaks not only to the ear but also to the mind, it cannot be assumed that the problem was simply one of fitting words and musical accompaniment. It seems rather that Sidney and his associates were struggling to investigate the fundamental puzzle of verse—how to relate intonation patterns to a regular verse structure. By 1600, perhaps largely as a result of the impetus given to development by the New Poets of the 1580s, poetry has come to be regarded as formally and functionally freed from its ties with music ; at the same time poets have succeeded in accommodating the inherent intonation patterns of spoken English to verse forms.

28. time. So Olney. Ponsonby and later editions read *tune*, which goes very plausibly with *words* here (cp. **100**/5 note). That **time** is the correct reading is indicated by Dicus' explanation in the cancelled *Arcadia* passage : in quantitative verse ' for every sem[i]brefe or minam, it had his silable matched unto it with a long foote or a short foote . . . and without wresting the word did as it were kindly accompanie the time ' (*Poems*, p. 390).

29f. more fit . . . to express . . . passions, where Sidney assumes the power of music to stir the emotions and thus achieve moral effects similar to those which were achieved by the Greek modes. Puttenham in *Arte*, pp. 84f., explains at greater length what was drawn out of this assumption in respect of verse composition : ' The poet using measured verse, places every verse, hauing a regard to his measure and quantitie only, . . . as to set one short meetre to three long, or four short and two long, or a short measure and a long . . . which maner of Situation . . . doth alter the nature of the Poesie, and make it either lighter or grauer, or more merry, or more mournfull, and many wayes passionate to the eare and hart of the hearer, seeming for this point that our maker by his measures and concordes of sundry proportions doth counterfait the harmonicall tunes of the vocall and instrumentall Musickes. As the Dorien because his falls, sallyes and compasse be diuers from thos of the Phrigien, the Phrigien likewise from the Lidien . . . mounting and falling from note to note such as be to them peculiar. . . .' Puttenham is talking about the placing of lines within a stanza, Sidney about the exact positioning of the word within the line, where syllables would need to be ' well-weighed ' to evaluate quantity, which would depend upon position. Much of Elizabethan discussion on quantitative verse ends in ineffectual attempts to establish the length of syllables in English words.

by the low or lofty sound. Cp. Dicus' distinction of ' a high note fitt for great matters ', and ' a light foote fitt for . . . amorous conceytes ' (see 26ff. note) ; and Puttenham's ' lighter or grauer, or more merry, or more mournfull ' poesy (see above). According to rhetorical teaching on delivery, volume, tone, and pitch were to be modulated according to the nature of the discourse ; cp. *Ad Her.*, III, xi, 19–xiv, 25. The phrases suggest that the Elizabethans were beginning to discern the real nature of pitch in intonation. In English speech ' the very high and very low pitches . . . are brought into play only in moments of strong emotion ' (Roger Kingdon, *The Groundwork of English Intonation* (London, 1958), p. 2).

30. The latter, i.e. modern rhymed verse, which, according also to Puttenham (*Arte*, p. 76), has ' a certaine tunable sounde ' of its own.

34ff. Truly the English, etc. This marks one of the most emphatic statements of the new-found confidence with which Sidney's generation of writers viewed their native language. ' The suddenness with which writers began to recognise the eloquent nature of the mother tongue enables us to date the turning point not earlier than 1575 nor later than 1580 ' (R. F. Jones, *The Triumph of the English Language*, p. 211).

37ff. The basis for these observations seems to be Sidney's rules for scansion (derived apparently from the so-called Rules of Archdeacon Drant (see Smith, i, 89f.)) written in the margin of St John's College Oxford MS I. 7, and reproduced by W. Ringler (*Poems*, p. 391). The fourth rule reads : ' Bicause our tonge being full of consonantes and monasillables, the vowell slydes awaye quicker then in Greeke or Latin, which be full of vowells and longe wordes ; yet are suche vowells longe as the pronunciation makes longe. . . .' And the fifth : ' Elisiones, when one vowell metes with another, used indifferently as thadvantaige of the verse best serves . . . and like scope dothe Petrarche take to hym self sometymes to use. . . .'

37. **Dutch,** ' German '. On Sidney's difficulty with German see his letter to Languet, February 1574 : ' Of the German language . . . I absolutely despair. It has a sort of harshness . . .' (*Works*, vol. iii, 84).

p. 141

2. **antepenultima.** The term is used also by Puttenham (*Arte*, pp. 71, 115, etc.) and by 17th c. prosodists.

5. **rhyme.** Modern accentual verse ; cp. **140**/21ff. note.

8. **caesura.** Sidney adapts the classical term to the requirements of English. In Latin verse the caesura refers to the division of a metrical foot and in particular to the division of the foot in the middle of the line. Sidney regards it as *the breathing place* in an English long line. Gascoigne had left the employment of caesura ' at discretion of the wryter ' (Smith, i, 54). Puttenham (*Arte*, p. 75) thinks that ' in euery long verse the Cesure ought to be kept precisely ', but he conceives of it primarily as a rhetorical pause.

11. **masculine.** Sidney's use of the term as applied to rhyme ending in stressed syllables is the first recorded use in English ; similarly with **female** (or feminine) as applied to two-syllabled rhyme between words ending in unstressed syllables. As a poet, Sidney reintroduced feminine rhyme into English verse. See W. Ringler, *Poems*, Introduction, p. lvi.

15. **sdrucciola,** ' slippery ' (Italian), in application to rhymes in which there are several unstressed syllables after the last accent. In Sidney's example, *motion/potion* is a trisyllabic rhyme. The Italian term had a limited currency in 17th c. English discussion on prosody ; see *NED s. v.*

21ff. The conclusion to the oration is tripartite, as was usually recommended ; cp. *Ad Her.*, II, xxx, 47–xxxi, 50 : (i) A summing-up, 21–7 ; (ii) an **a**mplification invoking authorities, 27–**142**/9 ; (iii) an emotional appeal to engage the self-interest of the audience, **142**/10 to end. Sidney's purpose remains serious, but he assumes **a** comical solemnity.

25. **poet-apes.** Cp. ' Pindare's Apes ' in *Astrophil & Stella*, III, on which W. Ringler refers to the ' pindarising ' of the Pléiade. The metaphor of the ' poet-ape ' derives from Latin school verse of the late-medieval period ; see Curtius, Excursus XIX, pp. 538–40.

28. **even in the name of the Nine Muses** is to be taken with *I conjure* (27).

33. **the ancient treasurers of . . . divinity,** *viz.* those who kept the old mythology alive in men's memories. Cp. Aristotle, *Metaphysics*, III, iv, 12. His authority was often adduced on this point ; see Boccaccio, *De genealogia deorum*, XIV, viii, and Osgood's note, p. 163.

34. **Bembus.** See **131**/16 note. In this impressive parade of authorities it is scarcely necessary to locate this commonplace ; but cp. the argument of the first chapters of *Le Prose* by Pietro Bembo.

35. **Scaliger.** See **131**/19 note. His recurrent theme in *Poetices* is the wisdom to be won from the *Aeneid* ; but the reference here is precise. ' Certainly you cannot become a better man, or a man better adapted

to society from the precepts of any philosopher than by reading Virgil '
(*Poetices*, III, xix, p. 238).

37ff. Clauserus, the translator of Cornutus. L. Annaeus Cornutus (1st
c. A.D.), a Stoic pedagogue, teacher of the poets Persius and Lucan.
Much of his written work is lost. Conrad Clauser, a German humanist,
published a commentary and translation of his *De natura deorum
gentilium* (Basel, 1543). Sidney draws here upon Clauser's prefatory
epistle to his kinsman, Christoph Clauser. ' Who were these first
philosophers ? Hesiod and Homer, from whom all human philosophy
took its beginning, through whom the Holy Name was pleased to reveal
it : these presented the precepts of philosophy to us under the veil of
fables. Do you seek dialectic, or logic, and all the art of discourse ?
You will discover it in the fables of the poets. Do you seek physics or
natural philosophy ? . . . Do you seek ethics, all the divisions of moral
philosophy ? You will discover them amply set out in the fables of the
poets.'

p. 142

3f. mysteries . . . written darkly. In some medieval and Renaissance
thought about the nature of verbal composition a certain degree of
' darkness ' was regarded as essential to high poetry ; see H. J. Chaytor,
From Script to Print (Cambridge, 1945), pp. 68ff. ; Osgood's note to
Boccaccio's *De genealogia deorum*, p. 157 ; and W. Ringler's note to
Rainolds, *Oratio*, p. 74. Sidney invokes the venerable respectability of
this traditional belief to claim his audience's indulgence towards his
presentation of his own theory of poetry, which is of course quite
different.

5ff. Landino . . . a divine fury. Sidney makes similar use, to suit his
immediate persuasive purpose, of an authority and a high theory of
poetry (which he has already rejected ; see **130**/7ff. note). Cristoforo
Landino (1424–1504), one of the most influential Florentine humanists
of the Medici court, tutor to Lorenzo the Magnificent, author of
Disputationes Camuldulenses and Latin poems ; translator of Pliny,
commentator on Virgil, Horace, and Dante. Sidney's reference is to
his edition of the *Divine Comedy* (Florence, 1481), where in his Prologue
(vii) he deals with the Divine Fury. On the importance of this Prologue
in Renaissance thought, see A. Chastel, *Marcel Ficin et l'art* (Geneva
and Lille, 1954), p. 25 and notes.

8. make you immortal. From ancient times poets had promised an
eternity of fame to their subjects ; see Curtius, Excursus IX, pp. 476–7.
Renaissance poets became more insistent ; see Oliver Elton, ' Literary
Fame : a Renaissance Study ', *Otia Merseiana*, 4 (1904), 24–52 ;
Robert J. Clements, *Critical Theory and Practice of the Pléiade*, Chap. 3,
pp. 84–121. Erasmus in *Praise of Folly* (p. 119) remarked that it was
the characteristic foolishness of poets to make this promise.

10ff. An elegant anticlimax.

12. most fair, most rich, most wise, most all. Phrases such as were
addressed to many a dedicatee in ' a poetical preface '.

14. libertino patre natus, ' son of a freedman '. The phrase applied by
Horace to himself in *Satires*, I, vi, 6, in priding himself on the familiarity
of his patron Maecenas.
    Herculea proles, ' offspring of Hercules '.

16. Virgil, *Aeneid*, IX, 446. In the next lines an immortality of fame is promised to the dead friends Nisus and Euryalus.

17. In Dante's *Divine Comedy* Beatrice inhabits Paradise ; in the *Aeneid* Aeneas encounters his father Anchises in the Elysian Fields.

19. **cataract of Nilus.** Cp. Cicero, *Somnium Scipionis* (a work which with the commentary by Macrobius held an immense prestige in the Middle Ages), V, 13 : ' Filled with the sound of the music of the spheres, men's ears are deafened. No sense in man is duller than hearing, just as those people who dwell near the place where the Nile falls down from the great mountains to the regions called Catadupa, have no sense of hearing on account of the volume of noise.' Cp. also Seneca, *Naturales Quaestiones*, IV, ii, 5. Sidney's allusion embodies the notion of Pythagoras often appropriated by Renaissance writers that the orderly motion of the planets made cosmic music ; see Cicero, *Somnium Scipionis*, V.

23. **mome,** ' blockhead ', ' fool '. In fairly common use in 16th c. (cp. MnFr *môme*), but deriving apparently from the proper noun **Momus,** the son of Night and a personification of ill-tempered criticism. Cornelius Agrippa, *Vanitie of the Arts*, sig. Av, suspected that for his attacks upon the arts ' the peevishe Poetes will put me in theyr verses for Momus. . . .'

24. **Midas,** king of Phrygia, was awarded asses' ears because he adjudged the music of Pan better than Apollo's. See Ovid, *Metamorphoses*, XI, 146ff.

25. **Bubonax** is apparently Sidney's conflation of the two names Hipponax and Bupalus. The unusual physical ugliness of Hipponax (*c.* 500 B.C.), a satiric poet of Ephesus, was portrayed by the two sculptors, Bupalus and Athenis. Hipponax's counter-assault in verse was said to have driven the two sculptors to suicide ; see Pliny, *Natural History*, XXXVI, 12. A similar story is told of the poet Archilochus (7th c. B.C.) driving the daughters of Lycambes to death for shame. Cp. next note.

26. **rhymed to death.** After Sidney the phrase became common ; see Shakespeare, *As You Like It*, III, ii, 185. Ben Jonson in the Apologetic Preface to *Poetaster*, seems to be recalling the *Apology* :

> I could do worse,
> Armed with Archilochus' fury, with iambics
> Should make the desperate lashers hang themselves
> Rime them to death, as they do Irish rats
> In drumming tunes.

Cp. Campion (Smith, ii, 330). That the Irish used verse charms in the control of vermin was commonly attested. So Reginald Scot in *The Discoverie of Witchcraft* (1584), III, 15, reported that they ' will not stick to affirm that they can rime either man or beast to death '.

29f. In *The Pilgrimage to Parnassus* (ed. Leishman), p. 122, V, 533–4, Philomusus borrows the threat to the despiser of poetry :

> Noe Epitaphe adorne his baser hearse
> That in his lifetime cares not for a verse.

INDEX OF NAMES

INDEX OF NAMES

241